# Careers of Service in the Church

# CAREERS
# OF SERVICE
# IN THE CHURCH

A Description of Many Interesting
and Satisfying Vocations

*Benson Y. Landis*

*Published by* M. Evans and Company, Inc.,
New York, *and distributed in association with*
J. B. Lippincott Company, Philadelphia and New York

# CONTENTS

# PREFACE

This book interprets for young people and their advisers or counselors about one hundred careers or vocations in the Protestant churches, their boards and agencies, their interdenominational organizations, and church-related hospitals, educational and social-welfare institutions.

Brief pertinent information is given for every vocation—personal qualifications; education and training recommended or required; the usual functions or duties, particularly of those beginning their work; and sources in which further information may be found.

This volume is for young people facing the practical decisions about their life's work. It is equally for the practical use of their advisers. These include ministers of local churches; directors of religious education; chaplains in colleges, and other campus workers; teachers and counselors in schools and colleges; executives of national boards and organizations; officers of state denominational units, and state and local councils of churches; directors of Christian Associations; librarians; adult lay leaders in the churches; and, not least, parents.

The book begins with a general description of church employment, including the various ways whereby people are "called" or enlisted; and some conditions of church employment. These are followed by a list of college majors and of the careers that they may lead to; data on military service by young men; a consideration of the general status of women in church employment; and a discussion of the unique roles of ministers' wives.

Herein are descriptions of at least ten types of ministries of

9

ordained persons, both in local churches and in the many other organizations. Increasingly, local churches employ more than one minister.

Attention is given to the now numerous careers in which either ordained or unordained persons may be engaged, and to those for which unordained persons are especially sought.

Increasing specialization in church employment is evident in all fields. Foreign mission boards, for example, enlist ordained ministers for general local church work, also graduates of agricultural colleges, home economists, nurses, physicians, teachers in all types of schools and colleges, librarians, community center workers. And in the U.S. there is probably a higher degree of specialization than in vocations overseas.

For information on ordained ministries I have relied upon many publications of, and interviews with, officials of religious bodies, teachers and administrators of church-related colleges and theological seminaries, and, of course, talks with active people in the parish ministry, both men and women. For the vocations found both within churches and elsewhere, I have often been aided by the *Occupational Outlook Handbook,* 1963-64 edition, Bulletin No. 1375, of the Bureau of Labor Statistics, U.S. Department of Labor, Washington, D.C. 20210. For the personal qualifications desired I have interviewed officials of religious organizations, and studied their literature.

BENSON Y. LANDIS

# I
# General Information
# on Church Employment

## AN INTRODUCTION

Just as there are "varieties of religious experience" in the world, so ably described by the famous philosopher, William James, so there are now many varieties of careers or vocations in the churches and in church-related work. There are close to a hundred vocations, full-time employment either in local congregations, in the numerous state, local, and international agencies of the churches, or in institutions that are related to the churches—such as hospitals, schools and colleges, and social-welfare agencies, especially those for children and older people.

In the Protestant churches, emphasis has been placed on the priesthood of all believers, ordained or not. All members of a church are called upon to minister, are charged with communicating "the good news," the gospel, to reconcile men to God and to one another. The ordained and unordained people who give all their time to the various ministries and receive salaries carry the same responsibilities as the church members who volunteer for part-time or informal work. Those who work full time possess no special spiritual merit. They are simply people who have had training for their ministry or they are people who perform the same duties that exist in non-religious organizations. Often called simply "the first among equals," ministers are employed so that the work of the churches may be systematically done in a day of large-scale operations.

As will be seen in the discussion of the various vocations, church employment is becoming increasingly specialized. The system of having one ordained minister in full charge and bearing the burden of many different positions in his church is becoming outmoded for several reasons. One is that the average size of a given congregation is increasing, resulting in the need for more services on Sunday morning and in the increasing number of events during the week that call for a minister's attention. Although there are still many local churches in which the minister is the only full-time professional employee, the tendency today is toward a multiple ministry, as the tasks become too much for one man to handle by himself. There are now many positions formerly filled by the minister that are filled by lay people; also many that may be filled by either an ordained or unordained person.

## WHAT IS "DIFFERENT" ABOUT CHURCH EMPLOYMENT?

The practice of the presence of God can go on in a kitchen as well as before an altar, wrote Brother Lawrence, a Roman Catholic whose writings are read by Protestants. Thus a member of a Protestant church may witness to his faith in a factory, on an airplane, or in an office, as well as in a full-time church position.

The question is often asked, "What, then is different about full-time church employment?" This question may be answered first of all by saying what is *not* different. In church employment one faces the same issues, dilemmas, and difficulties that exist in secular careers. The decisions, the human relations, and the drudgery are similar to those found in non-religious occupations.

A man who is now working in a religious organization after having left a secular career expresses the difference between employments in this way. In spite of universal human frailty, in a religious community there exists a fellowship, a common devotion to ideals as well as to the achievement of the job at hand. A person is working with dedicated people, a dedication that is often contagious. There is mutual aid and sharing of suffering to a degree not found in non-religious organizations. And he states, there is determination and zeal to do good work in a religious organization, even though the salary may be lower than at a comparable job in a non-religious organization. (See What About Compensation?, below.)

## WHAT IS A CALL?

The "call" to commitment to a church vocation is often discussed. Because a call may not be as clear as Paul's experience on the road to Damascus, many people are uncertain or confused. According to the late H. Richard Niebuhr in his work *The Purpose of the Church and Its Ministry* (New York: Harper and Row, 1956), there are four calls.

1) The call common to all Christians—to heal, to set free, to reconcile, to witness, to communicate. All church members are called to be a servant people.

2) The call that comes gradually through participation in the work of the church, study in the church school, the counsel and advice of parents, ministers, and church officials.

3) The providential call that comes through awareness of God's creation and providence, through thankfulness for God's gifts, through inquiry concerning why God has given us this world and this life.

4) The call that is a deep, inner experience in which a person becomes convinced that full-time service is God's will for him. This call, said Dr. Niebuhr, is the more clear when one has considered the other three calls.

## WHAT ABOUT COMPENSATION?

"You will probably find salaries neither as high nor as low as elsewhere." This is a generalization often found, at least in effect, in much of the literature that the churches send to young people.

13

National averages are not available, and if they were, they would have little meaning because of the varieties of jobs and experience. In some denominations there are standards or minimum scales, not always enforced, for ministers. Some religious organizations accept or are covered by the Fair Labor Standards Act, providing now for a minimum wage of $1.25 an hour for workers in offices, printing, etc. Salaries in church-related social-welfare and educational institutions are surely not the maximum paid in such institutions, but they may compare favorably with those generally paid. Foreign missionaries have numerous provisions other than cash salaries, and are probably more secure financially than professional persons in the U.S. Salaries of office personnel in church work are not as high as the highest paid in industry, but, again, may compare favorably with many of those of other non-profit organizations. For jobs that are much the same in religious organizations as in the community generally, churches find themselves in competition with others for good workers.

The ordained ministry is called a low-income profession—if only cash salaries are considered. In a survey of 2,200 ministers in nine denominations in 1956 (the latest study of its kind) the average cash salary was just under $4,500 a year, but when allowances for rent, expenses, fees, and utilities were added, the *total compensation* was $5,827. This was slightly more than the average *cash* salary of teachers of all grades in the colleges of the nation that year.

The denominations included in the sample study were the Congregational-Christian Churches, the Evangelical and Reformed Church (both merged in the United Church of Christ in 1961), the American Baptist Convention, the Methodist Church, the Presbyterian Church in the U.S.A. (now the United Presbyterian Church in the U.S.A., by merger with United Presbyterian Church in North America in 1957), the United Lutheran Church (since merged with three other Lutheran bodies to form the new Lutheran Church in America in 1963), the Christian Churches (Disciples of Christ), and the Protestant Episcopal Church. These bodies are surely not representative of Protestant bodies generally; probably in the others the compensation is lower.

14

The above study revealed that salaries of ministers vary according to size of congregation—"the larger the membership the greater the cash salary." While the average cash salary was $4,500, that of associate or assistant ministers was $4,300, while that of senior ministers or heads of staffs was $7,250. Also, the larger the community the larger the cash salary of ministers. There were few differences among the regions of the U.S.

According to this same survey, the full-time directors of religious education were paid an average annual cash salary of $3,550; office-workers got an average of $2,765; sextons received $2,675. "Other parish employees" received annual salaries averaging $2,883. (See *The Church as Employer, Money Raiser, and Investor,* by F. Ernest Johnson and J. Emory Ackerman. New York: Harper and Row, 1959.)

The compensation of church employees is bound up with the "total economy" of the Protestant churches. The tradition has been to have large numbers of small churches, each with one pastor, and with a wife as an unpaid professional servant. That pattern is rapidly changing, particularly in suburbs and cities. [The situation can only change decisively on the conviction of lay people.]

The theory used to be that since church employees receive intangible satisfactions and rewards in addition to their salaries, that these salaries need not be as high as in other fields of work where money may be the main reward. More prevalent today is the opinion that people who have paid for professional or other vocational training, and who are expected to take refresher courses or to continue their education, should have compensation comparable with that in other professions. One denomination makes an announcement to this effect: "It is possible in most church careers to live comfortably but not luxuriously." There are also frequently "fringe benefits" in the form of insurance, retirement pensions, and social security—see below.

## SOME CONDITIONS OF CHURCH EMPLOYMENT

Church employment is not as "standardized" as that in other organizations. This is because of the differences of organizational

15

experience, with many small organizations, and a heritage of informality. Along with "bigness" in religion has come more standardization of personnel policies—to the gratification of some and to the consternation of others. Here note is taken of certain aspects.

Group insurance is, according to informed persons, coming to be widely available, with both employer and employee contributing.

Unemployment compensation, jointly administered by the federal government and the states, varies considerably from state to state. Religious organizations are not required to be covered, but in at least one state, New York, they may have voluntary coverage by paying the necessary tax on payrolls.

In the states with Fair Employment Practices Laws, prohibiting discrimination because of race, creed, color, religion, or national origin, religious organizations are exempted from the provisions. It is not considered "discrimination" if religious organizations give preference to their own members in employment.

Retirement provisions appear to be as varied as are religious bodies in the U.S. All major Protestant denominations have national systems for clergymen, which may include lay employees. There are also some separate pension boards for lay people. In most of these, participation of the local church is not compulsory. There are no comprehensive national statistics for any of the major faiths.

The following notes sum up interviews with informed persons:

In most religious bodies the pension systems are of the contributory type, with the local church or the denominational board (the employer) and the employee both making payments.

While age 65 is often fixed as the generally accepted age of retirement, the tendency is toward flexibility. Thus in many instances retirement is permitted at an age earlier than 65—with lower amounts of payment; also there may be employment by mutual agreement or on invitation of the employer beyond age 65, often on a year by year basis.

Pension plans usually have provisions for payments to beneficiaries who become totally disabled prior to the normal age of retirement.

Pensions paid to employees are in some instances supplemented by payments of portions of premiums of major medical insurance.

Denominational pension boards also offer to persons participating opportunities for voluntary payments in excess of the required payments, thus adding to the potential pension available on retirement. In some instances, the option of purchasing health insurance or other benefits is also available to a participant before retirement.

Church pension boards also at times offer advice with respect to Social Security provisions and the taxation of pensions.

A high proportion of clergymen of the U.S. have elected to be covered by Old Age, Survivors, and Disability Insurance, administered by the federal Social Security Administration through their numerous local offices.

*Social Security*

Employees of most non-profit organizations receive Social Security credits for their earnings. These, like workers in industry and business, pay Social Security taxes and have the protection and benefits provided by the national system of Old Age, Survivors, and Disability Insurance.

Employees of some non-profit organizations—and their employers—are required by law to pay Social Security taxes. Examples are civic organizations, labor unions, business and trade associations, fraternal orders, and farmers' cooperatives.

However, other non-profit organizations are permitted by law to decide whether or not they want to make Social Security available to their employees. The initial decision is the responsibility of the employers. These non-profit organizations are the religious, charitable, scientific, literary, and educational organizations that have been held to be exempt from income tax by the Internal Revenue Service.

If an organization in one of these groups voluntarily gives up its exemption from Social Security taxes, the present employees

17

who want Social Security credit for their earnings may start receiving it.

Two steps are then necessary:

First, those employees in favor are asked to sign a list on Form SS-15a. This list must include each concurring employee's home address and his Social Security number if he has one.

Second, the organization must formally record its exemption from paying Social Security taxes by filing a waiver certificate on Form SS-15. This waiver must be sent to the District Director of Internal Revenue accompanied by the list of the signatures of the employees desiring Social Security. Waiver certificates may be made effective at once, or even retroactive for up to one year before the certificate is filed.

Employees hired or re-employed after the filing of the necessary papers are automatically covered. They have no choice and they need not sign any papers.

Employees who did not elect Social Security at first may, under certain conditions, start receiving credits later. For information on this point the District Director of Internal Revenue must be consulted.

For general information on Social Security or for a Social Security card, consult your local office of the Social Security Administration.

Effective with the year 1936, this system of public insurance now covers almost all the working population of the U.S. Among exceptions are self-employed physicians, most federal employees (who have their own retirement plan), and casual migrant farm workers and domestic servants who work for one employer for only short periods. Some work for members of a family is also excluded. The system is administered by the Social Security Administration, Department of Health, Education, and Welfare, Washington, D.C. 20201 The Social Security Administration has over 500 local offices throughout the nation furnishing information and service.

Generally, both employer and employee pay an insurance contribution, technically a tax, on earnings up to $4,800 per person per year. Self-employed persons covered, such as those in small business, farm operators, fishermen, pay the tax themselves also on earnings up to $4,800 per year when they file their annual income tax returns. For purposes of coverage under OASDI, clergymen are regarded as self-employed. Also, they are only covered if they elect to be; see description of their situation below.

The rates of tax, according to present law, are as follows:

| Years | Employers and Employees both to pay (per cent) | Self-Employed pay (per cent) |
|---|---|---|
| 1963–65 | 3⅝ | 5.4 |
| 1966–67 | 4⅛ | 6.2 |
| 1968– | 4⅝ | 6.9 |

To qualify for benefits, a person must be in work covered by the law for a specified number of quarters, which means three-month periods in which there are earnings of $50 or more. The number of credits needed to secure benefits when a worker reaches age 62 depends upon the time when he started in covered employment. On the chart on page 20, the credits of quarters worked could be earned at any time after the year 1936.

The law provides three types of benefits:

Retirement benefits, monthly payments to qualified persons when they have reached age 62 and have "retired." One does not have to stop working completely to be "retired." Certain dependents can also get monthly checks when the qualified worker starts receiving benefits.

Survivors' benefits, monthly payments to (a) a widow if she is age 62; (b) children under 18; (c) children over 18 if they have been disabled since childhood; (d) a mother of children who are entitled to benefits if she is caring for the children; (e) dependent parents 62 years or over; (f) a dependent widower 62 years or over.

Lump sum, payable to either a spouse, or the person who pays

| Year in which you were born | Quarters of Coverage Needed | |
|---|---|---|
| | Men | Women |
| 1892 or earlier | 6 | 6 |
| 1893 | 7 | 6 |
| 1894 | 8 | 6 |
| 1895 | 9 | 6 |
| 1896 | 10 | 7 |
| 1897 | 11 | 8 |
| 1898 | 12 | 9 |
| 1899 | 13 | 10 |
| 1900 | 14 | 11 |
| 1901 | 15 | 12 |
| 1902 | 16 | 13 |
| 1903 | 17 | 14 |
| 1904 | 18 | 15 |
| 1905 | 19 | 16 |
| 1906 | 20 | 17 |
| 1907 | 21 | 18 |
| 1908 | 22 | 19 |
| 1909 | 23 | 20 |
| 1910 | 24 | 21 |
| 1911 | 25 | 22 |
| 1912 | 26 | 23 |
| 1913 | 27 | 24 |
| 1917 | 31 | 28 |
| 1921 | 35 | 32 |
| 1925 | 39 | 36 |
| 1929, and later. | 40 | 40 |

funeral expenses of a covered worker, or directly to a funeral director.

Disability benefits, monthly payments to a worker and his family if he becomes disabled. Disability benefits are paid only under specified conditions, as follows: A person must have worked in covered employment for five out of ten years prior to becoming disabled; he must be suffering from a disability of indefinite duration and be disabled to such an extent that he cannot work; he must, if he meets the above tests, wait for six months before drawing his benefits, which will then be the same as they would have been when he came to age 65.

Examples of monthly payments, as provided by the amendments to the Social Security Act in 1961 are on the following page.

A worker may begin earning Social Security credits, no matter how young or how old.

The Social Security card which workers in covered employment must secure on starting work becomes valuable property. If it is lost, application should be made immediately for a new one to a local office of the Social Security Administration.

It is wise to make a periodic check of the earnings credited to your account. One does this by mailing Post Card Form OAR-70004, obtainable from your local Social Security Office, to Social Security Administration, P.O. Box 57, Baltimore, Md.

EARNINGS AFTER BENEFITS BEGIN. After a worker becomes age 72 or over, he may earn any amount in covered employment and still continue to draw his monthly benefits.

A Social Security beneficiary between ages 62–72 can earn as much as $1,200 a year and collect full benefits. Only earned income is counted, not pensions, or interest, or dividends, or rents.

A beneficiary who earns more than $1,200 a year will give up $1.00 of Social Security benefits for each $2.00 that he earns, from $1,200 to $1,700. For every dollar that his earnings go over $1,700 a year he gives up a matching $1.00 of benefits.

An important exception is that no matter what a beneficiary earns in a year, he can still be paid a full benefit for any month in which he does not earn wages of more than $100 and does not actively work in covered self-employment.

(SOURCES: *Publications of the Social Security Administration,* Washington, D.C. 20203.)

SOCIAL SECURITY TAX—CLERGYMEN. By terms of the Social Security Act as amended, a clergyman is regarded as self-employed for the purpose of participation in the benefits of Old Age, Suvivors, and Disability Insurance. However, clergymen are not subject to

## EXAMPLES OF MONTHLY PAYMENTS BEGINNING AUGUST 1961

| Average yearly earnings after 1950 | $800 or less | $1,800 | $2,400 | $3,000 | $3,600 | $4,200 | $4,800 |
|---|---|---|---|---|---|---|---|
| Retirement at 65 or disability benefits | $ 40.00 | $ 73.00 | $ 84.00 | $ 95.00 | $105.00 | $116.00 | $127.00 |
| Retirement at 64 | 37.40 | 68.20 | 78.40 | 88.70 | 98.00 | 108.30 | 118.60 |
| Retirement at 63 | 34.70 | 63.30 | 72.80 | 82.40 | 91.00 | 100.60 | 110.10 |
| Retirement at 62 | 32.00 | 58.40 | 67.20 | 76.00 | 84.00 | 92.80 | 101.60 |
| Wife's benefit at 65 or with child in her care or child of living worker | 20.00 | 36.50 | 42.00 | 47.50 | 52.50 | 58.00 | 63.50 |
| Wife's benefit at 64 | 18.40 | 33.50 | 38.50 | 43.60 | 48.20 | 53.20 | 58.30 |
| Wife's benefit at 63 | 16.70 | 30.50 | 35.00 | 39.60 | 43.80 | 48.40 | 53.00 |
| Wife's benefit at 62 | 15.00 | 27.40 | 31.50 | 35.70 | 39.40 | 43.50 | 47.70 |
| Widow 62 or over | 40.00 | 60.30 | 69.30 | 78.40 | 86.70 | 95.70 | 104.80 |
| Widow under 62 and 1 child | 60.00 | 109.60 | 126.00 | 142.60 | 157.60 | 174.00 | 190.60 |
| Widow under 62 and 2 children | 60.00 | 120.00 | 161.60 | 202.40 | 236.40 | 254.00 | 254.00 |
| One surviving child | 40.00 | 54.80 | 63.00 | 71.30 | 78.80 | 87.00 | 95.30 |
| Two surviving children | 60.00 | 109.60 | 126.00 | 142.60 | 157.60 | 174.00 | 190.60 |
| Maximum family payment | 60.00 | 120.00 | 161.60 | 202.40 | 240.00 | 254.00 | 254.00 |
| Lump-sum death payment | 120.00 | 219.00 | 252.00 | 255.00 | 255.00 | 255.00 | 255.00 |

this specific self-employment tax on "income they derive from services as duly ordained, commissioned, or licensed ministers of a church unless they elect to be covered. . . ." Also, "members of religious orders and Christian Science practitioners are also exempt from the tax in connection with the discharge of their duties as such, unless they elect to be covered. . . ."

OPTIONAL COVERAGE FOR CLERGYMEN. "If you are a clergyman, Christian Science practitioner, or a member of a religious order who has not taken a vow of poverty, you may elect to be covered by the Social Security program by filing a waiver certificate, Form 2031, with your District Director of Internal Revenue. In order for your election to be effective, you must file the waiver certificate on or before the due date of your return for the second tax year in which you had net earning from self-employment as a clergyman, etc., of $400 or more. Complete instructions for filing the waiver certificate are furnished with Form 2031. You will not be permitted to withdraw the certificate after it is filed."

COMPUTATION OF NET EARNINGS UNDER OPTIONAL COVERAGE. "This specific self-employment tax applies to your net earnings for services performed as a minister, a Christian Science practitioner, or a member of a religious order. In determining your net earnings you should deduct all expenses attributable to your calling, such as stenographic help, transportation, etc. You must include as net earnings the rental value of a parsonage or rental allowance furnished you as part of your compensation and the value of meals and lodging furnished to you for the convenience of your employer. These inclusions affect only your self-employment tax liability and do not alter the status of these items for income tax purposes.

"If one spouse is not a duly ordained, commissioned, or licensed minister of a church, that spouse is not entitled to file the waiver certificate, Form 2031, to elect Social Security coverage, although she may be entitled to such coverage as an employee for services performed for which she is compensated. Such earnings are not to be included in the other spouse's self-employment income.

"Husband and wife missionary teams. If you and your husband are duly ordained, commissioned, or licensed ministers of a church and both of you are hired under the same agreement which provides that each of you is to perform specific services and both are paid jointly or separately, the self-employment income of each of you is what you actually receive under the agreement. However, if the agreement is with only one of you and the other performs no specific duties for which compensation is granted, the payment received under the agreement is self-employment income only to the one who is party to the agreement, even though the other spouse is also a duly ordained, commissioned, or licensed minister."

## Taxation

Lay employees are taxed in the same way as persons in other employments. Clergymen are taxed on their salaries and on the fees or offerings paid to them personally for marriages, baptisms, funerals, masses, etc. If a fee or offering is paid to the church, and not personally to the clergyman, it is not taxable to him. Quoting the Internal Revenue Service: "A home furnished a clergyman, as part of his compensation, is not income to him, if he is duly ordained, licensed, or commissioned as a minister of the gospel."

A cash rental allowance is not taxable to him to the extent that it is used to provide a home. Conversely, a cash rental allowance is taxable to him to any extent not used, in the year received, to provide a home. "The rental allowance may be either a separate payment or it may be part of a payment which also includes other compensation, provided the rental portion is properly designated by proper church authority before the payment is received.

"The employing church must take the action to properly designate the rental allowance as to payments made after December 31, 1962.

"Expenditures to provide a home include the amount spent for rent, to purchase a home, to provide furnishings for the dwelling, for appurtenance to the dwellings such as a garage, and for the cost of utilities. It does not include the cost of food or servants.

"If a clergyman owns his home, or is buying it, his rental al-

24

lowance is excludable from income to the extent he spends it as a down payment on a home, as mortgage instalment payments, for interest, taxes, repairs, etc., on his home. For example, if a minister, received a rental allowance [of $1,200] in . . . (a calendar year) and made a $4,000 down payment on a home in . . . (the same year), the full $1,200 is not taxed.

"Theological students serving as assistant pastors during a required internship leading to a degree, may not exclude a rental allowance from taxable income, if they are not ordained, commissioned, or licensed ministers.

"Ministers of music or education who are not duly ordained, licensed, or commissioned ministers of the gospel are not eligible for this exclusion even though they are performing some of the services relating to the office and functions of a minister of the gospel.

"If a minister receives only a salary from which he must provide his own living quarters, and if no part of his salary has been properly designated as a rental allowance, his total salary is taxed."

Under a recent ruling of the Internal Revenue Service (62-171) ministers employed in religious schools are entitled to tax-free housing allowances. This applies to persons if they teach secular subjects, but to qualify, a clergyman must also perform pastoral functions. The ruling applies to clergymen teaching in schools or colleges "which are integral agencies of religious organizations." (Apparently the ruling does not apply to teachers in religious schools independent of denominations.)

### Sick Pay for Clergymen

"If you are a priest, rabbi, pastor, or other member of a religious order and your salary continues during periods when you are unable to perform your duties because of illness or injury, you are covered by a sick-pay plan. You may qualify for the sick-pay exclusion (when computing income tax) even though you elect to pay the self-employment tax in order to qualify for Old Age, Survivors, and Disability Insurance—"

## Retirement Income

Usually pensions or annuities of lay employees and of clergymen are taxed as are all those of other persons. There is, however, in the instructions of the Internal Revenue Service this special word to retired clergymen: "If he [the clergyman] is not expected to perform any further services, payments from his congregation are not taxable, provided they are based solely on his financial position and needs and the financial capacity of his congregation. Such payments must not have been made under any enforceable agreement, an established plan, or because of past practice."

A few general provisions with respect to taxation of retirement pay are here summarized:

"If you did not contribute to the cost of your pension and it was fully paid for by your employer, usually you must pay tax on the full amount you receive each year.

"If you and your employer each contributed a part of the cost of your pension or annuity, only part of what you receive is taxed.

"The cost of your pension or annuity is the amount you have contributed to the plan, including amounts contributed by your employer which you were required to include in your income. . . .

"If you will recover your cost in three years or less from the date of your first pension or annuity payment, the amount you receive are not taxed until your entire cost has been returned to you. After that your entire pension or annuity is taxable. . . ."

A special retirement income credit is available to certain persons, clergymen and others, but it cannot be claimed by anyone receiving Social Security or railroad retirement benefits of $1,524 a year or more, or by persons having earned income of $494 a year if they are under 62 years of age, or $2,974 a year if they are 62 or older but under 72, or by non-resident aliens, or by persons filing tax returns on Form 1040A. Note that "interest, dividends, pensions,

26

annuities, capital gains, and rents generally are not earned income." Royalties received by an author are not earned income.

To qualify for a retirement income credit one must also have had earned income of more than $600 in each of 10 calendar years prior to the current year.

Many persons thus have "retirement income" but are not entitled to the special retirement income credit.

"The credit is 20 per cent of the lesser of:

(1) The retirement income you received during the year; or

(2) $1,200 minus the total of certain pensions and annuities and current earned income."

(SOURCES: *How Social Security Works For Non-profit Organizations and their Employees,* Social Security Administration, Washington, D.C. 20203, published in 1961.

On tax aspect of Social Security: *Your Income Tax,* 1964 Edition. Obtainable from your district Director of Internal Revenue, or from U.S. Government Printing Office, Washington, D.C. 20401. 40 cents a copy.)

## COLLEGE MAJORS AND CHURCH VOCATIONS

College students need to think carefully during their freshman and sophomore years about the "major" or area of concentration they will pursue during their junior and senior years. Indeed, the prospective student should give some thought to his field of study even before his entrance into college.

The following list of majors indicates church-related careers that would naturally follow from that particular major.

ART: Teaching in school or college; commercial art for publishers of religious books, ranging from catalogs to dust jackets to window displays; design and layout for religious periodicals and pamphlets; art work for production of visual-aid materials distributed by religious publishers.

BIOLOGY: Teaching in school or college; research; vocations connected with health and medicine in church-related hospitals in the U.S. or overseas; work as an agricultural missionary overseas.

27

BUSINESS EDUCATION OR ADMINISTRATION: Business management of a large church; service in business offices of religious agencies, including publishing houses and interdenominational organizations; accounting jobs; teaching in school or college; secretarial or bookkeeping jobs in church and other offices; bookstore management.

DRAMA AND SPEECH: Parish ministry; evangelistic work in missions at home or abroad; writing careers; teaching in church-related schools and colleges; direction of drama programs of national church agencies.

ECONOMICS: Teaching in church-related colleges and schools; business management in various organizations; actuarial and related work for church pension funds; positions on social action staffs of religious bodies and interdenominational organizations.

EDUCATION: Director of religious education in a local church; teaching in schools and colleges here and abroad; teaching in week-day religious education; work in a Y.M.C.A. or Y.W.C.A.; a position on the staff of a council of churches.

ENGLISH AND JOURNALISM: Public-relations or editorial work for religious organizations; teaching English in community centers, Y.M.C.A.'s, and Y.W.C.A.'s; the ordained ministry; staff writing on religious periodicals.

HISTORY AND GOVERNMENT: The ordained ministry; teaching in schools or colleges here and abroad; the college chaplaincy; other campus ministries; the chaplaincy in the Armed Services; staff positions in a council of churches.

HOME ECONOMICS: Management of cafeterias and dining rooms in church-related institutions and denominational and interdenominational organizations; teaching in schools and colleges here and overseas; work in dietetics and therapy in hospitals, or homes for older people; home demonstration work with missions abroad.

LANGUAGES: Translation and literary work in missions abroad; the ordained ministry; teaching in schools and colleges in the U.S. and abroad; service on staffs of international church agencies requiring use of several languages.

MATHEMATICS: Bookkeeping and accounting; statistical work;

research work; management of budget and finance offices; teaching in schools and colleges in the U.S. and abroad; actuarial work for pension funds.

MUSIC: Music director of a local church; editing hymnals; teaching in schools and colleges; development of music programs for radio and TV programs of religious organizations.

PHILOSOPHY AND RELIGION: The ordained ministry; chaplaincy service; teaching in school, colleges, and seminaries; service on staffs of Y.M.C.A. or Y.W.C.A.; executive work for local, state, and national councils of churches.

PHYSICAL EDUCATION: Work with Y.M.C.A. and Y.W.C.A.; direction of youth work in a local church; teaching in schools and colleges here and abroad; direction of athletic programs; work in summer camps and conferences.

PHYSICS OR CHEMISTRY: Teaching in schools; teaching and research in colleges; the health professions—all these in the U.S. and abroad.

POLITICAL SCIENCE: Teaching in colleges in the U.S.; staff positions on social-action agencies of denominations and interdenominational organizations; service on staffs of church relief agencies.

PSYCHOLOGY: Pastoral counseling; teaching positions majoring on counseling and guidance; teaching in colleges in the U.S. and abroad; the chaplaincy in institutions (prisons, hospitals, children's homes; institutions for older people, the handicapped, etc.); the industrial chaplaincy; work as deaconesses; social work here and abroad.

SOCIOLOGY: Research and statistical work for religious agencies; direction of relief work aboard; teaching and research in colleges and theological seminaries in U.S. and abroad; social-welfare work.

(The above is based on the following sources: "College Majors and Church Careers," by Elmer G. Million in *International Journal of Religious Education,* New York, N.Y. 10027; and *Cedar Crest College Bulletin,* Vol. 20, No. 6.)

## MILITARY SERVICE OF YOUNG MEN

"Many are called but few are chosen" by the Selective Service System, through which young men are found for military duty in the Armed Forces. Since the Universal Military Training and Service Act, as amended, contains numerous references to schooling, training, and occupation, and to recall of employed persons in the Reserve, a digest of the current regulations is given here.

Early in 1964 it was announced that about 1,700,000 young men were available for draft. Draft quotas were expected to be at the rate of about 10,000 a month. There was thus a vast supply to meet the demand. However, this was not the total demand of the Armed Forces. Actually several hundred thousand men were required annually by the several Armed Forces, but most of their needs were met by enlistment rather than by the draft. Military units actually rely on the pressure or prospect of draft to stimulate enlistments.

The Selective Service System, Washington, D.C. 20435, operates through local citizens' draft boards. There are also headquarters in all the states, and in the District of Columbia, New York City, the Virgin Islands, Puerto Rico, Guam, and the Panama Canal Zone, a total of 56. There are some 4,000 local draft boards each consisting of three or more civilians who serve without compensation. These are generally appointed on a county basis. There is an appeal board in each federal judicial district.

Through a system of deferments, many men are encouraged to continue or extend their education or vocational training. The Selective Service System has, for example, given tests to over 600,000 students. The results serve as guides to local draft boards in making student deferments. Shortages of scientists, engineers, teachers, and other vocations have been at least alleviated by deferment of such persons with skills regarded as in the national interest.

The Selective Service System is also responsible for maintaining the stability of the Reserve and of the National Guard. The System does not induct men into the National Guard, but makes deferments because of continued satisfactory performance in these units. For example six or more years of satisfactory service in the Ready Reserve qualifies a man, on discharge from that Reserve, for classification as IV-A, which applies to those who have completed service under the Universal Military Training and Service Act.

The Selective Service System is also responsible for securing when needed, a selective recall from the Standby Reserve, when this is authorized. This necessitates keeping current records on those in the Standby Reserve, consisting of 1,000,000 men and women. The system must make this recall with due regard to the economy of the nation, and to extreme hardship to dependents.

The law requires that all selections of persons for draft must be "consistent with the maintenance of an effective national economy." Thus an elaborate system of deferments has been devised. These sequences are listed below. Worth noting here is that in January, 1962, the System put into effect a new regulation to create the classification of I-Y, into which are put men rejected under current standards of the Armed Forces, but who are regarded as qualified for service in an emergency.

Physicians, dentists, and closely allied specialists are liable for service under the same categories as registrants in general. The President also has authority to order these persons to active duty involuntarily from the Reserve. The law also authorizes the Secretary of Defense to draft persons by profession. Many of these persons apply for reserve commissions and then give two years of active duty as is necessary. Only when too few people in these special fields obtain commissions, does the Secretary of Defense make a call.

The Selective Service System has since 1948 inducted well over 3,000,000 persons, of which all but a small percentage were for the Army.

The priority of draftable categories, established by executive order, requires local boards to draft all men in each of the following categories before proceeding to the next, in this order:

1. Delinquents (or draft dodgers) 19 years of age and older in the order of dates of birth, oldest first.

2. Volunteers under age 26 in the order of their volunteering.

3. Non-volunteers, unmarried, between the ages of 19 to 26.

3a. Non-volunteers, married, non-fathers, between the ages of 19 and 26.

4. Non-volunteers, married men 19 to 26 who have a child or children with whom they maintain a home, oldest first.

5. Non-volunteers, men over 26, whose liability was extended because of previous deferments, oldest first.

6. Non-volunteers, 18 years and 6 months of age to 19 years, oldest first.

## Classifications

The registrant is placed by the local board in one of the following classes.

Class I-A: Avaliable for military service.

Class I-A-O: Conscientious objector available for non-combatant military service only.

Class I-C: Member of the Armed Forces of the United States, the Coast and Geodetic Survey, or the Public Health Service.

Class I-D: Member of reserve component or student taking military training.

Class I-O: Conscientious objector available for civilian work contributing to the maintenance of the national health, safety, or interest.

Class I-S: Student deferred by law until graduation from high school or attainment of age of 20, or until end of his academic year at a college or university.

Class I-W: Conscientious objector performing civilian work contributing to the maintenance of the national health, safety, or interest, or who has completed such work.

Class I-Y: Registrant qualified for military service only in time of war or national emergency.

Class II-A: Registrant deferred because of civilian occupation (except agriculture and activity in study).

Class II-C: Registrant deferred because of agricultural occupation.

Class II-S: Registrant deferred because of activity in study.

Class III-A: Registrant with a child or children; and registrant deferred by reason of extreme hardship to dependents.

Class IV-A: Registrant who has completed service; sole surviving son.

Class IV-B: Officials deferred by law.

Class IV-C: Aliens.

Class IV-D: Ministers of religion or divinity students.

Class IV-F: Registrant not qualified for any military service.

Class V-A: Registrant over the age of liability for military service.

In 1964, as this book was being completed, President Johnson ordered that all persons subject to draft shall be examined at age 18, in the expectation that many of the physical defects discovered shall be corrected, so that many persons rejected shall become available later.

## STATUS OF WOMEN IN THE CHURCHES

The employment of women by local churches and church agencies is much affected by the general opinion of men and women with respect to the status and role of women in the churches.

Just as in society as a whole, women are fully recognized here and there in church life, but they are also in other ways still limited in their opportunities for participation. And this in spite of the fact that the latest federal Census of Religious Bodies found that among members of local churches there were five women for every four men.

"The tradition that 'women should keep silence in the churches' is still strong in some denominations—though, almost certainly, far less than a generation ago," Inez M. Cavert reported in *Women in American Church Life,* a study completed in 1948. The study was made under the sponsorship of the Federal Council of Churches at the request of the World Council of Churches.

33

A sample of church women in 21 denominations, including many of the larger bodies, was asked to respond to an opinion scale that included the following:

1. Running the church is a man's job.

2. Women may serve on the less important boards but not on the most important.

3. Exceptionally able women should have the opportunity to serve on any board for which they are fitted.

4. All boards should include some women.

In most of the 21 bodies only very small proportions of the sample of women gave assent to (1) "running the church is a man's job." However, in four large bodies over 16 per cent of the church women expressed this opinion.

Biblical references, that is, the writings of Paul in his epistles, and "tradition" are the main explanations of the persistence of the feeling that "women should keep silence" and that "running the church is a man's job." This was the situation in the U.S., even though the women missionaries sent out by the churches of the U.S. had often worked for the emancipation of women in the countries of the younger churches. Again, there is much opinion that the teachings of Christ have been influential in winning for women a new place in the world.

Paul's dogmatic statement in I Timothy was: "I suffer not a woman to teach." It is interpreted by some as his reaction to a practice in the early church allowing women to exercise this function, and his view of a situation in which recent converts were unfitted for this task. There were obviously few offices in the first churches of the apostolic era. There are writers who insist that from the first women held offices. Also, as recorded in Romans, Phoebe was a deaconess. (See Deaconesses.) But Paul, a Roman citizen, as well as a figure formerly prominent in Judaism, was evidently anxious to maintain the ancestral traditions of good order in ancient societies. He taught the traditional inferiority of women but seemed ready to allow the use of their zeal and ability in Christian work. But the racial, social, and sex practices of the ancient world no longer exist; women are not now looked upon as inferior beings, in the opinion of those who oppose the attention still being given to Paul's writings.

One response to discrimination against women has been the organization of separate women's organizations, ranging from those in the local churches to national denominational organizations, and a large interdenominational agency, United Church Women, which recently celebrated its 20th anniversary. From days of a century ago some women have insisted on working interdenominationally for missions and other interests. And in the local churches the old term "ladies aid" is disappearing, as women seek autonomy or full participation in parish life.

Another development has been the slow recognition by the churches that a higher proportion of women are being fully employed in industry and commerce than in previous decades. The women who work cannot attend the meetings of the Women's Society on Thursday afternoons nor the somewhat leisurely luncheons that precede them. One solution to this problem has been to have separate organizations for employed women; another has been to have women's organizations meet at a time convenient to employed women. 1263130

A current issue is whether women should be appointed or elected to policy-making boards in the same proportion as women are found in the memberships of the churches—at least 50 per cent. Apparently, in a few boards of a few denominations, recognition is being given to this as a principle and it is being implemented.

Women are being employed in considerable numbers for full-time service as:

1. Directors of religious education or Christian education. Some of these are designated as ministers of Christian education. In this profession there is, however, the familiar complaint of low status. (See Director of Religious Education.)

2. As pastors of rural churches in those denominations that ordain women. (See Ordained Women.) Although not welcomed to these churches the same way men are, these pastors often find that prejudice against them disappears when there is devoted service.

3. As teachers in church-related schools and colleges. (See Teaching.)

4. As administrators and in many other vocations of church-related institutions in the fields of health and social welfare. (See Social Workers.)

5. As workers with various skills in the migrant ministry. (See Mobile Ministry to Migrating Farm Workers.)

6. As secretaries and stenographers. (See Office Positions.)

7. In various other vocations herein described, including librarians, journalists, workers in student centers, nurses, X-ray and other medical technicians, weekday religious teachers, etc.

8. As foreign missionaries in the many specialisms now recognized or required for these various service. (See Missions Overseas.)

9. As deaconesses in a few bodies. (See Deaconesses.)

Other information on the status of women may be had from the national lay organizations of denominations; and from United Church Women, National Council of Churches, 475 Riverside Drive, New York, N.Y. 10027.

## THE WIVES OF MINISTERS

It has often been assumed in the Protestant churches, from colonial days on, that the minister's wife should be an unpaid servant of the congregation. She was expected to be teacher or officer in the church school, a member or officer in the Women's Society, interested in the young people's organization even though she might not attend, to be on duty and be informed of church affairs in the absence of her husband, to call on members with him, to attend church services regularly, and often to be at her husband's side. Today, some ministers' wives work for pay five days a week in order to give the children a college education, or for other economic reasons. The more urban the community, the less the minister's wife is expected to be an unpaid servant of the church.

There are other aspects of the life and work of the minister's wife that make her role probably more important to the career of

36

her husband than in any other occupation. It is essential that the minister's wife be genuinely—not perfunctorily—interested in the work of the church and of her husband. It is essential that she participate willingly in some of the activities of the congregation and of her husband. She may at times become an informal counselor of people, provided she does not become so deeply involved as to appear to take sides in the inevitable controversies. She may advise young people with regard to vocations, and may thus, it is hoped, use this and related books.

The minister's wife has most unusual opportunities to love, and share in the lives of people in the parish, and thus to receive their love in a usual way. If she is a woman of wisdom, she will know when to serve and when to say "No." Even the saying of "No" with charity may win for her the affection of large numbers of people. This is more than a diplomatic process; it is an intangible that is a characteristic of many personalities.

For the working wife, whose name may soon be legion, there is even more of a problem if she is a minister's wife. Work is considered necessary so that Johnny may stay in college, or may go to college. But a working wife of a parish minister disrupts the historic pattern of congregational life. Thus the working wife may be blamed or praised in a congregation, even though now theoretically "her life is her own." She is still expected to show interest in the life and work of the congregation, and of her husband. This has to be on a selective basis or, it may result of moving the meeting of the women's society from Thursday afternoon when working women cannot attend, to another hour that is convenient.

The minister's wife has opportunities to have an educational role. She may have access to publications of the church at large beyond that of many of the members. Thus she may review books or pamphlets or call attention to them. Actually there are many ways whereby she may improve religious knowledge and literacy, particularly of the women of the congregation.

The minister's wife has the opportunity to be a leader in social action and the related educational activities. With knowledge of movements and causes, she can present them to the congregation or parts of it. This may be a function that no one else will perform if the minister's wife does not.

Finally, it is in the very personal and intangible social role of the minister's wife that she contributes to the church and her husband, and often determines the fate of the latter's career. Such personal traits as openness, genuine friendliness, broad concerns, deep sympathy, love of people, a willingness to share, an authentic cooperative attitude—all these are mentioned as assets of the minister's wife.

# II
# Descriptions of Vocations

## ACCOUNTANTS

Accounting is a large field of employment, particularly for men, who hold 90 per cent of the jobs in this field. Many denominational offices, church-related colleges, hospitals, and social-welfare institutions employ accountants. Of all accountants, about 17 per cent become C.P.A.'s (Certified Public Accountants). They have passed special examinations and met requirements for education and experience, as determined by state boards. The majority of accountants in church employment work for relatively large organizations with offices in metropolitan areas.

Accountants compile and analyze financial records and prepare the necessary auxiliary reports. The latter include profit-and-loss statements, balance sheets, studies of costs, and reports for tax purposes.

*Private* accountants handle the financial records and make the necessary reports of organizations which employ them on a salary basis.

*Public* accountants are independent; they work on a fee basis for any organization wishing their services. Public accountants usually specialize in auditing, which consists of careful review of financial reports and records on which they are based, and then giving opinions as to the reliability of the reports. They may also give expert advice on tax matters or, especially in the case of religious organizations, on tax exemption.

Accountants in any type of employment may become specialists in systems and procedures of keeping records, making reports, budgeting, cost accounting and control, auditing, or taxation problems.

PERSONAL QUALIFICATIONS. Obviously, interest in handling numerical data and in reporting and presenting it, are primary essentials in this profession. Patience, accuracy, and thoroughness are also necessary. Clarity of expression when making data public is a great asset. An accountant must also know how to confer and cooperate with officials of church agencies, their volunteers, and at times with government officials. For *general* personal qualifications expected by religious and church-related agencies, see Office Positions.

EDUCATION AND TRAINING. A number of educational institutions offer training in accounting: colleges and universities, junior colleges, private business schools, private accounting schools, and correspondence schools. One may become an established accountant from any of these. A Bachelor's degree with a major in accounting is valuable, especially because it is required in some positions. A Master's degree is a still greater asset.

Some colleges offer their students practical training programs whereby they may acquire first-hand experience, by cooperation with either accounting or other organizations.

More than half the states restrict the title of "public accountant" to those who are licensed and registered, with the standards varying from state to state.

All states require that the title of "Certified Public Accountant" be given only to those who hold a certificate issued after examination by the state board of accounting. Usually two years of practical experience is also necessary before a certificate is issued. All states use a standard examination for the certificate that is furnished by the American Institute of Public Accountants.

Persons without experience are generally assigned responsibility for elementary or routine work, and may be regarded as "juniors" for two or three years. They then usually advance to semi-senior positions, and senior positions, in large offices or accounting organizations.

Some accountants are required to travel to regional or branch offices.

OTHER INFORMATION. The opportunities for women are reported to be expanding although tradition makes accounting firms reluctant to employ them. Women with college training have better opportunities to enter the field than those without.

For general information on accounting as a career write to The American Accounting Association, School of Commerce, Madison, Wis. 53706. For associations in public accounting and in the specialized fields, see the list in *Occupational Outlook Handbook*, 1963-64 edition, published by the U.S. Department of Labor, Washington, D.C. 20210.

# ADVERTISING WORKERS

People who plan and prepare advertisements for various media, those who sell space or radio time, and others in related jobs, are called advertising workers. In religious organizations they are employed full-time mainly by periodicals with relatively large circulations, and by the larger church-related publishers, colleges, and social-welfare institutions. In many of the smaller organizations part-time work may be available, or advertising work may be combined with other duties.

Advertising workers include copywriters, artists who prepare illustrations, layout specialists who arrange copy and illustrations, sales people, and their supervisors and executives. In small offices, and at times in large organizations that have small advertising offices, one person may have to do everything; or the special jobs may be shared by two or three persons.

PERSONAL QUALIFICATIONS. One essential in advertising work is an absorbing interest in language, written and spoken. Others are a liking for solving problems; constant interest in people, ideas, and

41

programs of religious organizations; tact and ability to take criticism (fair or unfair). For *general* personal qualifications see Office Positions.

Beginners, particularly women, may at times start as stenographers and secretaries, and then shift to advertising work if they demonstrate talent and ability. Others begin as "junior" copywriters or sales people. Most beginners must seek jobs directly with employers rather than through agencies.

EDUCATION AND TRAINING. Employers of advertising workers increasingly prefer college graduates who have had liberal arts curricula or a major in journalism or business administration.

Volunteer work on high-school or college papers is often helpful. Young people can acquire experience in writing advertising copy or in selling space in these papers. Summer jobs in selling and interviewing are sometimes available. Many people shift to advertising work from other occupations, and some successful advertising workers have had no special training and no college courses.

OTHER INFORMATION. For more information on advertising work as a career write to:

Advertising Federation of America, 655 Madison Ave., New York, N.Y. 10021.

American Association of Advertising Agencies, 200 Park Ave., New York, N.Y. 10017.

## BOOKSTORE MANAGERS

Church publishing houses operate a number of bookstores that need managers. Their general duties are to study markets and to select and purchase the necessary titles and related materials. The same general personal qualifications summarized below under Business Administrators or Managers apply to this vocation. In addition, the educational background recommended and the duties to be performed are quite similar to those of a business administrator.

However, bookstore managers also need a good knowledge of the "book trade." Religious bookstores tend to handle so-called "secular" titles, as well as those specifically labeled religious. The rise of the paperbound books has brought with it new opportunities and problems.

Bookstore managers should be familiar with religious periodicals, not for their sale in a store, but to note book reviews and to spot books receiving wide public discussion.

During recent years sales of religious books, measured in terms both numbers sold and dollar volume, have been increasing. Not all of this business is handled by religious bookstores, but many of them have large numbers of steady purchasers.

Bookstore managers also need to be aware of titles in religious education for sale to Sunday-school teachers, and of books that may appeal to lay people as well as to ministers. Many religious books are purchased only by ministers, but religious books in special fields, such as those written for children, seem to be increasingly important.

Young persons can secure positions as clerks in bookstores, a job which may lead later to management for those qualified.

## BUSINESS ADMINISTRATORS OR MANAGERS

Business administrators or managers are employed in several hundred large local churches, large denominational boards and agencies, and large interdenominational organizations. This vocation is a relatively recent one in the churches, and is probably a direct result of "bigness" in religion. In local churches, a business manager or administrator is usually employed when the financial resources become available, when the staff of professional workers is large and diversified, or when business management duties overwhelm one or more of the ministers on the staff. Appointment of a church administrator in a parish adds to the personal resources of a staff, facilitates systematic handling of business aspects, and aids the staff in serving the members. In church boards and the larger interdenominational organizations, a business administrator is usually employed when the staff becomes specialized, and the function cannot, or should not, be handled by one with other duties.

PERSONAL QUALIFICATIONS. The business manager or administrator is called upon to cooperate with other staff members and to arrange efficient administration, with such functions as may be assigned by agreement (see "What Do They Do?" below). The business manager is a "representative" of the church to the public, whether he is so designated or not. He is also the servant of the members or trustees and comes frequently into contact with them. Especially is he called upon for effective cooperation with the officers of the various organizations; in addition, he also helps these officers in their relationship with other agencies.

The church administrator must be a patient diplomat. He may have to explain why the Lincoln Room cannot be used by the men's club on a certain night. Resolving the inevitable small conflicts between the various groups in the church is part of his job. Changing minds and plans constantly need his tactful attention. Diplomacy is especially vital in the relation between the church and other community organizations who may wish, for example, to hold meetings in the church or to cooperate with the church in some endeavor. The church administrator is generally responsible for handling these delicate relationships.

A competent administrator will have to watch his working hours more carefully than if he held a nine-to-five job five days a week. Duties can be arduous in church work—the church is generally open seven days a week and many church events take place in the evening.

What has been said above applies particularly to business administration of a parish, but is pertinent to business duties in church-related national organizations.

EDUCATION AND TRAINING. For people planning a career in business management, a Bachelor of Science degree with a major in business administration, now offered by many church-related and other colleges, is recommended as a minimum. Graduate study at a school of business of a large university is also highly recommended for proper training.

Knowledge of current church programs, local and national, is always valuable. Some of this can be secured in undergraduate and graduate study. It can also be acquired by attendance at certain of the numerous church conferences, held throughout the nation.

Some theological seminaries give instruction in business management, intended mainly for ministerial students who will have business duties when they enter the pastorate.

Independent study and reading, summer schools and evening courses, provide additional resources.

Knowledge of economics, mathematics, religion, psychology, or philosophy is recommended by some liberal arts colleges for courses leading to a Bachelor's degree in business administration.

WHAT DO THEY DO? Since business administration is a relatively new vocation in the churches, the functions are probably less standardized than those of the older vocations. In local churches, the functions are usually determined by officers of the congregation, including the trustees and the senior ministers.

Among the better-known functions are the following:

Responsibility for administration of the building or buildings. In a large parish, or in a religious organization that owns or operates its own buildings, this can involve many things. Supervision of insurance coverage may be one item. A church naturally carries fire insurance, and often insurance for public liability. Responsibility for everything related to heating, lighting, and relations with the municipality for such utilities as water, sewerage, and sidewalks may be part of the administrator's job. He may also have to handle tax matters on buildings not used exclusively for worship, on admissions charged for events, on liability, if any, for sales taxes.

Social security for lay employees, and private pension plans for employees, may require the business administrator's attention.

Engagement of personnel for maintenance of buildings will probably be handled by the business manager.

Other important matters may include:

Scheduling of meeting places for church organizations and others wishing to use the buildings. This may include determining charges for services to non-parish organizations.

Supervision of caterers, or operators of kitchens, for the numerous occasions when people meet in church at a luncheon, or supper.

Supervision of the purchase of all supplies, including printing.

Supervision or handling of office procedures and records involving the business functions of a parish.

Supervision of volunteers that assist in performing business services, such as giving time at information desks on Sundays or other days.

Supervision of cleaning and laundry operations.

In short, the functions may include everything directly concerned with the smooth operation of an institution.

OTHER INFORMATION. There is a National Association of Church Business Administrators (formerly National Association of Church Managers) with voluntary or unpaid officers, with an office at this writing at Boston Avenue Methodist Church, Tulsa, Okla.

## COMMERCIAL ARTISTS

Commercial artists are employed by religious publishing houses, other boards and agencies that bring out printed matter or visual-aid materials, and interdenominational agencies.

Illustrations designed to attract readers or users and to stimulate interest in a product or service are found in religious magazines, books, and other publications and materials. The drawings in them are prepared by commercial artists.

This commercial art includes various skills. Some artists, for example, concentrate on layout and design of a finished advertisement. While this seems routine, it is an essential part of the total process. The majority of commercial artists—including those employed full or part time by religious organizations—do the entire job of illustration or advertisement from drawing board to proper layout.

Most commercial artists employed by religious organizations are in offices in the larger cities. Many women find opportunities in this field.

46

PERSONAL QUALIFICATIONS. Interest and ability in art are the elementary essentials. Training in the techniques is also necessary. Skill in draftsmanship, creative imagination, and artistic judgment are other requirements. An artist employed by a religious organization should have a deep interest in the rich heritage of religious art, much of which was created for the purpose of instructing people in religion. The artist of today may or may not make practical use of the religious art of the past, but it is an asset to be familiar with it. For general personal qualifications see Office Positions.

EDUCATION AND TRAINING. Two types of study are recommended for a career in commercial art. First, thorough education in the fine arts—painting, sculpture, architecture—as well as the study of other liberal arts courses. Second, by specialized courses in commercial and applied art. Such instruction is offered in art schools or institutes that emphasize this aspect of art study.

Entrance into an art school usually requires a high-school diploma, but occasionally an art school may accept a student who has submitted satisfactory examples of his work. The course of study, which may include some general academic work, is usually for two or three years. A certificate is awarded on completion of the work. However, a growing number of art schools, notably those connected with universities, require four or more years of study and give the Bachelor of Arts degree on satisfactory completion of the work. The degree is usually that of Bachelor in Fine Arts (B.F.A.). For this degree, instruction in liberal arts subjects such as English and history are given in addition to that in the specific art subjects.

It is possible to secure a limited training in commercial art in some vocational high schools and by learning on the job.

WHAT DO THEY DO? As said above, most commercial artists spend all their time on the drawing board—sketching, lettering, retouching photographic prints, preparing charts or maps, cartooning, or still other assignments. If the office is relatively large, there is division of labor, and there are employees who concentrate on layout, or planning the selection and arrangement of illustrations and lettering, determining colors, etc. Some specialize in lettering or the making of sketches and drawings.

Employment by religious organizations may be on a part-time basis, or by contract for a certain job of work.

In a small office, even a beginner may spend all his time on the drawing board; in larger offices, beginners are given the more routine or elementary assignments.

Experienced personnel may become art directors or designers, although there are as yet relatively few such positions in religious agencies. Art directors may also purchase the work of independent or free lance artists.

OTHER INFORMATION. For information on art training and employment, write to the National Society of Art Directors, 115 East 40th St., New York, N.Y. 10016. A list of the special schools in art and design is published by the National Association of Schools of Art, 50 Astor Place, New York, N.Y. 10003.

## COMMUNITY CENTER WORKERS

A number of denominations encourage the organization of community centers, or neighborhood houses, or settlements. First established in cities, they are now being formed, because of need, in small towns and rural areas. These centers engage in many services to individuals and families in the areas. The services vary as greatly as the numbers of such centers. The central purposes are everywhere the same, however: to work with people, to strengthen family life, to improve living conditions in neighborhoods—"all in the spirit of Christ."

Community centers are supported by local, district, or national board funds, depending upon the situation. National support is often given in the early years of an organization. These centers are administered by local churches or by special boards or committees set up by church women and others, often in cooperation with interested lay and professional people from the community. The committees or boards are asked to aid the employed staff to develop interest in, and support for, the program, to find out what are the critical community needs, to formulate policies, to plan programs of work.

Some centers concentrate on developing cooperation among groups and members of different races. Others try to bridge the gaps between economic or cultural groups. All demonstrate the love for people which has been the prime concern in home missions work of religious bodies. Thousands of people find new purpose and meaning in daily life as they take part in these programs.

PERSONAL QUALIFICATIONS. Paid directors and other workers on the staffs, "who have a sincere and genuine love for people and who are eager to help them develop their minds and personalities," are needed from time to time, says one denominational agency. "Trained men and women are needed who can transform the techniques of successful social work into a vibrant and personal way of life. Young people are needed who are challenged by the opportunity in day-to-day informal relationships, to build Christian character, and to develop the spiritual potential within the people whom they are serving."

Most of the men and women employed in these centers are not ordained. An interest in the problems of minority groups, of the neglected and handicapped, of low-income families is essential. This must be accompanied by a commitment to help meet their needs by the highly personal methods that are vital in this kind of work.

EDUCATION AND TRAINING. A Bachelor's degree, including courses in sociology, psychology, recreation, arts and crafts, Bible, and religion, is recommended. Also valuable is such informal preparation that comes with leadership in camps of children or young people, vacation church schools, work camps, and summer employment for college students as is arranged from time to time by boards of home missions. Visits to such centers, conversations with staff members, personal reading of home missions literature all add to the education of workers in this field.

WHAT DO THEY DO? Among the many activities reported are these: The workers teach English; arrange clinics; teach in nursery schools and kindergartens; conduct day-care services for children;

organize clubs and interest groups for all ages; carry on vacation Bible schools; arrange family nights; lead recreation activities.

The work of some centers is determined by their special functions, for example, among delinquent youth, handicapped children, older people, families with long-standing "hard-core" problems. In these centers professionally trained case workers are employed. (See Social Workers.)

One person, reflecting on two years of work in a center, said her experiences were marked by the following satisfactions: The joy of belonging to the community center staff; playing with the tots in the day-care program; skating with teenagers; guiding the activities of children in clubs; associations with the senior citizens; opportunities for personal cultural enrichment and spiritual growth.

OTHER INFORMATION. Further information can be secured from denominational boards of home missions; administrators of church-related colleges; administrators of schools of social work. Boards of home missions often have knowledge of openings, and assemble personnel information from applicants. Decisions regarding employment are usually made by local boards or committees.

## COUNCILS OF CHURCHES

Councils of churches, whether they are international, national, state, or local, generally offer the same wide range of vocations as denominational agencies.

These councils emphasize cooperation among religious organizations, which in turn select representatives who formulate and control the policies and programs of the councils. Many office positions are available in the organization of the councils. People trained in religious education and with a background of some church experience are generally preferred. Other opportunities are for training in interdenominational institutes as either Sunday-school teachers or officers of the cooperating organizations. (See Religious Education.)

Councils also employ trained personnel in the various fields of social welfare, research, radio and TV programs. Also needed are business managers and chaplains, who serve in one or more hospitals or institutions.

The executives of councils of churches are, with exceptions, ordained ministers who have had experience in pastorates or in religious education or administration of mission programs in the U.S. or abroad. (See Ministries of Ordained Persons.) Probably the proportion of professionally trained lay persons among the executives is increasing.

Councils of churches probably employ women to the same extent as their constituent organizations. (See Ordained Women and Status of Women in the Churches.)

# DEACONESSES

Paul wrote in Romans 16 of "Phoebe, a deaconess of the church at Cenchreae, [a town near Corinth], that you may receive her in the Lord as befits the saints, and help her in whatever she may require of you, for she has been a helper of many and of myself as well." This is the ancient origin of the office or order of Christian deaconess. In the 3rd century of the Christian era, deaconesses served mainly by caring for the sick. In Constantinople in the 4th century there were 40 deaconesses. But after the year 600 there is little mention of deaconesses in the Roman Catholic Church.

The office of deaconess was fostered in Germany by the Lutheran Pastor Theodore Fliedner at Kaiserswerth Hospital and Training School, where deaconesses were trained as nurses, beginning in 1836. At this place Florence Nightingale, a wealthy English girl, became Probationer 134 and received the training that she used to nurse the British soldiers in the Crimea in 1854. Later Miss Nightingale founded a School of Nurses at St. Thomas' Hospital in London. In 1864 the officials of Kaiserswerth reported 1,592 deaconesses in 386 fields of work in Germany.

Employment of deaconesses in a formal way began in the Church of England in 1861, among English Methodists in 1888, and by Methodists in the U.S. in 1888. The Methodist Church has thus just celebrated 75 years of service by deaconesses.

51

In the U.S. today, deaconesses are formally engaged in full-time service mainly in the Methodist Church, Lutheran bodies, and the Protestant Episcopal Church. In many other denominations, deaconesses are appointed in local churches only for volunteer performance of relatively simple tasks.

Deaconesses of the Lutheran and Episcopal bodies wear a traditional or special garb, but Methodist deaconesses no longer do so.

PERSONAL QUALIFICATIONS. Personal religious faith is the basic qualification. One aspiring to be a deaconess must be convinced of the world's need of Christ; she must have an authentic desire to share and communicate her faith and to minister to the needs of others. Good health, emotional stability, resiliency, love of people, and adaptability are also important. Age limits are set by the religious bodies.

EDUCATIONAL REQUIREMENTS. A Bachelor's degree from an accredited college plus specialized training in Bible and religious education are being recommended. For those wishing to teach, a certificate from a state department of education is necessary in addition to a Bachelor of Arts degree. For nurses, certification as a Registered Nurse, as well as the Bachelor's degree is required.

FIELDS AND TYPES OF WORK FOR DEACONESSES. In local churches, deaconesses serve as pastor's assistants, directors of Christian education, church secretaries, music directors, parish visitors, directors of youth or children's work.

In settlements and community centers, deaconesses serve as head residents, directors of social activities, kindergarten teachers, juvenile court workers, social case workers, secretaries, bookkeepers.

In educational institutions, deaconesses occupy any position for which they have the education, training, and experience, including deans and other administrators, professors and instructors, counselors, secretaries, matrons, dieticians, etc.

In hospitals, they are needed as nurses, dieticians, social workers, bookkeepers, and leaders of worship.

In social agencies, they serve as case workers, house parents, counselors, secretaries, and superintendents.

In missions overseas they are found in the numerous positions, detailed in this book on "Missions Overseas."

In denominational and interdenominational agencies they work in secretarial, field work, and executive positions, depending on their education, training, and experience.

OTHER INFORMATION. The Woman's Division of Christian Service of the Methodist Church, 475 Riverside Drive, New York, N.Y. 10027, provides educational grants for specialized study to young women who have been accepted as deaconess candidates in that denomination.

Officials and agencies of the Lutheran Churches and of the Protestant Episcopal Church should be consulted by members of these bodies.

# DIETICIANS

Dieticians are people trained to plan and supervise the preparation of well-balanced meals for the purpose of maintenance of good health or of the recovery of health. They are employed in considerable numbers in church-related hospitals, social-welfare institutions, educational institutions, and in large offices of religious organizations that maintain cafeterias, lunchrooms, restaurants. About one-half of all dieticians of the nation are employed in hospitals.

Many young women choose this as a field of study because of their interest in foods and homemaking, and leave the profession because of marriage and family responsibilities. It is largely a woman's occupation, although men are entering it in small numbers for work in large establishments. Many home economists (which see) become dieticians.

PERSONAL QUALIFICATIONS. Among the personal requirements are physical stamina, the ability to cooperate with other people, the capacity to plan and organize, a real interest in science—especially chemistry and mathematics. For the general personal qualifications expected by religious agencies, see Nursing and Physicians.

53

EDUCATION AND TRAINING. The preparation generally recommended for professional work in this field is four years of college plus one year as a dietetic intern. Study in college should include foods and nutrition, management of institutions, bacteriology, chemistry, physiology, psychology, sociology, and economics.

Young persons who wish to test their interest in the field will do well to try to secure summer experience in a hospital department of dietetics.

A college graduate who meets specified academic requirements is elegible to enroll in one of the 59 dietetic internship programs approved by the American Dietetic Association. About 500 people are enrolled annually under these approved programs. Recently, there have been more internships available than were accepted. Numerous scholarships and loans are available for study in this field.

Internships are offered in three kinds of organizations: (1) Hospitals where food service and therapeutic dietetics are emphasized. (2) Business establishments which emphasize food service. (3) Nutrition clinics which emphasize nutrition education and therapeutic dietetics. Interns acquire on-the-job experience under supervision of a trained person. They also spend time in the classroom and work on special projects. Interns may in many instances be provided with room and board, and even laundry service, without cost. They also usually receive a monthly stipend.

The American Dietetic Association's requirement for membership is one year of internship, or three years of work experience if one year of the service has been supervised by a member of the Association.

Some junior colleges and vocational schools offer two or three years training in dietetics, but this is not considered as acceptable preparation for *professional* work. Usually those completing these programs may secure employment as supervisors of food service.

Graduate study may lead to the more responsible and advanced positions in research, teaching, or administration.

WHAT DO THEY DO? Professionally trained dieticians work in one of four major areas.

*Administrative dieticians,* who are the largest group, administer and direct food-service programs. The majority of these work in hospitals. Others work in social-welfare institutions, educational institutions, and large office organizations. The dieticians apply the principles of good nutrition to large-scale meal planning, cooking, and service. They also select and supervise food-service workers, administer budgets, and cooperate with others in the health services, e.g., physicians and nurses.

*Therapeutic dieticians* are usually employed in hospitals and clinics where they plan food service, including the special foods required by many patients. They instruct patients in the use of special diets, and confer with their families concerning the preparation of diets after the patients leave the hospital. There are dieticians who work only with the "out-patients" of hospital clinics, including expectant mothers and others with unusual needs.

*Teaching dieticians* are employed in hospitals, colleges, and universities where they conduct classes in a variety of subjects: dietetics, foods and nutrition, diet therapy, menu planning, budgeting, and institutional management. The persons taught include medical students, student nurses, dietetic interns, and many others. They give intensive supervision to the interns, conduct informal conferences, and offer in-service training to food-service workers.

*Research dieticians* are those with long experience and training who conduct experiments or other projects. These may be specifically on the dietetic needs of older people, or may be part of broader projects in which physicians and others participate.

OTHER INFORMATION. Information on approved colleges and dietetic internship programs, scholarships available, and opportunities in employment, may be had from the American Dietetic Association, 620 N. Michigan Ave., Chicago, Ill. 60611.

# HOME ECONOMISTS

Home economists are employed by church-related schools and colleges both for teaching and food services, and in social-welfare agencies where they may become dieticians (which see), or counselors for neglected and handicapped persons, particularly in the care of children and older people.

Home economists have a common interest in improving home products, services, and activities. Home economists are often closely related to other vocations. They may draw knowledge and skills from such disciplines as chemistry, physics, bacteriology, art, economics, psychology, and teaching.

Home economists gather their information from a variety of sources. They frequently make thorough tests of food and other products, and evaluate the tests of others in their profession. Some write regularly for magazines or occasionally for newspapers or other media. Experienced people may be called upon for radio and TV programs. Home economists are also often asked for advice in the planning of new buildings to be used as college dormitories.

Like many other vocations described in this book, home economics is becoming a specialized field. Thus home economists may specialize in foods, clothing and textiles, equipment used in homes, household management, child care, or family relations and development.

Historically, home economics has been one of the women's fields, but a growing number of men are entering it as teachers or counselors or in connection with the equipment of large institutions.

PERSONAL QUALIFICATIONS. Home economists generally have jobs that call for ability to work with people of varied standards of living and social and cultural backgrounds. They should have the capacity to inspire cooperation in other people. Poise, perspective, and a real interest in people are called for. For general personal qualifications see the notes herein under teachers of biology, economics, sociology, or on psychologists.

EDUCATION AND TRAINING. A Bachelor of Art's degree with a major in home economics is the minimum essential for a professional career in this field, and for many jobs a Master's degree is required.

Many colleges and universities offer a degree with a major in home economics. The curriculum usually includes courses in nutrition and foods, clothing and textiles, home management, family life, household equipment, child development, art and design. In addition liberal art subjects such as English, psychology, economics, chemistry, physiology are recommended. Those wishing to specialize in a branch of home economics should choose their field of concentration carefully. Those wishing to teach are also required to take courses in education, which will lead to their certification by state departments of education.

WHAT DO THEY DO? General or introductory courses in home economics are taught in many secondary schools, generally in those with girls as students. Newly graduated women with a B.A. and the necessary courses in education may qualify for teaching such courses.

In colleges, home economists often combine teaching and research, for which a Master's degree is usually required and for which a Ph.D. may be recommended. Home economists also supervise food services in educational institutions.

In social-welfare agencies, home economists are enlisted for advice and consultation on family budgets, proper diets, and clothing. They may give personal counseling to children and older people.

Experienced persons qualify for full-time research or for administration of research and teaching.

OTHER INFORMATION. Further information on home economics as a career and on graduate fellowships available may be had from American Home Economics Association, 1600 20th St., N.W., Washington, D.C. 20009. A list of educational institutions granting degrees in home economics is found in a bulletin, *Home Economics in Degree-Granting Institutions,* published by the U.S. Department of Health, Education and Welfare, Washington, D.C. 20201.

# HOUSEKEEPERS

Housekeepers have responsibility for the many kinds of duties involved in keeping various rooms, lobbies, halls, and equipment of hospitals, social welfare and educational institutions clean and attractive. In most institutions they supervise maids, housemen, and other employees. Many housekeepers are women. In the larger institutions they may have assistants for particular buildings or floors in dormitories.

PERSONAL QUALIFICATIONS. Many housekeepers are mature women, near the retirement age. Their maturity is regarded as an asset. Although they may deal with patients or students only indirectly or occasionally, the position requires mature judgment, high standards of personal conduct, an authentic interest in people, and the ability to cooperate with others. There is a "public-relations" aspect to housekeeping. Good housekeeping is as important as other aspects of the running of institutions.

EDUCATION AND TRAINING. No specific educational standards have been formulated for housekeepers. Training can be obtained in some universities which offer short courses in summer, in cooperation with the National Executive Housekeepers Association. These courses include housekeeping procedures, personnel management, interior decorating, and the use and care of fabrics and equipment.

At several colleges curricula in hotel administration include courses in housekeeping; the general study of hotel administration will be of value to persons becoming housekeepers in church-related hospitals, college dormitories, and social-welfare institutions.

WHAT DO THEY DO? In smaller institutions the housekeepers may not only supervise those who do cleaning, etc., but also do some maid's work themselves.

In the larger institutions the head housekeepers are mainly administrators. These must have charge of budgets, purchase supplies, have knowledge of fabrics and the way they should be cleaned, and at times, do, or arrange for, interior decoration. They train new employees, and supervise the staffs so that they work efficiently. They order repairs, take inventories, and make periodic reports on conditions of rooms and equipment. They confer from time with the general administrators of the institutions.

OTHER INFORMATION. Further information may be had from administrators of hospitals, colleges, boarding schools, and social-welfare institutions. Decisions regarding employment are made by the responsible officers of these organizations.

General information is also available from National Executive Housekeepers Association, Kettering Memorial Hospital, 3535 Southern Blvd., Kettering, Ohio.

# JOURNALISTS

Persons with training or experience in journalism are employed on staffs of religious periodicals, and of public-relations offices of religious organizations. Boards of missions, home and foreign, also employ a considerable number of people whose main duty is writing. Boards of religious education of the Protestant churches publish extensive curricular materials that are used in the denominational Sunday schools. During the past generation there has been an expansion of the staffs of public relations (which see), also called communication, information, publicity, interpretation. Thus for persons with the proper training here are expanding fields. Many women have opportunities in these vocations.

PERSONAL QUALIFICATIONS. Writing ability and interest in the processes of writing and publishing are prerequisites. However, the personality of a writer determines his style more significantly than technical training, no matter how proficient that may be. There are many opportunities to test writing ability and interest, in high school, indeed, even in the lower grades. School publications thus enable one to experiment. Other characteristics frequently mentioned as helpful are a good memory, initiative, resourcefulness, persistence, and an instinct for what interests or will attract potential consumers. Skill in typing is a good part of preparation, because many writers have to do their own typing. For some jobs a knowledge of photography is essential, because photographs are increasingly used in religious journalism and related fields.

EDUCATION AND TRAINING. Some people with real native ability become reporters or writers of consequence with little or no education beyond high school. Increasingly, however, employers will only consider persons with a college education, or with a graduate degree in journalism. In college one should concentrate on courses in English, also, if available, specialized courses in writing. Other valuable subjects are history, psychology, economics, political science, sociology. Some 150 colleges offer courses of study that lead to the Bachelor's degree in journalism. This kind of specializing is highly approved in many circles, while in others a well-rounded curriculum in liberal arts is thought just as desirable.

The special courses leading to a Bachelor's degree in journalism are generally taken in the third and fourth year of college—courses such as reporting, copy-reading, editing, feature writing, the history of journalism. A number of colleges also offer a Master's degree in journalism, but the number offering Doctor's degrees is very small.

FOR BEGINNERS IN RELIGIOUS JOURNALISM. Frequently young people just out of college are offered positions as editorial assistants or as writers in the more elementary tasks of a religious publication or board. These tasks may include attending conferences, taking notes on speeches, and then writing simple accounts for early publication. As editorial assistants, they may be given such tasks as copy-editing and proofreading, or later, the reviewing of books and pamphlets. They may be asked to do more difficult assignments, such as writing important articles that carry a by-line. Promotion to assistant or associate editor or to head of a special department may follow.

Churches have become increasingly aware of the value of "mass communication." They are striving to use the varied means offered by these media. Thus journalists are being called upon in large numbers to reach more people and promote more programs by means of mass media.

TYPES OF EMPLOYMENT. Among the numerous fields open to journalists, in which the Protestant churches employ persons, are the following.

Religious periodicals. Probably the most numerous opportunities offered to young journalists are those on the staffs of religious periodicals of which there are many. Most of them are small enterprises maintained by a few devoted souls. The small periodicals offer full-time employment only to small numbers of people. These periodicals also frequently do not pay contributors for articles. Larger periodicals offer employment to beginners and also provide for division of labor on their staffs. The positions vary from elementary reporting of conferences and events to conducting book-review departments that must report on serious and erudite works in philosophy and theology. Full-time copyreaders and proofreaders are also employed by the larger periodicals. The Sunday-school publications require people with writing skill and interest in religious education.

Most religious periodicals are subsidized in one way or another. The denominational periodicals survive by grants from board treasuries and also by the practice of many local churches of paying for a subscription to a periodical for all members who contribute to the local church budget.

Radio, TV. Journalists sometimes transfer to writing for radio or TV from other fields; recently, writers have been able to start careers in this rapidly developing field. This work is highly technical and specialized, and so far, there are few employed full time. Many church-related radio and TV programs are produced by drawing upon the unpaid services of clergymen, officers of church boards, and lay people. Special training is recommended, and is offered both by colleges and universities and in short-term institutes under church auspices. (See Radio and TV Broadcasters.)

OTHER INFORMATION. Salaries in religious journalism are not as standardized as, for example, those in the daily newspaper field where the American Newspaper Guild has negotiated minimum rates of pay based on experience and providing for annual increases. In religious journalism, starting salaries are undoubtedly lower in the smaller cities and on the journals with relatively small circulation than they are in the larger cities and with the larger periodicals or church boards.

Information on church-related colleges offering courses or degrees in journalism may be secured from the boards of education of the larger religious bodies, or from the institutions themselves.

For information on religious journalism in your denomination write to the editor of your denominational organ or periodical.

For general information on the Protestant religious press write to Associated Church Press, 875 N. Dearborn St., Chicago, Ill. 60610.

For information on public relations write to Religious Public Relations Council, 475 Riverside Drive, New York, N.Y. 10027.

## LIBRARIANS

A library is a center at which books, pamphlets, periodicals, manuscripts, clippings, reports (and sometimes recordings of music and copies of paintings) are gathered, housed, and made available to readers and users. Librarians are professionally trained persons who select, purchase, and maintain these materials, and also advise and assist those who need and use them. Librarians are employed in church-related colleges and secondary schools, theological seminaries, denominational boards and agencies, interdenominational organizations, etc.

In a small library, the librarian must usually perform a variety of tasks. In a large library, one librarian may perform only one function or may concentrate on one area of subject matter.

PERSONAL QUALIFICATIONS. The value of a library depends largely on the librarian's skill, knowledge, initiative, and personality. A deep interest in religion, plus a deep interest in the persons served, are great assets. The librarian with a good memory of the special interests of people will be able to be useful in ways that a person running a routine job cannot. Interest in, and ability to manage, certain extra-curricular activities, such as exhibits, are valuable also. Librarians who know the special needs of persons often give invaluable help to authors, research-workers, and teachers. The personal attitude of a librarian can stimulate or discourage reading.

EDUCATION AND TRAINING. In order to qualify as a professional librarian, a student must complete a course of study in a graduate library school. This calls for four years of study for a Bachelor's degree, plus a year or more of specialized study in library science for which a Master's degree is conferred. A Ph.D. is an aid for those who may wish to teach in a graduate library school, or those who combine teaching with a college library position.

In order to enter a graduate library school, one must meet the following requirements: A degree from an accredited four-year college or university; a good academic record as an undergraduate student; a reading knowledge of a foreign language. Many library schools prefer liberal arts undergraduate study, and may be especially interested in students with majors in literature, the arts, social science, physical or biological sciences. Skill in typing is a useful tool for a librarian.

Graduate study focuses attention on principles of librarianship, organization and administration of libraries, history and function of libraries in society. A student may also concentrate on one major area of librarianship, such as school or college libraries.

Most library schools confer a Master's degree in library science only after three full semesters of resident study, or two semesters plus a summer session.

Some students are permitted to attend library schools under co-operative work-study programs, thus combining their academic study with practical work experience in a library.

Librarians in schools under state inspection must be certified as librarians and as teachers, and are therefore required to take courses in education in addition to those in liberal arts and librarianship. In a few states, librarians in colleges and universities must be certified by the state department of education.

WHAT DO THEY DO? In the larger libraries, there are two principal kinds of work: services to readers, and technical duties. All who render services to readers, including reference librarians and children's librarians, work constantly and closely with the users. Specialists who process books, such as catalogue or order librarians, are often without contacts with those who use the library.

In the smaller school and college libraries, where there may be only one professional employee, the librarian must perform many services.

Librarians are often called upon to compile short reading lists on special subjects, or even lengthy and somewhat technical bibliographies. They may be asked to supply annotated lists of new acquisitions for posting or for publication. They may be asked to write articles on books, or book reviews. Ability to express oneself through the written or spoken word thus counts in a librarian's favor.

Some college librarians combine library work with teaching one or more classes, usually in the ways and means of using library facilities.

Part-time positions in libraries are increasingly available, and some of these are taken by students.

Experienced librarians are eligible for appointment as administrators of the staffs of large libraries.

OTHER INFORMATION. Decisions with respect to employment are made by the officers of church-related schools and colleges, and by those denominational boards and interdenominational agencies that maintain libraries.

On the profession in general, consult publications of The American Library Association, 50 East Huron St., Chicago, Ill. 60611.

# MEDICAL TECHNOLOGISTS

Most medical technologists are women and most are employed in hospitals, many in church-related hospitals.

Medical technologists work in laboratories where they have responsibility for making many chemical, microscopic, and bacteriological tests. The technologists generally work under the supervision of a physician, usually a pathologist, that is, one who specializes in the nature and causes of disease. The tests performed are for the detection, diagnosis, and treatment of disease. Some technologists work as assistants to physicians engaged in research in clinical sciences.

Among the well-known tests made by medical technologists are blood counts, urinalysis, and biological tests of the skin. They examine with microscopes samples of body fluid and tissue. These are "cultured" to discover the presence of micro-organisms (bacteria or fungus). They are then analyzed for chemical content or reaction. Medical technologists also determine types of blood, match blood samples, measure the time of blood coagulation and sedimentation, measure basal metabolism, analyze water, milk, other foods, and products for presence of bacteria.

Those who work in the laboratories of relatively small hospital laboratories must perform many different kinds of tests. In the larger hospitals, technicians may specialize even though they are prepared to perform various tests. Among the specialists are those in bacteriology, parasitology, biochemistry, virology, and cytology. Others assist researchers on new drugs. Experienced technicians are eligible for appointment as administrators or technical chiefs of a laboratory.

PERSONAL QUALIFICATIONS. The tests made by medical technicians are increasingly relied upon by physicians in diagnosis. Thus accuracy is of first importance. Accuracy, with speed, may provide life-saving information in some cases. Thus the medical technologist needs not only skill in performance, but also some theoretical knowledge of the field. It is even necessary, at times, to make a test in the course of an operation. Then, especially, will the technologist be called upon for both speed and accuracy. A medical technologist with the necessary knowledge to recognize the unusual and to make correct observations has become an invaluable worker in the health service field. Interest in science and in serving the sick are both desirable. For general personal qualifications emphasized by church-related institutions, see the notes under Nursing and Physicians.

EDUCATION AND TRAINING. There are 757 schools of medical technology approved by the Council on Medical Education and Hospitals of the American Medical Association. These are all in or affiliated with hospitals. Students must usually complete three years of college, study for 12 months or more additional in a school approved by the A.M.A. The academic requirements generally include chemistry, biological sciences, and mathematics. A certificate in blood-banking is awarded by the A.S.C.P. (American Society of Clinical Pathologists) to those who have completed its requirements and have had a year of training and experience in blood-banking. The A.S.C.P. also awards a certificate in chemistry and one in microbiology to those having a Bacherlor's degree with a major in chemistry or microbiology plus one year of laboratory experience in their respective fields.

The increasing complexity and specialization of medicine has resulted in ever rising standards of training in this field. Many hospital employers will consider only applicants with four years of study. Other hospitals and clinics will consider only persons with a college degree.

The cost of training, aside from maintenance, is relatively low. Most A.M.A. approved schools do not charge tuition, and most also pay stipends to students.

A few universities offer advanced courses for those who wish to teach or to engage in some highly specialized branch of the field.

A few states require licenses for medical technologists and other laboratory personnel.

OTHER INFORMATION. Information on opportunities for employment and on schools of medical technology approved by the American Medical Association may be obtained from:

Registry of Medical Technologists of the American Society of Clinical Pathologists, Box 44, Muncie, Ind.

American Society of Medical Technologists, Suite 25, Hermann Professional Building, Houston, Tex. 77025.

## MEDICAL X-RAY TECHNICIANS

A high proportion of all medical X-ray technicians are women, and many of these are employed in hospitals. Church-related hospitals also employ these technicians.

Medical X-ray technicians have a number of duties in connection with the use of X-ray equipment. Their duties fall into two categories: diagnostic and therapeutic.

Most X-ray technicians do diagnostic work—taking X-ray pictures of parts of the body in order to diagnose disease. In addition X-ray equipment is used to discover foreign matter in, injury to, or malformation of, parts of the body. Technicians must learn: to put patients into the required position; to protect the parts of the body not being X-rayed by means of a lead plate; to use devices to prevent a patient from moving; to arrange proper voltage, current, and exposure, and controls so that film of good quality is available for study and interpretation by a physician. They also at times assist physicians in fluoroscopy or other special kinds of X-ray work. They may prepare opaque materials to be swallowed by the patient so as to secure proper visibility of parts of the anatomy in the X-ray process. Fluoroscopy is done by physicians.

The other X-ray technicians do therapeutic X-ray work. These operate the equipment needed for treatment of some diseases, especially cancer and infections of tissue. After placing the patient in the proper position, the technicians operate equipment from an adjoining room, as ordered by a physician. The technicians also help the physicians known as radiologists in preparation for use of radium and other radioactive materials, including those involved in "atomic medicine."

There are technicians who do both diagnostic and therapeutic work, all under the supervision of a physician.

Technicians may also process film and keep records of services given to patients, although in large hospitals these duties are handled by an assistant. In some hospitals the X-ray technicians are called upon to operate other kinds of diagnostic equipment, for example, that used to test basal metabolism. Usually the technician is expected to examine equipment in order to keep it in order, and at times to make minor repairs.

While medical X-ray technicians work in pleasant and sanitary conditions, special care must be taken to protect them from exposure to the rays. They use various safety devices, including lead aprons, special gloves, and other shields. Technicians are required to have frequent blood counts, and to give special attention to their diet and securing fresh air and sunshine. Constant progress is being made in the entire protective process.

PERSONAL QUALIFICATIONS. A person in this field must surely be accurate, thorough, and precise. Because the technicians often have contacts with the injured and ill, they must be patient, sympathetic, and cheerful. They must exercise their responsibilities with neatness and dispatch. Since the job requires standing most of the working day, good health is necessary.

Varieties of skills in relation to the whole process are assets for advancement to teaching or supervision. For general personal qualifications see the notes under Nursing and Physicians.

EDUCATION AND TRAINING. There are many schools of X-ray technology, and they are located in all regions of the U.S. Most of these offer a training program of 24 months; although some have courses of 12 or 18 months. A few schools require 36 and even 48 months of resident study. A few grant a Bachelor's degree.

The programs of study with the highest standards are those of the 715 schools approved by the Council of Medical Education and Hospitals of the American Medical Association. These programs are conducted either by hospitals or by medical schools affiliated with hospitals.

Most approved schools require that applicants must be high-school graduates, while a few require one or two years of college work or graduation from an approved school of nursing. One school will only admit registered nurses. Generally, applicants between the ages of 18 and 30 are given preference.

The cost of training in approved hospital schools is relatively low, aside from expenses of maintenance. Most of these schools do not charge tuition, and most pay their students a stipend.

High-school study of physics, chemistry, biology, mathematics, and typing is desirable.

In the technical schools the curriculum usually includes anatomy, physiology, physics, radiation protection, darkroom chemistry, medical ethics, principles of radiographic exposure, film critique, radiographic positioning, equipment maintenance, and administration of a department.

The American Society of X-ray Technicians offers refresher courses annually to enable technicians to improve their skills and to acquire new knowledge in the field.

Training is offered in vocational and technical schools—other than that in approved hospital schools. However, persons wishing employment in hospitals will have the best opportunities for employment if they study in approved schools in hospitals or in medical schools related to hospitals.

OTHER INFORMATION. The Woman's Bureau, U.S. Department of Labor, Washington, D.C. 20210, publishes material on the outlook for women as medical X-ray technicians.

General information on the field and on approved schools may be had from:

The American Society of X-ray Technicians, 537 S. Main St., Fond du Lac, Wis.

The American Registry of Radiologic Technologists, 2600 Wayzata Boulevard, Minneapolis, Minn. 55405.

## MINISTRIES OF ORDAINED PERSONS

A GENERAL INTRODUCTION. There are many ministries for which ordained persons are needed in the Protestant churches and their boards and agencies, their interdenominational organizations, and church-related educational and social-welfare agencies.

About 3 per cent of the ordained Protestant ministers are women.

There is probably no profession in which the role of the wife is as important as in the career of the minister.

Most ministers still serve in local churches in which there is but one full-time employee—the minister himself. And there are ministers who also have other occupations.

Increasing numbers of congregations have a "multiple" professional ministry, with division of labor among the members of the staff, and with all the advantages and problems of cooperation among them. More and more local churches have two or more services on Sunday morning, a break with precedent that has come with the rise of numerous large congregations.

There are now various specialties for which ordained persons are engaged. There is a mobile ministry for migrating farm workers (in which both ordained and other persons are serving). There are ministries overseas. There are "university pastors." There are

69

ministers of Christian education and ministers of music. There are ministers who give full time or much time to counseling with individuals both within and outside of their congregations. There are several distinct types of chaplains.

There are many positions in church agencies which may be filled by either an ordained person or a professionally trained lay person.

All of these ministries are considered in a group of articles that follow this Introduction.

THE NEED FOR ORDAINED MINISTERS. Needs for ordained ministers vary from denomination to denomination. A few denominations have a relatively high proportion of pulpits vacant, but the vacancies are often in small congregations which find it difficult to assemble the financial means to support a professionally trained minister and his family. On the other hand, some pulpits of large and well-established local churches are vacant for many months because of the difficulty of finding experienced persons capable of carrying the varied and heavy duties that must be performed in administration of a staff and a large organization. There is need for ordained ministers who can serve well in declining populations as well as those who can handle the difficult tasks in mushrooming suburbs.

There is reported to be a general need of men and women willing to serve as associate or assistants in large churches. Often the associate or assistant has few opportunities to preach sermons, and this is considered a handicap. But systematic attention to the young peoples' organizations, involving little preaching, may be as important as formal preaching at the Sunday morning service.

There is need for persons willing to concentrate on the special problems of churches in the centers of large cities; and for those willing to serve widely scattered families away from centers of population.

There is need for ordained ministers who can concentrate on service to the rapidly rising college populations.

There is continuing need for ordained persons to serve in missions overseas.

DUTIES OF ORDAINED PERSONS. A young minister who alone is pastor of a local church is called upon to perform many functions —many more than most lay people realize. He is expected to lead or conduct worship services, including the preaching of sermons; preside at meetings of church committees or arrange for such meetings; administer the sacraments (among Protestants, baptism and the Lord's Supper); perform marriage ceremonies; conduct funerals; visit the sick and the well; counsel with individuals as time may permit; have general responsibility for religious education; enlist and train teachers in the Sunday school; prepare copy for the weekly church bulletin; send items to the local newspaper; cooperate with community organizations; express an interest in the public school; be the general supervisor of parish life and organization, including such matters not mentioned above as music, stewardship, home and foreign missions, world relief, social action. His work brings him into contact with physicians, including psychiatrists, lawyers, police, and social workers. He is thus in contact with people wherever they are. He is involved in the greatest joys and tragedies and problems of human beings. There is much evidence that people in trouble or need first consult a minister rather than any other professional persons. These are the functions of the pastor who is general practitioner, somewhat like the so-called family doctor. His functions are considered in more detail below.

The more specialized ministers, such as chaplains, university pastors, directors of religious education, are called on to perform fewer of these duties than is the single pastor of a local church. Likewise, when there is a multiple ministry there are usually divisions of labor.

WHAT KIND OF PEOPLE? "God does not call people into the ministry who do not have the capacity to fulfill it," reads a portion of a paper on the ordained ministry issued by one denomination. An experienced minister writes that the ministry "takes all there is of" a person, adding that the ministry needs "clear-minded, convinced, daring" young persons—not idealists interested only in social reform, or the dreamy, always pious person.

"Those who are absolutely, prayerfully committed to whatever portion of God's will they know thus far" have already experienced "a call," says John Oliver Nelson of Yale Divinity School. There is usually "no special heavenly vision," no "hearing a voice," he goes on. "For a man to be called of God does mean having a constant concern, recurring again and again, to make his life count in the Christian scheme of things."

Again, "thoroughly educated" men and women are needed. They should surely not be any less thoroughly educated than doctors or lawyers. Performance of the tasks of the ministry requires a disciplined mind, and continuous study. Rigorous intellectual training is as necessary as evangelical passion and compassion.

As for other personal qualifications, the following are often mentioned: interest in communication; ability to communicate; emotional stability; academic competence above average; sound physical health; a love of people; a willingness to learn and to grow; a deep sense of obedient service to God.

EDUCATIONAL REQUIREMENTS. These are generally a diploma from an accredited high school, plus four years of study leading to a Bachelor's degree from an accredited college and three years leading to a Bachelor of Divinity degree from a recognized theological seminary. In some instances "the educational equivalent" of a three-year course leading to the Bachelor of Divinity will be accepted.

For majors at college the American Association of Theological Schools recommends English, philosophy, or history—not religion —because courses in religion in colleges involve loss of other important pre-seminary studies. The statement on pre-seminary studies of the Association is here quoted in large part:

I. The Function of Pre-Seminary Studies

College courses prior to theological seminary should provide the cultural and intellectual foundations essential to an effective theological education. They should issue in at least three broad kinds of attainment.

1. The college work of a pre-seminary student should result in the ability to use certain tools of the educated man:

(a) The ability to write and speak English clearly and correctly. English composition should have this as a specific purpose, but this purpose should also be cultivated in all written work.

(b) The ability to think clearly. In some persons this ability is cultivated through courses in philosophy or specifically in logic. In others it is cultivated by the use of scientific method, or by dealing with critical problems in connection with literary and historical documents.

(c) The ability to read at least one foreign language and in some circumstances more than one.

2. The college work of a pre-seminary student should result in increased understanding of the world in which he lives:

(a) The world of men and ideas. This includes knowledge of English literature, philosophy, and psychology.

(b) The world of nature. This is provided by knowledge of the natural sciences, including laboratory work.

(c) The world of human affairs. This is aided by knowledge of history and the social sciences.

3. The college work of the pre-seminary student should result in a sense of achievement:

(a) The degree of his mastery of his field of study is more important than the credits and grades which he accumulates.

(b) The sense of achievement may be encouraged through academic concentration, or through 'honors' work, or through other plans for increasingly independent work with as much initiative on the student's part as he is able to use with profit.

## II. Subjects in Pre-Seminary Study

The following is regarded by the Association as a minimum list of fields with which it is desirable that a student should have acquaintance before beginning study in seminary. These fields of study are selected because of the probability that they will lead in the direction of such results as have been indicated.

It is desirable that the student's work in these fields of study should be evaluated on the basis of his mastery of these fields rather than in terms of semester hours or credits. That this recommendation may help the student faced with the practical problem of selecting courses, however, it is suggested that he take 30 semester courses or 90 semester hours of approximately three-fourths of his college work in the following specific areas:

English—literature, composition, speech and related studies. At least 6 semesters.

History—ancient, modern European, and American. At least 3 semesters.

Philosophy—orientation in history, content and method. At least 3 semesters.

Natural sciences—preferably physics, chemistry and biology. At least 2 semesters.

Social sciences—psychology, sociology, economics, political science and education. At least 6 semesters, including at least 1 semester of psychology.

Foreign languages—one or more of the following linguistic avenues to man's thought and tools of scholarly research: Latin, Greek, Hebrew, German, French. Students who anticipate postgraduate studies are urged to undertake these disciplines early in their training as opportunity offers. At least 4 semesters.

Religion—a thorough knowledge of the content of the Bible is indispensable, together with an introduction to the major religious traditions and theological problems in the context of the principal aspects of human culture outlined above. The preseminary student may well seek counsel of the seminary of his choice in order most profitably to use the resources of his college. At least 3 semesters.

Of the various possible areas of concentration, where areas of concentration are required, English, philosophy and history are regarded as the most desirable.


III. The Nature of This Recommendation

The Association wishes to point out two characteristics of the list of pre-seminary studies it is recommending:

First, this is a statement in minimum terms. We make no attempt to list all the work which it would be profitable for a student to do. It is thus possible to include many other elements in one's college courses, while still working in what the Association regards as the first essentials.

Second, the emphasis is on a 'liberal arts' program because, in the judgment of the Association, the essential foundations for a minister's later professional studies lie in a broad and comprehensive college education.

INFORMAL PREPARATION. Everyone considering the ministry should investigate the actual work of a minister or of several ministers. How does a minister spend his time? Of what significance, for example, is it that one minister calls at three hospitals every day—in addition to all his other duties? Ask your minister about his attitude toward his preparation and what he recommends.

Work diligently in a local church, participating in not one but several activities.

Study the needs of the world on your own, particularly the community in which you live, and consider how a minister may help to meet its needs.

Assess your own potentialities, your assets and weaknesses, and compare them with what are needed in the ministry. Usually one cannot do this alone. Counsel from within a church or a school will help.

"Seek guidance, human and divine, in making your decision," says an informed church official.

DISADVANTAGES. A minister is often a person actually alone, although surrounded by people, because many people are very formal and reserved when in the presence of a minister. Some say only the things they think he will like to hear, while others actually keep a minister at arm's length. Not everyone welcomes a pastoral call.

A minister's work is often irregular and very hard to organize. Most ministers work long hours and work hard most of those hours. Some ministers testify that they find it difficult to arrange for time for study, prayer, recreation, family life—even for reading and study of the Bible.

Although a minister is an employee, he often finds that it is he

75

who must discipline himself. Frequently he does not have a minister to turn to, although he is in need of one. This situation is changing, however, and some ministers do consult with other ministers. In some communities, a minister becomes known as a "pastor of ministers."

The minister's wife and family are frequently under public gaze and criticism. It is often hard for them to have normal privacy. (See The Wives of Ministers.)

HOW TO ENTER THE MINISTRY. The steps towards becoming a minister differ greatly within the denominations. Generally, an early informal contact with a minister is desirable for advice. In some churches, a student in college becomes an applicant seeking the ministry. This is usually recommended by the junior year in college, not earlier.

After graduation from seminary there is an examination before ordination by an ordaining body or person.

SALARIES OF MINISTERS. There are few national averages of cash salaries paid to ministers. Some of these national averages are meaningless because there are so many types of ministers, including part-time and temporary persons.

The ministry is known as one of the low-paid professions considering the amount of professional preparation required.

In 1956, in nine denominations a large sample of ministers reported average cash salary of $4,436. However, they estimated their total compensation at $5,827 (including cash, salary allowances, fees, perquisites, and estimates of the rental value of dwelling furnished). These denominations were the Methodist Church, Congregational Christian Churches, Presbyterian Church in the U.S.A.; United Lutheran; American Baptist; Church of the Brethren; Disciples of Christ; Evangelical and Reformed; Protestant Episcopal. These bodies probably paid higher salaries than most other bodies. However, the average figure of total compensation, $5,827, was in excess of the average *cash* salary paid to college teachers of that year. It was not a poverty figure.

It is often said that the salary of the minister is one of the last items to be considered in a local church when annual budgeting time rolls around, even in an affluent society. Many laymen do not know the salary of their minister, and do not seem to inquire. On the other hand there are other factors and forces at work: Some denominations recommended minimum salaries. Some state units of denominations are at work. And there are concerned lay people who express their opinions. Again there are those who volunteer to work in depressed communities or other difficult situations or even dangerous situations, without much reference to salary, because they are committed ministers who wish to witness in such areas and try to meet the needs of the people there.

## Ministers with Multiple Duties

Continuing a pattern of organization brought from the Protestants of Europe, the churches in the U.S. have in the past formed small congregations with the minister as the only employee, or the only professional employee. This pattern of numerous small congregations differs markedly, incidentally, from Roman Catholicism, which has emphasized large parishes, usually with several priests in charge.

This Protestant pattern is today usually observed in most of the numerous rural communities of the U.S., which still have a high proportion of the local churches of the nation. It is also found in numerous small city parishes. One factor that affects the situation is that in areas adjacent to theological seminaries, many students serve rural churches part-time, for pay, while carrying on their seminary studies. As a result the student gets some financial help, while the congregation receives a very limited pastoral service. An important part of the pattern, too, has been the practice to regard this minister's wife as an additional unpaid professional servant. This has been a sort of unwritten agreement. The practice is changing, more in urban than in rural communities. (See Wives of Ministers.)

This is the conventional picture of the ordained minister and his profession. Many people think of the ministry only in terms of the single professional employee with many duties—whereas one of the purposes of this book is to detail the many and varied kinds of work open to ordained and unordained persons.

The single professional employee is required to fulfill a number of functions, many of which only bear obliquely on his responsibility as a man of God. A minister cannot do everything and must divide his time, deciding which job to emphasize one week and which to ignore or neglect because of other priorities. A minister working alone is generally responsible for the following eight functions. It is easy to see that with a larger and larger congregation this minister could use some specialized help.

1. *Preacher.* In the public mind, a minister is primarily a preacher; indeed, in many parts of the U.S. he is still popularly called just that. Along with preaching are the other elements of worship—conduct of a liturgy in the liturgical churches or the arrangement of the order of worship where the form varies, administration of the sacraments (among Protestants these consist of baptism and the Lord's Supper), and the conduct of funerals, both of members and non-members.

2. *Pastor.* Thought of as the "priestly" function of the Protestant minister, this responsibility entails not only a perfunctory calling on, or visiting with, members and non-members of his congregation, but also systematic counseling for troubled or confused people, as well as dealing with difficulties within church groups. A minister working alone obviously does not have as much time for this aspect of his work, even if he feels it is extremely important. Some ministers, of course, feel it is unwise to practice too much counseling since he may be regarded as "taking sides" in controversies because he consults with one faction more than the other.

3. *Main supervisor* or administrator or executive officer of the parish or congregation. As a minister, he may not be so designated or so regarded or so recognized, but the simple fact is that he has this function. And the larger the congregation the more important the function. In these days, for example, much new building is going on. A lay committee may decide many things in relation to it—but who executes the decisions? Often the minister. The minis-

ter may supervise the record-keeping, the music program, the services of the part-time sexton, and the entire religious education program—see Religious Education, below. And, in addition, many ministers serve more than one congregation.

4. *Director of religious education.* Although the officers of the Sunday school are lay people, the minister must supervise other aspects of religious education. He may be asked to teach the men's or adult group—a good many Protestant adults go to Sunday school. Or, the minister's wife may be elected the superintendent of the school or may be asked to teach a class of girls.

5. *Public relations officer.* Again, as a minister, he is probably not so designated or recognized. But he is often "the writer" in the congregation, and it is he who is most often called upon for news of church and community affairs. The minister may try to train or enlist lay people for this task, and is apparently having increasing success.

6. *Money-raiser.* While lay people are assuming more and more responsibility for the task of raising money, the impetus and encouragement must come from the minister. He will undoubtedly be asked to mention the "cheerful giver" during one of his sermons just before the "every-member canvass."

7. *Chief contact* with community organizations. He is expected to support and be familiar with the programs of such diverse groups as the Visiting Nurse Association, the local Foreign Policy Association group, people promoting Human Rights Day or UNICEF, and the United Fund. Often he must support these worthy causes in sermons or at least in notes in the weekly bulletin.

8. *Building superintendent.* This admittedly is a function that is temporary, but new buildings are constantly being erected to house growing congregations and Sunday schools. While most of the work of the choice of architecture and actual construction is settled by lay committees, the minister must be sure the decision reached is a careful and wise one.

DECISIONS REGARDING EMPLOYMENT. Such decisions are usually made locally even when a national or state officer makes a recommendation.

## Senior Minister or Pastoral Director

More and more churches have what is called a multiple ministry. The chief reason for it is the increase in the average size of churches. In many instances, particularly in growing suburbs, the number of members is so large that employment of more than one minister becomes necessary. A connected development is an increasing tendency in Protestant Churches to hold two or more identical worship services on a Sunday morning—a trend surely opposed to the prevailing tradition of even a generation ago.

This multiple ministry demands or implies division of responsibility. The usual duties of associates and assistants are described below. Here will be indicated the main responsibilities of the pastoral director or the senior minister. He probably usually goes by the latter title, but the former is more indicative of his functions.

The senior minister must be more of an executive or at least to give more time to executive duties, than the general practitioner or the associate ministers. He is usually a person who had been a working minister before he became the head of a group or staff of professional persons.

PERSONAL QUALIFICATIONS. Because the multiple ministry is something relatively new, many ministers have not yet had experience with the system and have to learn to adjust as they perform their duties. As ministers, they may seem to have more status than non-ordained staff members with whom they work. Sometimes staff cooperation is not readily achieved. The personal responsibility of the senior minister is therefore great. Above all, he needs the talent, tact, and ability to elicit cooperation between himself and brother or brethren. Other duties include preaching the sermon at the principal Sunday morning service. The roles and priorities of other ministers in that and other services often become issues of first importance to them. The senior minister obviously must be an experienced man, both in pastoral service and in handling personalities.

EDUCATION AND TRAINING. The education and training generally required are the same as those of all ministers—except that any experience or personal traits that help a man to carry out executive duties will be useful. To repeat the usual ministerial requirements:

A Bachelor's degree from a liberal arts college. (See above the suggested pre-seminary studies recommended by the American Association of Theological Schools.)

Three years of seminary training.

In addition, a few ministers who are or who are to become pastoral directors may find it useful to study in graduate schools of business or in schools of public administration. There is as yet, no school of church administration, except that seminary teachers show increasing awareness of the need. Summer schools, workshops, and refresher courses offer opportunities to discuss the special roles of the senior minister.

WHAT DO SENIOR MINISTERS DO? First of all, congregations expect the senior minister with a staff to have the same knowledge and skills as a minister carrying out all church duties by himself. He is expected to know how to conduct all of the worship services, to counsel effectively, and in general to fulfill all the functions described in the discussion of the minister with multiple duties.

The most important task of the senior minister is to work out, by agreement or experiment, which functions his colleague or colleagues will perform, and which will be handled by him. Overlapping of duties is obviously unavoidable—attendance at the annual meeting of the men's brotherhood and of the women's society will be expected of all church ministers. On the other hand, separate and well-defined functions are filled by associate or assistant ministers. Supervising religious education, calling upon parish members, visiting the hospital to comfort the sick are examples of duties performed by one or more of the ministerial staff. Often the associates or assistants will work with young adults and youth and have special responsibilities for their meetings, conferences, and outings. How often shall the colleagues preach the sermon at the principal Sunday morning services? Generally, the senior minister makes this decision.

Critical in the smooth performance of a church organization is the executive function, involving not only agreements regarding division of duties among staff but also supervision of what may be called the business side of the church. This may include handling insurance in various forms, social security for staff, denominational provisions for retirement of staff, use of church building by other than church organizations, contacts among organizations in the church, and, if building operations are in process, cooperation with architect and contractor. Unfortunately, the minister may not have had any training or experience in business. Some seminaries are aware of this need, and are reportedly adding courses in business management to their curriculum. (Some large churches now employ full-time business managers. See Business Administrators or Managers.)

OTHER INFORMATION. Decisions about the appointment of senior ministers are made by the local congregation.

Further information may be had from denominational boards, theological seminaries, and the Department of the Ministry, National Council of Churches, 475 Riverside Drive, New York, N.Y. 10027.

## Associate Ministers

The ordained associate minister, man or woman, works in a church where there is at least one other minister, usually the senior professional officer. The increasing size of congregations and the consequent increase in duties has led to a greater demand for the added trained help that associates can provide.

The associate minister usually performs two duties. First, he takes over the functions of the senior minister in the latter's absence. Although the associate rarely preaches regularly, preaching is usually one of the functions he assumes when the senior minister is not present. It is interesting to note that the general lack of preaching opportunity is one of the greatest handicaps to the office of associate minister and accounts for high mobility among this group. Ordained ministers have been trained to preach and to have complete charge of a congregation. To perform substitute duties or to have less responsibility than they have been taught to assume may lead to dissatisfaction.

The second and more rewarding function of an associate is to take full charge of one or more of the many organizations found in a large church. For example, full-time service as the director of religious education (see Religious Education) or sole responsibility for young people's groups seems to lead to greater satisfaction than when this function must be combined with other services. An associate may spend all of his time on the organization of social events or he may organize men's work in the congregation. Thus, there are many opportunities for an associate to use his talents and initiative.

OTHER INFORMATION. It is the rule in many denominations that the senior minister may choose his associates. Therefore, the authorities of the local church usually act on appointments on the recommendation of the senior minister. Information about vacancies may be secured through the appointment officers of theological seminaries or from national, and particularly state, denominational officials. Salaries of associates are generally lower than those of senior ministers. Also, while there is not the same provision of housing for associates, there is increasing opinion that this provision should be made.

## Counseling Ministers

As already pointed out, all ministers do some counseling—if only because they cannot avoid giving some time to this function. Here we will describe ministers who devote all their time to counseling.

Counseling ministers are employed in relatively few churches, mostly because not many churches have the resources to make such service available. There is, however, a growing number of special counseling centers that are appearing in all parts of the nation. These provide employment for the talents and training of the minister who has taken special courses in counseling, whether at the seminary or graduate school. In addition, clinical training in mental hospitals is sometimes available.

PERSONAL QUALIFICATIONS. As in other specialized ministries, the general personal qualifications are the same as those of the ministry elsewhere—except that there are certain accents and emphases that are required. One must not only like and love people—one must have a real willingness to listen to people. A counseling minister will be exposed to all the insecurities and disturbances and, at times, the seemingly insoluble problems of people. He will be listening to people and encouraging them to understand their situations, but he will *not* be preaching a sermon. This is not to say that the counseling minister will not sometimes preach a sermon at a formal worship service. One famous clergyman says in his autobiography that his sermons were simply an aspect of his counseling, which was his major occupation.

EDUCATION AND TRAINING. The general requirements are a Bachelor's degree and three years of study at a seminary leading to the B.D. (Bachelor of Divinity). In undergraduate study emphases on psychology and social sciences generally are recommended. In seminary, specialized study of pastoral counseling, including perhaps a year beyond the usual three-year course, is desirable. In addition, there are opportunities for summer or full-year chaplaincy experience in mental hospitals, where students work under the supervision of a full-time experienced institutional chaplain (see Chaplains in Institutions). Disciplined and continuous study while on the job is especially needed in this most difficult field. Workshops and summer courses often offer opportunities to exchange experiences and to keep up with some of the always newly developing knowledge in psychology and pastoral counseling.

WHAT DO COUNSELING MINISTERS DO? While there is no one precise pattern of work, generally the full-time counseling ministers make formal, one-hour appointments with people who seek help. Counseling by discussion of problems among people in small groups seems to be on the increase. Both types of counseling are in great demand.

It may be well to indicate here what counseling ministers are not. They are not psychiatrists, or even amateur psychiatrists. They may work in close cooperation with psychiatrists, learn from them, or at least from time to time confer with them. They may attend courses in which psychiatrists are teachers.

The counseling minister is simply systematically carrying on, or extending, the historic pastoral function of the clergy. He does this mainly by encouraging persons to talk about the problems or handicaps or tensions that bring them to his office. Beyond merely listening to their problems, the minister seeks to have the people themselves offer their ideas concerning the adjustments or solutions (or alternatives) desirable in their situation. From here on, the methods of counselors differ in their emphases on "direct" or "non-directed" counseling. At any rate, quick and dogmatic clerical advice is not recommended, nor is a pretense of super-wisdom. The goal is to instill a humble desire for re-education in those being counseled.

Pastoral counselors are confronted by people troubled about such problems as choice of, or adjustment in, a job; pre-marital and marital situations; personal conflicts and tensions as wide as humanity itself; homosexuality; old age; housing; and, especially, religious doubts and resources. In all his counseling he makes use of the resources of religion, either indirectly or directly, by recommending certain kinds of reading or worship.

The pastoral counselor may have no other choice than to recommend that a counselee go to another counselor, either a psychiatrist or social worker, or another clergyman.

While counseling about vocations, the minister does not take the place of the specially trained vocational adviser found in many high schools, colleges, and elsewhere. The minister will find it good to know that there is such a vocation as "electronic computer operator," but he cannot be expected to know the details of this or most other of the more than 700 occupations discussed in the *Occupational Outlook Handbook,* 1963-64, of the U.S. Department of Labor.

The full-time counseling minister may also have time and opportunity to present, particularly to young people, the careers within the Protestant churches presented in this volume.

OTHER INFORMATION. A number of theological seminaries now offer special full-time training in pastoral counseling or pastoral psychology as part of study toward the Bachelor of Divinity. Their announcements should be consulted. Frequently the teachers of these courses may be consulted about the training offered.

A special resource is the periodical, *Pastoral Psychology* (monthly except July and August), Manhasset, N.Y. in which special courses in pastoral counseling are listed from time to time.

Among those arranging clinical training is the Council for Clinical Training, 475 Riverside Drive, New York, N.Y. 10027.

For general advice and information, write to the Department of the Ministry, National Council of Churches, 475 Riverside Drive, New York, N.Y. 10027.

## Ordained Women

Women are recognized in the ministry in some 80 Protestant bodies. About 3 per cent of active ordained ministers are women. They may be ordained, or licensed, or given some special status. Among the large denominations that ordain women for the ministry are the United Presbyterian Church in the U.S.A.; the Methodist Church; American Baptists; Disciples of Christ; and the Unitarian and Universalist Association. Apparently all but a few of the Protestant theological seminaries admit women, some admitting more women than there are jobs in the denomination.

The following positions are open to ordained women:

Directors of Christian education;

Associate or assistant ministers;

Employees on church boards, denominational and inter-denominational;

Teachers in church-related schools and colleges;

Teachers or assistants in theological seminaries;

Writers, journalists, editors for religious periodicals and other publications;

Missionaries in various posts overseas.

In all these fields ordained women are consistently welcomed. (Most of these positions are described elsewhere in full detail.)

Ordained women occasionally serve as pastors of local churches, but only the small, and particularly, the rural congregations are open to them for pastorates. An ordained woman usually serves in a church which employs her as the only professional employee. This is a situation of long standing. Explanations are as follows: Custom or tradition (but there were also traditions against ordained women in other positions for which they are now welcomed). Ordinarily, a local church will accept a woman as pastor only when the officers are sure no man is available. Women are not regarded generally as "pulpit orators," and many churches feel they must have a pulpit orator to bring in the people and, among other things, thus help raise the budget. It seems that many men do not want a woman pastor for the same general reasons (usually unstated) as they do not wish a woman physician. Many women feel the same way, although the reasons may be either unclear or unspecified.

The vocation of pastor is still not widely open to women, however well qualified. The situation is gradually changing. There are a number of ordained women, for example in rural communities of New England, who are well-recognized pastors of local churches, and against whom all prejudice seems to have melted away after their devoted and sacrificial labors became evident to their congregations. Large numbers of young women are studying for the ordained ministry. The church may soon have to recognize the equal ability of some qualified women and take steps to correct the present prejudice against women ministers.

The above has been purposely realistic about the employment situation in the pastorate. Women can be ordained to the ministry and work in considerable numbers in all the vocations other than that of sole or senior minister in the local church.

PERSONAL QUALIFICATIONS. Women candidates for the ordained ministry need to present the same personal qualifications as are outlined for men. In addition, it is generally recognized that women offer to the ministry qualities not shared by men. Women bring to the ministry those special talents for healing that they bring to nursing or medicine, for example. Also, women have a deeply personal attitude toward their work. (This is sometimes called a disadvantage in administrative posts, where one must apparently not be too personal or sensitive.) But in the ministry the deeply personal element is an asset, particularly in contacts with youth and older people. Women also have a tendency toward direct, social action. They are not tempted to call expensive consultations of experts who will tell them how difficult a task is; rather, many of them are accustomed to hearing about human needs and doing something practical about them. Also, in many local churches women are known for their abilities to raise budgets in rather simple and direct ways.

EDUCATIONAL QUALIFICATIONS. The educational qualifications of ordained women in the ministry are the same as for ministers in general. Women should probably pay special attention to public speaking, psychology, counseling, and social science as part of their training.

OTHER INFORMATION. In addition to advice available from denominational church boards and seminaries, information may be obtained from:

United Church Women, National Council of Churches, 475 Riverside Drive, New York, N.Y. 10027.

Association of Women Ministers, 6630 Chew Ave., Philadelphia, Pa.

## Town and Country Pastorate

The town and country pastorate, often defined as a church in towns with up to 10,000 people (and the rural pastorate, in communities up to 2,500 people) have certain special characteristics. In some denominations most ministers go directly from the seminary to churches in small communities. Indeed, some ministers serve nearby rural churches part-time while they are theological students. This is also a pastorate in which ordained women may serve.

The economic and social situation in small communities has been rapidly changing. For one, the population of many rural counties declined between 1950 and 1960. Also, rural communities are now more diverse than a generation ago. Many people now live in small communities far away from their places of work.

People who live in the country but do not work there are a new and special group, and they often do not mingle freely with older residents, particularly not with farmers. Having to deal with separate community groups makes the pastor's job more complicated and more difficult than a generation ago. Factories may be located in rural areas. This brings industrial workers and their families into these communities for the first time.

Rural schools have been consolidated on a grand scale, resulting in larger schools than a generation ago and in the transportation of pupils—even those of the first grade—far from their homes. While consolidation is generally approved because it permits a more specialized instruction, compared with the old one-room school—the process also often results in loss of community ties and in a more impersonal atmosphere in schools. Thus churches are called upon to provide a center of fellowship where the personal and community ties may still exist and be strengthened. The minister in a rural community usually works alone. He has to do without many of the social and health agencies available to his city colleague.

PERSONAL QUALIFICATIONS. The general personal qualifications have been given above in the general introduction to the Ordained Ministry. But some of these need to be underlined for the rural, or town and country, pastor. In this pastorate the minister is expected to know all the people in the congregation, as well as many others in the community. Since life is still on a more personal basis in these communities than in larger centers, the ministry must be on a more personal basis too. Thus this pastor calls on people frequently. Being a good and considerate neighbor is an integral part of his pastorate.

When this minister counsels with people, he must use his own experience and judgment. There is no readily available psychiatrist to whom he can refer people. The only help he does have is a physician, usually a general practitioner. For the handicapped or dependent, he does not have the resources of specialized social workers. He should, however, be fully aware of current national programs. Public assistance for the aged, the blind, and dependent children, must be available to all residents of the nation. Benefits and information are usually secured through offices at county seats. Church-related hospitals and institutions for children and aged cooperate actively with rural ministers in meeting the needs of their parishioners and others.

This minister must face the plain fact that he "serves in a thousand ways," and like the country doctor is expected at all times to be available to his people. And the thousand ways often interfere with continuous and disciplined study, and with the process of preparing the sermon for the Sunday morning service or services. For these ministers frequently serve more than one parish or congregation. The Protestant churches reported 289,892 local churches (parishes, congregations) and 223,807 pastors in 1962 (*Yearbook of American Churches,* 1964).

EDUCATION AND TRAINING. One needs as much education and training for a rural pastorate as for any other. Four years of college at a liberal arts institution are generally recommended. A Bachelor's degree at an agricultural college has been part of the preparation of a few rural ministers. Summer courses at agricultural colleges are frequently recommended. The college course should be followed by three years at seminary leading to the B.D. At some seminaries there is supervised field work in rural communities. There are a few "rural internships" available through seminaries and boards of home missions interested in special training for rural work. Informal personal preparation can be made by reading much of the literature on the rural or town and country church.

WHAT DO THESE MINISTERS DO? Like all general practitioners, this minister is called upon to determine his priorities day by day among his main and incidental functions. He is the leader of the parish in every way. He is called a "preacher" rather that a minister by people in many parts of the U.S. Thus he conducts worship in all its forms. He is the general supervisor of the life and work of the parish, especially of religious education, music, lay church organizations, including young people's, and use of the building. He has the opportunity to train lay leaders and to delegate important duties to them. He may be expected to be interested in local library service, social services, and the work of the Farm Bureau, the Grange, the Farmers Union, and the numerous cooperatives for marketing, purchasing, credit. He counsels with individuals in hospitals, in his study, and in the homes of the people. He is his own public-relations director, and he writes copy about the church for the local newspaper and the weekly parish bulletin.

OTHER INFORMATION. Further information may be had from seminary teachers and administrators; denominational boards of education and of home missions; the Department of the Ministry, and the Department of Town and Country Churches, National Council of Churches, 475 Riverside Drive, New York, N.Y. 10027.

## Chaplains in the Armed Services

A military chaplain is an ordained and practicing minister who is expected to be capable of performing all the duties of a pastor of a local church. He is appointed by one of the branches of the armed services, is paid by the government of the U.S., is an officer of an Armed Service, and is subject to the same full military discipline as any other officer.

A military chaplain is also, it may be truly said, a unique servant of the members of the Armed Services. Every chaplain carries not only his own prayer book or equivalent—he also carries the prayer books of other faiths. For example, a Protestant chaplain who is of Southern Baptist heritage and training, must also carry a Roman Catholic and a Jewish prayer book. He must be prepared to minister, particularly in emergencies on board ship or on a field of battle, to Protestant, Roman Catholic, or Jew. The same rules apply, of course, to Roman Catholics and Jews in their ministries to Protestants. This kind of cooperative ministry has been the rule of the Armed Services, and it is willingly practiced.

Another unique aspect of the military chaplaincy is the use of one assembly room for formal worship—with rotating altars and other equipment. By pushing a button one can be ready for a Roman Catholic mass; by pushing another button another altar comes into place for a Protestant service; and so on for a Jewish service. This is another kind of interfaith cooperation.

(Several denominations, it is understood, that do not have an *ordained* ministry, have been granted the privilege of appointing chaplains, who are under the same regulations and perform the same duties.)

Military chaplains are appointed in numbers corresponding to the proportion of members of a denomination in the population. This is never an altogether neat or precise process, because some denominations from time to time do not have applicants to meet the "quota" assigned or desired by the armed services.

WHAT DO MILITARY CHAPLAINS DO? A chaplain ministering to the men and women of the Armed Services is expected to know, and to be able to perform, the functions of a pastorate as described in the introductory material above. That is, he conducts formal worship services in the chapels available or at other places. He is also general counselor on subjects too numerous to mention. In this connection he is frequently confronted with advising a person who is affiliated with a religious body of which the chaplain has never heard. Here the chaplain needs such aids as the annual *Yearbook of American Churches,* Mead's *Handbook of Denominations,* Landis' *The Clergyman's Fact Book* or some similar source. Many adherents of religious bodies are not well informed about the beliefs and doctrines of denominations of which they are members.

The military chaplain must have frequent contacts with other officers of the Armed Services and with the American National Red Cross. The Red Cross, a voluntary organization, has specialized on facilitating contacts or communication between members of the Armed Services and their families and other relatives. The same is true of the United Service Organizations, which maintain numerous centers of recreation, education, and religious services in communities adjacent to military installations, at the request of the U.S. Department of Defense.

The military chaplain has unusual opportunities to encourage members of the armed services to continue their education by correspondence and related methods.

Also, a number of young men, after completing their military service, consider going into the ministry or other church careers. At this point, the chaplain as advisor can be of special help.

Incidental duties may include organizing handball or volleyball tournaments.

EDUCATION AND TRAINING. The basic or general education or training for the chaplaincy is the same as that for the ministry in general: a Bachelor's degree at an accredited liberal arts college, plus three years at a recognized seminary leading to a B.D. degree. In addition, special training is offered from time to time by the Armed Forces, which should be attended by all considering chaplaincy service. Frequently extensive travel is involved in the course of chaplaincy duty.

Not every local pastor can, or should be, a military chaplain. Some pastors will not become part of the Armed Services for reasons of conscience. From time to time, some idealist proposes that the churches should pay the salaries of chaplains and that they should not be officers in the services subject to military discipline. But nobody knows how the huge sums of money involved could be secured, in the light of all the other current demands on the various church treasuries.

SEMINARY STUDENTS AND ARMY AND NAVY CHAPLAINCY. The Army and Navy both have plans whereby certain qualified students at recognized theological schools and seminaries may be commissioned as second lieutenants in the Staff Specialist Branch Reserve. On graduation and ordination they are commissioned as first lieutenants in the Chaplain's Branch. Further information may be had from Chief of Chaplains, Department of the Army, Washington, D.C. 20310; and from Office of Chief of Naval Chaplains, Bureau of Naval Personnel, Department of the Navy, Washington, D.C. 20350.

OTHER INFORMATION. You may consult with the chaplaincy agency in your denomination (only the larger ones have special organizations), or with the official of your denomination who has responsibility for contacts with the military chaplaincy.

The interdenominational Protestant agency with special responsibility is the General Commission on Chaplains and Armed Forces Personnel, 100 Maryland Ave., N.E., Washington, D.C.

## Chaplains in Institutions

The chaplaincy in institutions is a new and developing specialized area of service. Here the ordained minister works with people who are under trying and difficult circumstances, when compared with those in communities. New applicants are needed every year to meet the religious needs and problems of those who are in distress because of physical and emotional illnesses, disturbances, maladjustments.

The institutions that employ or are furnished with ordained ministers who serve as chaplains, include:

> mental hospitals, generally maintained by the states;
> the federal prisons and other penitentiaries;
> jails and workhouses of counties and municipalities;
> the larger general hospitals;
> hospitals for narcotics;
> reformatories;
> training schools;
> correctional institutions;
> children's centers;
> veterans' hospitals.

The employer varies with the type of institution. For example, the Federal government employs the chaplains who serve in the Federal prisons. The state governments pay the salaries of chaplains in the larger mental hospitals. County and municipal governments pay for chaplaincy services in some of the institutions they support.

Chaplains in institutions are also provided from funds of denominational boards, of councils of churches, and of corporations. In some instances the services are rendered on a part-time service. For example, a city council of churches may employ an ordained minister for half of his time, to be spent calling on persons in the general hospitals of the city.

PERSONAL QUALIFICATIONS. It must be evident that only ordained ministers with certain personal qualifications and interests should apply for, or attempt to perform the functions of these specialized ministries. Full-time service involves "institutional living," which is far different from living in ordinary communities. An interest in personal counseling as well as in conduct of worship services seems essential.

EDUCATION AND TRAINING. The requirements for full-time service in these specialized areas are more lengthy than those of others, according to the Department of the Ministry of the National Council of Churches. They include:

a Bachelor's degree from an accredited college;

graduation from a theological seminary;

practical pastoral experience;

endorsement by an authorized denominational official, and evidence of good standing in the denomination.

One year of clinical pastoral training is advised, according to the standards of the National Advisory Committee on Clinical Pastoral Education, as necessary for this specialized ministry. Clinical pastoral training offers to the student or pastor practical application of what he has learned. He lives and works in an institution, under the supervision of an accredited chaplain. During this year the student or pastor will experience all phases of institutional living. He will be confronted with problems in pastoral counseling, preaching, visitation, and practical applications of the theology he has acquired. In a year of trying to help and to understand people, their illnesses and handicaps, a student will gain in self-knowledge as well as learning more about the practice of his work.

At times financial assistance for persons seeking clinical training is available. Scholarship aid may come from a local church, a denominational scholarship program, foundation grants, etc. Many institutions provide room, board, and laundry during training in residence.

WHO NOMINATES OR RECOMMENDS? Nominations of a candidate is usually made by a group of church people, or a council of churches near the institution, or a denominational agency, or by the Department of the Ministry of the National Council of Churches.

A nominating agency needs a formal application, an endorsement of good standing from an ecclesiastical agency of the denomination in which a man is ordained, references, interviews, and a satisfactory statement from a clinical training agency indicating completion of requirements.

OTHER INFORMATION. Further information may be had from your denominational officials, theological seminaries, clinical training agencies, local and state councils of churches, and the Department of the Ministry, National Council of Churches, 475 Riverside Drive, New York, N.Y. 10027.

*Chaplains in Industry*

A relatively small number of ordained men are employed as industrial chaplains in the U.S. This is obviously a recent development. These men are employed by corporations or other businesses in order to conduct meetings and to do counseling with employees. They work in one or more factories, offices, or other establishments among the persons there employed.

PERSONAL QUALIFICATIONS. The general personal qualifications expected of ministers—see various descriptions above—are also expected of industrial chaplains. They deal constantly with people and their problems. A like and love of people, an authentic desire to listen, a wish to communicate, an effort to understand the special problems or stresses of people in business and industry, are especially desirable. Considerable skill in public speaking is also required because the meetings held are usually relatively brief and are conducted in factories or other places of assembly that do not resemble the sanctuary of a local church. Disciplined and continuous study of the developments and issues of industry, management, and labor also seems essential.

EDUCATION AND TRAINING. The general education and training are those expected of other ministers. These include a Bachelor's degree and three years of seminary study leading to a B.D. The education of an industrial chaplain should include the study of economics in college or later; participation in special workshops or field trips or seminars, or any educational events on the economics of modern industry. This may involve study of the role of government in the economy, the role of the consumer, and related questions.

WHAT DO INDUSTRIAL CHAPLAINS DO? The activities of industrial chaplains seem to fall into three categories: conducting religious services in factories; counseling with individuals concerning religious and related problems; personal participation in recreational, social, and other activities.

OTHER INFORMATION. See the general introduction to the Ministries of Ordained Persons, above.

An industrial chaplain is hired by the officers of the corporation which plans to employ him.

Further information may be had from United Church Men, National Council of Churches, 475 Riverside Drive, New York, N.Y. 10027; also the Department of the Church and Economic of the National Council at the same address.

## College and University Chaplains

College and university chaplains are ordained persons engaged either by educational institutions to serve all the students, or as employees of denominational church boards of education to serve the students of an institution affiliated with that denomination.

College chaplains require the high school, college and theological seminary education and training of ministers generally, as outlined above, but also benefit by special work in such subjects as the history of church work with young people and students, educational methods, group work or "group dynamics," and personal counseling.

When on the job, college chaplains do many things. They may conduct personal interviews with students; raise money; promote get-acquainted or "mixer" parties; organize formal seminars on current issues, including theological matters; conduct formal worship services for students Sunday mornings or evenings, or other occasions; offer invocations and benedictions at university con-

97

vocations and other functions; talk over religious perplexities of students and faculty; come to know many students and faculty; become a resource, or center of information on religious knowledge; promote interdenominational and interfaith activities on the campus.

The common interests of denominations are nowhere more evident than among the students of colleges and universities. The unique aspects of denominations do not make much of an appeal to many modern students. Yet there are searchers for religious truth among the inquiring minds of college students.

In order to work in the college field, a minister must realize the basic differences between college and church. The college encourages broad intellectual inquiry to an extent that many local churches do not. Thus the college chaplain works in an atmosphere that is far removed from the conventional local church. The subjects for discussion in a student group are often far different from those in local churches.

Having said that the two are not the same, one can go on to say that the church may serve the college and the college may serve the church, each in its own authentic way, maintaining its own integrity. It is easy to say that a particular college exists to serve the church. This is only partly true. The college exists to serve society and owes great debts to the institutions of society including the church. But most colleges do not exist to serve only the church. Likewise society owes debts to the institutions of higher learning, and is obligated to pay that debt in ways that preserve the independence and integrity of the institutions of higher learning.

OTHER INFORMATION. If a chaplain is needed for an entire student body, he is hired by the institution. If a chaplain is to serve only those students affiliated with a particular denomination, he is chosen and employed by denominational boards in consultation with local groups. Salaries of college chaplains probably compare favorably with those of ministers generally.

(See also Other Campus Ministries, describing student work done by a variety of denominations, often cooperatively.)

## Other Campus Ministries

Large numbers of men and women, ordained and unordained, are constantly engaged in religious and church-related programs among students of colleges and universities, on denominational and interdenominational bases. These vary from the part-time service of a minister of a local church in a community with a college to large formal interdenominational arrangements at many large universities. They also differ from the expected work of one denomination with students in a denominationally affiliated college, to carefully worked out arrangements at tax-supported institutions. In general, religious work with students is old and well-established, and the larger denominations advise with respect to personnel in this kind of service. This is also a vocation in which there has often been the tradition that the minister's wife is an unpaid professional servant, with all the burdens, issues, and problems implied (see The Wives of Ministers).

PERSONAL QUALIFICATIONS. The general personal qualifications called for in this ministry are essentially the same as those of the other ministries previously described. But there are special talents that are needed for good work in this field. The personal dimension of the ministry is very important. The personality of the minister does—and should—influence the program. Skill in organizing small groups is of first importance. Also, the campus minister, like the college chaplain (see above) works constantly in an atmosphere in which freedom of inquiry, and interest in science, are probably much more evident than in community parishes generally. This campus minister usually works with both sexes, but they are of a fixed age group—not with all ages and occupations. He also works among young persons who have interest in actions of service or courage as expressions of faith. He may work with people who prefer jazz to the music of Johann Sebastian Bach. Whether he wishes it or not, he becomes an informal counselor—or a formal one—giving a good deal of time to this function. And whether he thinks he has time for it or not, he is compelled to read—not only the Bible and commentaries thereon, but possibly also something

99

of the writings of Martin Heidegger, the German philosoper. He encounters agnostics and skeptics, and meets philosophers and scientists who have only marginal interests in religion. He may also encounter scientists more eager to discuss the relation of science and religion than some clergymen of his acquaintance. He meets Roman Catholics and Jews, as well as Protestants.

EDUCATION AND TRAINING. The general education and training are the same as for other ministers: a Bachelor's degree followed by three years of seminary study leading to a B.D. (For the unordained people on a college staff, a Bachelor's degree plus graduate study in religion, religious education, and social science are desirable.) As noted in the personal qualifications above, there are certain emphases or accents called for in training. For example, study of methods of education, "group dynamics," history of church student work, some of the recent trends and developments in higher education, current discussion of the relation of faith and learning, psychology, sociology, and economics—all are desirable.

WHAT DO CAMPUS MINISTERS DO? A campus minister inevitably becomes a counselor of individuals. He conducts worship, perhaps not always at the Sunday morning service, but at other times or occasions. He promotes or conducts study of religion, often as a supplement to what is offered at the educational institution.

Drawing on the experience of one campus minister: His office was small but bright and attractive in the center of the campus. It included a battered piano; a bulletin board where summer jobs could be announced; a hamper for clothes on their way to a relief agency; many ash trays; and in a corner a small altar and a cross. To this room one midnight came three students asking the minister to arbitrate at once a feud that threatened to tear the campus apart —the minister could and did arbitrate that conflict. The walls of the room are exposed to moral tragedies, unhappy hasty marriages, the deceits, dishonesties, pretenses, and failures that are part of campus life; also to the glories and satisfactions of student life.

Early in the morning (6:00 A.M.) small groups of six or eight students came to kneel in prayer, then read such works as those of Thomas à Kempis, the Bible, and the Danish theologian-philosopher Sören Kierkegaard.

At noon, the minister conducted chapel, in a larger room, where varieties of religious experiences were permitted expression. Here the Book of Common Prayer was used one day, and a lady evangelist with command of only bad grammar held forth the next. The chapel room was also used as a discussion center. Among those discussing were sixty professors, including all department heads. Among them was an agnostic professor of English who said Christian students had an appalling ignorance of the Bible.

In the course of one year, the campus minister pinpointed some 50 campus Christian leaders. He recruited over 30 for summer work projects, and when they returned from these to the campus they were of great help to him.

He felt that here he had had an unparalleled opportunity for intellectual development, for creating and experiencing genuine fellowship, for endless variety of work, for encouraging Christian family life. He also said he had more freedom than faculty members at the unnamed institution which he served. (See: *A Manual for United Campus Christian Projects,* published by the Commission on Higher Education, National Council of Churches, New York.)

OTHER INFORMATION. Funds for employment of campus ministers may come from several sources, and the extent varies by denomination: Local churches, state conferences, conventions, or dioceses; national boards. Frequently all budgets must be approved by national boards, particularly if they have a part in the financing. Final prerogatives with respect to decisions of employment are usually lodged with local committees.

For "principles of denominations on policy, personnel, and finance as related to United Campus Projects" see the Appendix in the title mentioned above, "A Manual for United Campus Christian Projects."

The prevailing opinion in church boards seems to be that campus ministers should work under conditions of employment recommended for other ministers with respect to salary, vacation, expenses for conferences and professional meetings, allowances for operation of an automobile, insurance, pension rights and payments, Social Security, etc.

101

(See also College and University Chaplains, Y.M.C.A., and Y.W.C.A.)

For further information consult a campus minister, your denominational agency for Campus Christian Life or equivalent (usually in the Board of Higher Education); or the Commission on Higher Education, National Council of Churches, 475 Riverside Drive, New York, N.Y. 10027.

## MISSIONS OVERSEAS

Protestant churches of the U.S. maintained 26,390 missionaries overseas in 1960, a gain of about 80 per cent in 10 years. Members of the Protestant churches gave in 1959 some $170,000,000 for foreign missions, or about $2.75 per member. These 26,390 missionaries from the U.S. comprised over 60 per cent of the total number of foreign missionaries—42,250—sent by all the boards in the "sending nations" to lands other than their own. Four well-known denominations each maintained over 1,000 missionaries abroad—The Methodist Church, Seventh-day Adventists, Southern Baptist Convention, and The United Presbyterian Church in the U.S.A. Both men and women are sent abroad as missionaries.

Missionaries are trained for their tasks. Most of the vocations fall into such groups as the following:

Evangelists, who often supplement native pastors of local churches; usually ordained;

Directors of religious education and related work;

Teachers in theological seminaries, frequently ordained persons;

Teachers in schools and colleges;

Physicians, nurses, dentists;

Social workers, or social-welfare workers;

Agricultural missionaries;

Home economists and dieticians;

Community center workers;

Also, some of the more recent vocations such as librarians, radio programmers, business managers, superintendents of construction and maintenance of buildings.

Thus missionaries do "many things," and missions, like other church organizations, are becoming increasingly specialized and are changing rapidly. The fundamental and extensive change is that the *national* church agencies are rapidly assuming responsibilities. One denomination, the United Presbyterian Church in the U.S.A., has renamed its board of foreign missions the "Commission on Ecumenical Mission and Relations," and its missionaries have the title of "fraternal workers."

PERSONAL QUALIFICATIONS. The personal qualifications are conditioned by the situations in which missionaries work. The countries traditionally called "mission fields" are now the "developing nations" marked by rapid social change. The "newer churches" or "younger churches" of these nations are becoming conscious of independence and resentful of outside influence. The task of the missionary is an increasingly difficult one.

He (or she) must have a willingness to master at least one foreign language. He must have the physical and mental reserve to do hard work for long hours. He must be flexible enough to adjust without shock to a culture far different from his own. He will see day by day some of the most evident needs—physical, social, and spiritual—among the people to whom he is sent. He will probably find race problems there as well as at home. He will have to learn how to face criticism, whether fair or unfair.

What of "the call" to mission service overseas? This is like the call to the ministry or the call to teach in a church-related college. To some persons it is dramatic and sudden—something akin to Paul's experience on the road to Damascus. Others come to a call through nurture of the family, the Sunday school, the local church, the college—to these it is a matter of growth. Anyone who thinks seriously of the great needs of the people of the world, and of his talents and study in relation to them, has already experienced a call.

All persons in the church, not only missionaries abroad or the full-time servants of the churches at home, are called upon to dedicate themselves and their daily work to God. For the prospective missionary there should be two main drives: his own experience of God, so full of meaning that he feels he must share it with mankind, and a spirit within him so sensitive to human need that he is moved toward fulfillment of that need.

There are both special opportunities and unusual problems involved in mission service abroad. Maintaining family life, rearing children, educating children, may all be more complicated and difficult abroad than at home.

EDUCATIONAL REQUIREMENTS. A college education for lay people and theological seminary training for pastors are generally the minimum requirements. A person with many years of academic training ahead of him should select his courses carefully.

For example, study of anthropology is strongly advised. Anthropologists have frequently studied the more primitive societies among whom missionaries work. Missionaries on furlough often give special attention to readings in anthropology, because this social science has documented the cultural characteristics of people among whom they work, or of people resembling their constituents.

Language courses may sometimes be taken in summer sessions or at theological seminaries. But most of the languages the missionaries must know are not taught in the regular curricula of colleges and seminaries. They are taught in the field, or in special courses set up by boards of foreign missions in the U.S. Usually a training period of one to six months is required before proceeding overseas.

A person expecting to be an agricultural missionary, for example, will usually be required to study, probably for four years, at an agricultural college. There is one of these colleges in every state in the U.S. A physician should take all of the courses necessary for medical practice in the U.S. Nurses should take the training expected here of registered nurses.

HOW ARE MISSIONARIES APPOINTED? The boards and societies of foreign missions have their own procedures. There are, however, some general methods that apply.

Boards like to make contact with prospective missionaries during the early years of college.

One should discuss the matter first with the minister of the local church. Through him, or on his advice, contact may be made with the foreign mission board. The board will respond to inquiries by mail, but will regard a personal interview as more valuable. The board, which constantly receives information from abroad concerning workers needed, may advise students regarding desirable studies in college or the theological seminary.

The student who is seriously interested in missionary work will probably be asked to file in writing information about himself with the board during the last two years of formal study. This may be an application blank, requiring information on personal health, references, and even giving instructions regarding a psychological test. Academic records must be filed. Photographs may have to be sent. Arrangements for an interview may be discussed.

If there is a vacancy in the field, in a position supported by the board, the application will be thoroughly studied. If the information filed is satisfactory, the applicant will be regarded as an approved candidate.

Traditionally, the boards have asked for life commitment, although today, many boards are offering short-term appointments, ranging from one to five years. If there is life commitment, furloughs or sabbatical leaves are granted after stated periods of from three to seven years. While on furlough, a missionary may be expected to have a thorough physical examination, to undertake formal study to continue his education, and to speak in local churches about his work.

NEW SHORT-TERM ASSIGNMENTS. Increasingly, foreign mission boards are offering short periods of service, either to students or to experienced specialists.

For students, this service was stimulated in large part by the Student Conference on the Christian World Mission in 1959. Examples of short-term service are here cited:

The Junior Year Abroad is offered as an overseas study plan by one board. This enables juniors in colleges to live abroad as students and to become involved in the church and the life of another country. Students in their sophomore year who have participated in campus religious programs are invited to make application to their board (between October 1 and March 1 of that academic year). An applicant must have the cooperation of his faculty

105

adviser, and must be able to pay his own expenses, much as he would if he remained in his college—about $1,500 to $2,000 a year. The student will receive aid from his board in transferring credits from the U.S. to an institution abroad; in obtaining passport, visa, insurance, and transportation. The board will give advice regarding study materials, housing abroad, and conferences abroad while he is studying there. As of a recent date one board was offering arrangements for junior years of study in Ghana, Nigeria, Sierra Leone, Brazil, Lebanon, Pakistan, India, the Philippines, Mexico, Chile, Japan, Hong Kong, Germany, and Switzerland.

A Frontier Internship in Mission of two years abroad is offered by one board, to mature and dedicated college students who wish to interrupt their study in the U.S. for these years, and to graduates of colleges and theological seminaries. The arrangement was made because students in the U.S. requested opportunities to serve abroad. The "frontiers" named by the students are non-geographical, as follows: Technological upheaval, racial tensions, new nationalisms, modern secularism, universities abroad, militant non-Christian faiths, communism, responsibilities of statesmanship, and displaced, uprooted, and rejected populations.

A student going abroad on an Internship usually maintains some contact and cooperation with missionaries and fraternal workers of various denominations. He agrees to live for these two years at a "subsistence level"—that is, equal to the economic resources of fellow workers in accordance with standards of the area. It is a level lower than that of the missionaries already in the field, one about the level of student nationals in the nation. Study is a necessary part of the internship, indeed, a regular study and worship discipline is required. The programs of the Interns vary greatly, depending in part on their own initiative, sensitivity, and concern. Some are in "multi-racial" student bodies. One Intern writes that a "university campus anywhere is a frontier." Another does medical work, still another teaches. In general they practice fellowship with people in the area, because they think it is necessary for the communication of the Christian gospel.

Special Term Missionary is the title used by another board to designate those young people between the ages of 21-28 willing to share the life of people with whom they will work for periods of three years outside the U.S. (There are also the same kind of assignments in the U.S., including Puerto Rico, for periods of two years.) Graduates must be committed Christians, active church members, graduates of accredited colleges, and above average in academic achievement. They must be emotionally mature. They must be single and agree to remain single during the period of service.

These young men and women work with youth in dormitories, social centers, youth fellowship, Bible classes, and athletic activities. They train and work with adults in Christian education, family life, hygiene, and literacy programs. They work with children in day nurseries, community centers, church schools, children's homes, and rural centers. They teach formal courses at mission schools and colleges in English, Bible, science, art, music, home economics, physical education, argriculture, and library science. They assist in medical education and health service by broadening the church's healing ministry, and aid in training others in these fields. They serve as boys' hostel managers and social workers.

Applicants must agree to an intensive seven-week study of cultures, linguistics, and the Christian faith, given in June and July at the expense of the board. The board provides travel to and from the appointed country. Salary for work abroad will be the same as that of the life-committed missionaries, including provision of housing, medical care, social security, and retirement pension benefits.

SOME CONDITIONS. It has been said the the *essential* methods of conducting church work, broadly defined, are the same in India as in Indianapolis, with this difference: the missionary in India probably has more secure arrangements and provisions than the pastors or teachers in Indiana. The churches make various provisions for their missionaries overseas, rather than emphasizing cash salaries. Housing, medical care, and travel expenses are provided. In many instances education of children will be paid for by the home mission board. Retirement pensions are generally available, and, in many instances, social security coverage. Missionaries are not able to save much from their modest cash salaries.

A development worth noting is that at times people in middle life may be accepted for service overseas. Also, one denomination will frequently accept laymen from another body. A recent example is that of a middle-aged physician who is a Congregationalist, after having had ties with the Church of God, and who went abroad for the United Presbyterian Church. On assignment overseas, one often finds more hearty and generous cooperation among denominations than in the home town. Walls between denominations built up in past years have been gradually crumbling—not all walls, but enough for one to notice.

Also, the new or younger churches of Asia, Africa, and Latin America have begun to send out missionaries to other lands. The industrial and wealthy West is no longer the sole sender.

DESCRIPTIONS OF MANY POSITIONS. As previously stated, the services abroad are generally the same as those performed by paid servants of the church in the U.S. General descriptions of these vocations will not be repeated here. Only brief notes follow, with references to the more thorough accounts elsewhere. In general, prospective overseas workers need some special skills or knowledge beyond that necessary for work in the U.S. Illustrations of types of work and of workers follow (recognizing that there is much overlapping among the categories).

*Church Development and Evangelism.* For this work ordained persons with the degree of Bachelor of Divinity are generally needed, but lay evangelists, and musicians are also employed at times. Ordained ministers may serve as pastors of one or more established churches, or they may be called upon to organize new churches in the area to which they are assigned. They may do much evangelism by radio, and by visiting the people, as well as preaching in churches or elsewhere, as the opportunity arises. People between the ages of 22 and 35 are often preferred, although age limits can be waived. (For training of missionaries abroad, see notes above under Education and Training, and for fuller descriptions see Ministries of Ordained Persons.)

*Directors of Religious Education, and Related Work.* In missions abroad persons with training in religious education may work in the larger local churches but usually train others in districts and thus encourage the development of Christian education in many churches and centers. The usual educational requirements are a college degree, graduate study in Christian education, or a Bachelor of Divinity. Single women are often preferred for this work.

*Teaching in Theological Seminaries.* The number of Protestant theological seminaries abroad is increasing, and in many instances teachers from the U.S. are enlisted. Obviously those who have studied theology or taught it in the U.S. are those qualified. They may be asked to teach the Old Testament, the New Testament, Christian ethics, Christian education, church history, Bible translation, and other disciplines customarily taught in seminaries of the U.S. Both short-term and regular appointments are made by some boards.

*Teaching in Schools and Colleges.* In elementary schools single men and women, and married couples are accepted. Some boards make short-term appointments. Usually a college degree with a teaching certificate is the minimum educational requirement. Some boards desire persons with training or experience in Christian education in the U.S. before going abroad. (See Teaching in Elementary Schools.)

For secondary schools, single men and women, and married couples, are recruited. As in the U.S., teachers are needed who have preparation in high-school subjects, and, as at home, a teacher may have to teach more than one subject. The usual minimum educational requirement is a college degree, with a state certificate for teaching high-school subjects in the U.S. Both short-term and regular appointments are made by some boards, and the more technical educational requirements are waived in the case of short-term appointments. (See Teaching in Secondary Schools.)

In colleges, single men and women, and married couples are recruited for teaching subjects much the same way as in the U.S. In the larger institutions, there is more specialization and research. (See Teaching in Colleges and Universities.)

*The Health Service Vocations.* The foreign mission boards maintain, in whole or in part, numerous hospitals, clinics, and other health centers, where physicians, nurses, medical technicians, and physical therapists are employed, as in the U.S. Abroad, the church-related health agencies employ dentists and pharmacists to a greater extent than in the U.S. As with other vocations abroad, skills and knowledge, above that needed in the U.S., are required. Some positions require persons with experience. (See articles on Physicians, Nurses, Medical Technologists, Physical Therapists.)

*Social Work.* For social work abroad, mainly women are recruited. The functions are the same as in the U.S. The work is less specialized than in the U.S., but there are trends towards specialization. Some boards require eligible applicants to have both a college degree and a graduate degree in social work. (See Social Workers.)

*Agricultural Missions.* Agricultural missionaries sent abroad are generally male graduates of American agricultural colleges. They have started many projects under missionary auspices abroad, including demonstration farms, other farms, rural service centers, and extension programs. They have encouraged cottage industries, administered loan funds, and assisted in organizing credit unions and other cooperative associations. Land settlement has been guided. They have sought to train local leaders for improvement of food production and distribution, and for the broad purpose of helping people to help themselves.

*Home Economists and Dieticians.* The duties and educational requirements are much as in the U.S. Women are recruited for these vocations. (See Home Economists and Dieticians.)

*Community Center Workers.* Women are needed to direct centers in rural and urban communities, for informal educational, recreational, and vocational activities. (See Community Center Workers.)

(See also Librarians, Radio and TV Broadcasters, Business Managers.)

# MOBILE MINISTRY TO MIGRATING FARM WORKERS

During the past 44 years an extensive mobile ministry has been carried on among migrating farm workers. Begun by church women through the Council of Women for Home Missions, it is now carried on nationally by the Division of Home Missions of the National Council of Churches. State and local councils and local committees are responsible for many of the numerous local programs. Although begun and supported originally by church women, the ministry is now a program with participation by men and women ordained and unordained.

In 1920 a group of church women heard of a report by the Interchurch World Movement, a temporary organization, of the great needs of the people who "followed the crops." They were described as among the most neglected of our citizens. Poorly paid, they were outcasts in the communities where they worked. They once helped to plant crops and to harvest them, but recently they have been engaged mainly in harvesting. Many of these workers followed regular cycles year by year, starting in the South where crops ripened first and moving to the North. The workers and their families were being denied education and health services, and they were generally not invited to attend the churches near the fields where they labored. Many were Negroes.

The response of the church women was one that is characteristic of women's organizations in the churches: They decided to do something immediately. (They did not delay by consulting with experts concerning the difficulties.) They determined that, as a beginning, a few women should be employed to work among these migrant workers. Out of the early work of the pioneers, a varied program with many facets emerged that is described below under "What Do they Do?"

In 1962 the mobile ministry was active in 36 states, with the number of projects in each state varying from one each in four states to more than 200 in others. The total number of salaried staff workers was 426. In addition, 169 persons received only their living expenses, making a staff, national, state, and local, of

**111**

595. The number of migrant people participating regularly in the programs was 48,500, but some 132,650 were reached by "mass programs." Thus about 181,500 people were reached out of about 800,000 migrants in the 36 states. Assisting the paid workers were 9,513 volunteers, mainly from local churches. There were 32 state committees and 242 area and local committees (also unpaid), with a total membership on these committees of 3,476 persons.

PERSONAL QUALIFICATIONS. In order to engage in this mobile ministry one must be willing and able to be with the people who do seasonal work in the fields, harvesting all sorts of fruits and vegetables. Machinery has been developed for harvesting many crops, but its use varies according to place and crop. Beans, for instance, can be harvested by machine. But many migrants and their families do the "stoop labor" necessary for harvesting such crops as cauliflower, asparagus, cabbage. They remain in one area only until the harvest is completed.

On the eastern shore of Maryland, as an example, there is extensive cultivation of truck crops in large fields. Many workers are brought in, usually in groups enlisted by crew leaders. And to the extent it is possible, workers of the migrant ministry are there among them while they work. A migrant minister, man or woman, may sometimes work in the fields for no pay, putting crops into the baskets of the workers, as one means of coming to know something about these people. Some of the workers have come to the U.S. from Mexico and the Caribbean area.

The ministers must, of course, come in contact with the employers—who usually, but not always welcome the migrant ministry. They encourage communities to make educational and health services available to the temporary residents. A knowledge of state laws in regard to housing and sanitation is valuable; at times they may need to ask for the enforcement of these laws.

This ministry is one of the unusual among the specialized ministries, calling for courage, perseverance, and resilience, as well as for knowledge of the economy, social conditions, and religion and theology. Formal training in theology is not required of all workers, but an interest in worship and counseling is called for.

The "backgrounds" of members of the seasonal or temporarily employed staff include theological seminary students, foreign missionaries (on furlough or retired), specialists in Christian education, nurses, teachers in public schools, dieticians, college professors, college chaplains, child-care specialists, and homemakers.

EDUCATION AND TRAINING. A Bachelor's degree at a liberal arts or agricultural college is usually the minimum for regular employment, although students are employed for numerous summer jobs. Experience with student organizations or the group work of the Y.M.C.A. and Y.W.C.A. counts in working with these groups of families.

A small portion of the regularly employed workers have had seminary training and experience in a local pastorate before entering the migrant ministry.

Training and experience in methods of modern religious education are essential because much time may be spent with groups or classes of children while the parents work in the fields.

Knowledge of, and training in, social work, increasingly called social-welfare work, are helpful. But most migrant ministers have to learn some things in the field by experience.

WHAT DO THEY DO? The kinds of "direct service" most frequently mentioned in the 36 states reporting are: Worship services in camps; family nights; vacation church schools; child-care centers; "make-up" schools; clinics; hospitality centers in towns near farms on which migrants are employed.

The migrant minister may conduct formal worship of a Sunday morning if a meeting place is available. He will encourage the seasonal workers to attend church service in the community, and will ask the local churches to invite them and welcome them.

Workers in the migrant ministry frequently cooperate with voluntary community agencies, including parent-teacher associations, associations of growers, Chambers of Commerce, Red Cross, Salvation Army, medical societies, service clubs, Y.M.C.A., Y.W.C.A., and numerous public or tax-supported agencies.

Some of the persons in the migrant ministry are supervisors and executives. They help to enlist personnel for their sections, and

113

raise funds from state and local sources. These are persons who have had previous experience in the migrant ministry or related pursuits.

OTHER INFORMATION. Further information may be had from state councils of churches in areas where many seasonal farm workers are found; also from the Division of Home Missions, National Council of Churches, 475 Riverside Drive, New York, N.Y. 10027.

# MUSIC DIRECTORS

Local churches, church-related colleges in the U.S. and abroad, theological seminaries, and other institutions employ persons increasingly known as directors of music. In the past the position has been known as "organist" or "choir leader," and in the smaller local churches these persons have usually been part-time employees or volunteers. In the larger local churches the position is a full-time one and may even be designated as Minister of Music, a title reserved for persons with advanced training and considerable experience. Whether so designated or not, the position offers experience in a ministry through music.

There is always need for good music leadership in the local churches and other institutions mentioned above. Some churches of necessity combine the position of director of religious education with that of director or minister of music. This arrangement has rather varied results, and church officials recommend that such a combination be only temporary, leading to two positions to be occupied by persons with professional training.

Indeed, large local churches with the means occasionally have two professional persons sharing the music leadership. The first is a director or minister of music who is responsible for planning the entire program of music and is the executive leader. The second one is an associate in the ministry of music who is the organist assisting the director in making the music program and in executing it. Such persons necessarily must have competence in education and liturgy, both broadly defined.

114

PERSONAL QUALIFICATIONS. A person engaging in a ministry of music, no matter what the title, should realize that music, like poetry, conveys to people by an emotional reaction something that cannot be said. Many people in a congregation are helped as much by music as by any other portion of a worship service. Dedicated people who seek a creative life and a challenging program, who have an interest in the church and its total mission, and a sincere love of people are needed. Physical fitness along with maturity in emotional judgments and a desire to help other people grow; knowledge of Christian education, including good teaching procedures; commitment to disciplined, continuous personal study; and awareness of the relation of hymnody and liturgy in the history of the Christian Church—all these are desirable.

EDUCATION AND TRAINING. A Bachelor of Arts degree with a major in music or music education, or a Bachelor of Music degree with a major in sacred music, are regarded as essentials for beginning a career in music direction. There are other kinds of approved preparation. (1) A four-year liberal arts program plus a year of graduate study leading to a degree in music. (2) Attendance at a specialized school of church music. (3) Graduate study combining theology and church music, leading to a Bachelor of Divinity degree and training in church music, which would enable a person to be in a formal sense a Minister of Music. Courses in psychology, speech, English, sociology, religion, and related subjects are recommended, in addition to specialization in music.

Music workshops are often organized by denominations for persons with responsibility for music leadership. They provide continuing education or "refresher courses." At one such, recently held, eighty-five persons gathered for intensive study of the place of music in the church program. They heard a paper on "Music in Worship," engaged in a music-reading session in which they were introduced to new anthems, considered the role of music in Christian education, and saw a large display of published anthems and other music among which they could browse.

WHAT DO MUSIC DIRECTORS DO? The duties vary with the training of the director, the situation of the local church, and agree-

115

ments concerning the role with the minister and officers of the church. The range, previously intimated, may be listed. These persons serve as organist, choir leader or director, and among their duties are the organizing and training of children's, youth and adult choirs. They organize special musical programs in the church, such as "hymn festivals," and the special music of meetings of men's or women's organizations. They may become supervisors of assistants or associates. They may be "Ministers of Music" in the full and formal sense. These functions refer to those in the local churches.

In schools and colleges these people may also be organists and choir directors and arrange special musical programs or events. In addition they may teach music. In large institutions, with division of functions, some become supervisors of associates and have primary responsibility for planning programs and executive duties.

OTHER INFORMATION. Decisions on employment are made by local churches and by the colleges and other institutions employing music directors, or others of somewhat similar title.

Large denominations have boards with offices that furnish information on vocations for which persons are needed, and other specific advice.

Many college and seminary administrators can advise regarding preparation for the position of music director.

Directors of music in local churches will often advise concerning training and give opportunities to volunteers—who seek experience in, and knowledge of, the work.

## NURSES

The relationship between nursing and the institutions of religion are ancient in origin. The earliest formal nursing was developed by the first hospitals, many of which were closely associated with churches. The experience with nursing in the Protestant churches of Western Europe was brought by immigrants to the U.S. Here, many hospitals are church-related and conduct schools of nursing.

Many thousands of registered nurses are employed as part of the professional staffs of Protestant church-related hospitals. Some of these work only part time. The demand for nurses is currently great in all institutions that employ them.

In the U.S., the number of nurses, more than 500,000, almost all women, is second only to the number of women employed in teaching. Nursing also is the largest of the major health-service vocations.

Registered professional nurses give service to patients either by direct care, or by supervising allied nursing personnel, including practical nurses, nurses aides, orderlies, etc. Professional registered nurses are primarily responsible for carrying out instructions of physicians, and are thus important members of professional medical teams. The general concerns of nurses are, however, not confined to care of the sick. They are also responsible for encouraging preventive practices and promoting good health. Nurses are trained to administer medicines under a physician's instruction; to observe, record, and evaluate symptoms, progress, and attitudes of patients; to provide proper physical and emotional environments for patients.

PERSONAL QUALIFICATIONS. A woman interested in a nursing career in a church-related hospital should first of all be convinced of her genuine interest in people and of her aim to minister to the sick. Nurses must be in good physical and emotional health. They are asked to be cooperative, patient, dependable, understanding, sympathetic.

Many high-school students may learn about nursing and test their own interests toward the duties of the profession by joining one of the Future Nurses Clubs, organized in about one-eighth of the nation's high schools. These clubs usually arrange for volunteer work in hospitals. If the program is well supervised, the student will have an experience that tells much of what nursing is about. Even where there is no high-school club, volunteer work may often be arranged.

EDUCATION AND TRAINING. There are many training programs in the numerous schools of nursing of the nation. Graduation from a high school is required for admission. Some schools also require evidence of competence in science and mathematics as part of the admission standards. Some schools accept only students who have been in the upper third or upper half of their class in academic attainment. Many schools admit persons between the ages of 17 and 35 only, but because of the critical need for trained personnel, the upper age limit is frequently suspended.

The traditional nursing-school program operated by many hospitals is for three years, leading to a diploma.

Programs leading to a Bachelor's degree require four, sometimes five, years of study in a college or university.

Somewhat recent "associate degree" programs are offered for two years in junior and community colleges.

In all training programs both classroom instruction and supervised practice in nursing are included. The subjects offered are usually anatomy, physiology, microbiology, nutrition, psychology, and basic nursing care. For supervised practice, students are assigned to various hospitals or other health services, where they may learn the elements of care for different types of patients. In some college nursing programs, students are also assigned to public health agencies which require visits to homes. Some "general" education is combined with specific nursing instruction in all schools of nursing.

The educational expenses in schools of nursing vary from no cash outlay to over $2,000 a year per student. In certain schools operated by hospitals, it is estimated that the services performed by students in the hospital compensate for all or a large part of the costs of training. Colleges and universities, of course, charge all of their regular fees and tuition rates. Tuition at junior or community colleges is usually lower than at institutions requiring dormitory residence. Scholarships and loans for nursing education are frequently offered by nursing schools, colleges, and community organizations.

LICENSING. A license for professional nursing is required by every state. In order to obtain a license a nurse must pass an examination given by a state board and must have graduated from a nursing school approved by the state board. State boards licensing

118

nurses use uniform examination forms prepared in cooperation with the National League for Nursing (see address below) but each board decides its own passing grades. A nurse may be registered in more than one state, either by taking a separate examination, or by acceptance or endorsement of a license secured in another state. Fees for examination or endorsement are reported to range from $5.00 to $30.00.

*Hospital Nurses.* These are the largest group of nurses and they are almost two-thirds of all professional nurses. They are employed not only by hospitals but also by related health institutions such as clinics, homes for the aged, and the like. They are usually "general duty" nurses, performing the more skilled bedside duties. These include care of a patient after an operation, assisting in blood transfusions and intravenous feeding, and giving medicines. General-duty nurses may also assign their more routine duties to auxiliary hospital personnel, including practical nurses, nurses' aides, and orderlies. General duty nurses may be promoted to more advanced positions, including supervisor, head nurse, assistant director, or director of nursing services. For the more advanced positions, a Bachelor's or Master's degree is usually required.

*Private-duty Nurses.* These nurses, perhaps 15 per cent of all in the profession, serve both in hospitals and in patients' homes, usually in situations calling for a good deal of independent judgment. When they work in hospitals, they are paid directly by the patients or their families. They give individual care when constant or near constant attention is needed. Because of shortages of personnel, group plans have been worked out whereby one nurse can sometimes care for as many as four patients requiring special care but not constant attention.

*Public-Health Nurses.* These are employed by both tax-supported and private community agencies, including the *visiting nurse* associations in which many Protestant churches and people are often participants and supporters. Their duties vary greatly, and may include part-time or periodic home nursing care, the giving of treatments as prescribed by a physician, and participa-

119

tion in community health education programs such as mass X-rays and immunizations.

*Nurse Educators.* Employed in the church-related hospitals that operate nursing schools, their primary duties are to teach the nursing students, to assist them in putting theory into practice, and to recommend facilities needed for adequate training. They may also conduct short or "refresher" courses, or in-service training for nurses who already have some experience.

(There are other specialized fields of nursing such as general duty office nurses, nurses in industry, nurses in state mental hospitals, and nurses in government hospitals for veterans.)

*Practical Nurses and Auxiliary Nursing Workers.* Practical nurses and auxiliary nursing workers are being employed in increasing numbers because of prevailing shortages among professional or registered nurses. They perform many of the less complicated tasks, and thus enable the professional nurses to concentrate on the duties requiring greater skills and knowledge. A proportion of the practical nurses are licensed, and they may perform more tasks than the unlicensed. Hospitals employ a high proportion of the practical nurses of the nation. Most of these nurses are women, but the number of men is reported to be increasing.

There were some 700 practical-nursing training programs in operation in 1962 compared with only 11 in 1930. These were programs approved by state boards of nursing. Entrance requirements vary greatly, with most schools requiring an applicant to have at least two years of high school and to be under 25 years of age. Candidates for admission must usually take a physical examination and psychological tests. An increasing number of high schools offer approved programs. The courses in most schools are for one year.

Among auxiliary nursing workers are nurses' aides, generally women, and orderlies and hospital attendants, mostly men. These workers are not licensed and are usually trained in hospitals on the job. Their duties require less skill than most of those of the practical nurses.

OTHER INFORMATION. The demand for professional nurses is such that the employment outlook is most favorable. Everywhere there are efforts to have good employment conditions, including Social Security coverage, regular vacations, and reasonable hours.

For information on education, Future Nurses Clubs, and related matters communicate with the National League for Nursing, Committee on Careers, 10 Columbus Circle, New York, N.Y. 10019.

On practical nursing write to the National Association of Practical Nurse Education and Service, 475 Riverside Drive, New York, N.Y. 10027; and National Federation of Licensed Practical Nurses, 250 West 57th St., New York, N.Y. 10019.

## OCCUPATIONAL THERAPISTS

An occupational therapist determines and directs or carries out the recreational, educational, and vocational activities designed to meet a patient's specific needs, after a physician makes a diagnosis and gives an outline of the course of treatment. Many occupational therapists work in church-related hospitals, where they are members of medical teams. A medical team may include physicians, nurses, social workers, physical therapists (all of which see), and others.

A large majority of occupational therapists are women. They work not only in hospitals, but also in nursing homes, homes for the aged, and child-care agencies. Some work for institutions but visit in homes those patients not able to attend clinics or workshops. In hospitals they work with those general medical and surgical patients that need the special skills of the occupational therapist.

PERSONAL QUALIFICATIONS. Because occupational therapists work with the injured, the ill, the handicapped, and the dependent, the personal qualifications needed include emotional stability, physical stamina, a cheerful personality, a liking for direct work with people, an authentic interest in medical service, and an objective attitude toward disabilities. Experienced people also mention as assets manual dexterity and ingenuity. For the general personal

121

qualifications expected of persons employed in church-related positions, see the articles herein on Nurses and Physicians.

EDUCATION AND TRAINING. Generally recommended for entry into this profession is graduation from a college or university offering an educational program in occupational therapy approved by the Council on Medical Education and Hospitals of the American Medical Association. The number of such programs is limited. In 1962 only some 30 colleges and universities gave courses leading to a Bachelor's degree with a major in occupational therapy. In these courses there is an emphasis on the sciences related to health service and on the occupational skills necessary. For professional registration by the American Occupational Therapy Association, supervised practice in a hospital or other health agency for nine or ten months is also required. Some colleges permit their students to secure this experience during summer months or during their last year at college.

Some approved schools will accept college graduates who have majored in other fields, and then give a certificate in occupational therapy on completion of special training.

Those who have completed college and supervised practice are then eligible to take the standard examination given every six months by the American Occupational Therapy Association. Successful completion of the examination results in authorization to use the title O.T.R. (Occupational Therapist Registered). Some hospitals will only employ an occupational therapist who is registered.

Five universities offer a program leading to a Master's degree to registered O.T.R.'s. People already in occupational therapy may earn the Master's degree in such subjects as guidance, counseling, education, psychology, or a social science. They are then qualified for teaching, research, and executive work. Some institutions also offer in-service or refresher courses annually for occupational therapists, thus enabling them to learn about new knowledge and skills.

WHAT DO THEY DO? Therapists without experience or with little of it are often offered positions as members of staffs, and may thus advance to senior therapists after a few years of satisfactory work. Experienced therapists also become eligible to direct staffs in the larger hospitals.

Occupational therapists may use several kinds of treatment in order to achieve the rehabilitation of patients. The aim of rehabilitation may include the elimination of boredom during a long illness or recuperation from injury; the restoration of physical or emotional stability; development of self-sufficience in ordinary daily living; assistance in the performance of specific tasks or jobs.

In the past, occupational therapists have often taught such arts as weaving and working with clay and leather. Recently, therapists have added work in specific industrial and business skills, such as typing, and use of tools or power machines. At times the therapist supervises volunteers, confers with others in health services, and consults with parents or other relatives of patients.

Therapists with thorough experience may be asked to become teachers of medical students, and of student and graduate nurses. Others assume administrative work in education.

OTHER INFORMATION. The Woman's Bureau, U.S. Department of Labor, Washington, D.C. 20210 publishes information on the outlook for women in occupational therapy.

Detailed information of the field, on colleges offering training, and on scholarships available may be had from the American Occupational Therapy Association, 250 West 57th St., New York, N.Y. 10019.

## OFFICE POSITIONS

Two-thirds of the more than 10,000,000 persons engaged in all clerical and office vocations are women. One out of every four office workers is a typist, stenographer, or secretary. About one-third of all the women of the nation who work have office jobs.

Employee turnover is especially high among office workers. Many work for only a few years, and then leave in order to stay at home, or to marry, or to care for children. In a recent year one out of every four office positions became vacant, according to a study

123

made of several hundred large corporations. In one large eastern religious organization, the turnover was privately reported to have been 42 per cent in one recent year.

Workers in this group do a large amount of record-keeping and communication required in modern offices, including those of religious organizations. Many are bookkeepers and office-machine operators.

EDUCATION AND TRAINING. The minimum educational requirement for starting in most office positions now is usually graduation from high school or a business school that gives the necessary training. Beginners will find that instruction in business subjects in high school, including the operation of modern business machines, is helpful in becoming established in office positions. Part-time employment while in high school and summer jobs while in school are good experience.

Many employers, including religious organizations, give tests to applicants for office positions. For jobs requiring typing and transcribing, there will be tests in these skills. Increasingly, other abilities are tested. These include reading comprehension, spelling, grammar and arithmetic. Evidence of ability to cooperate with other people will enable persons to hold jobs.

Although high-school graduation is regarded as a minimum, a college graduate can qualify at once for the more difficult office positions. College graduates also often have opportunities to advance to professional or administrative positions. For example, a secretary with a college education may qualify for appointment as an administrative assistant, or as an editorial assistant, or as a writer.

In some organizations, seniority is important in the advancement process. Often the more important clerical positions are filled by promotion of people already employed in the office. An operator of business or other machines may become a supervisor or may train new employees to handle the office machines.

PERSONAL QUALIFICATIONS. "I once had a secretary who was a saint," one church official recently remarked. "I had one who became a philosopher," another said. While the proportion of saints and philosophers may be as small among office workers as in the world in general, personal attitudes and interests of office workers are of great significance in religious organizations. While, like the professor of literature in his classroom, an office worker is not ordinarily expected to preach evangelistic sermons while on the job, nevertheless religious organizations expect and put a high value on such as outgoing friendliness, reverence for life, some knowledge of, and interest in, religious organizations and in religion, among their office workers.

Many religious organizations give preference in appointments to some office positions to members of the local churches of their denomination or of their constituency. This is recognized as a basic right of religious bodies, and is understood to be in accord with the Fair Employment Practices Laws of many of the states.

Many religious organizations endeavor to have interracial office staffs, although public discussion of this issue indicates that this is a policy that is neither universal nor always willingly adopted.

The full-time office secretary in a local church is in a peculiar sense a representative of the institution to members of the church and to the public. The person occupying this position is also usually required to be responsible for all or most of the duties of a secretary. (See Secretaries, below.)

General personal qualifications of office workers also usually include manual dexterity, initiative, discretion, and care in personal appearance.

*Typists*

More than 95 per cent of all typists in the nation are reported to be women. Skill in typing is not only the basic requisite for a full-time position as a typist, but is also a necessity for work as a stenographer and (usually as a) secretary.

Typists usually spend most of their time making typewritten copies of handwritten, typed, or printed materials. They may also type various lists or to set up statistical tables or properly rearrange previously written matter. The more skilled and experienced typists are called upon to handle the more complex or involved drafts. They may also be expected to understand simple statistical or printing (including proofreading) terms, and abbreviations; to compile matter from various sources; to plan arrangements of complicated sources.

An increasing number of offices are purchasing electric typewriters to replace the standard ones. A special kind of typing sometimes required involves the use of special keyboards for transcribing coded instructions for electronic data-processing machines.

Many typists are also expected to do filing, answer the telephone, cut and proofread mimeograph stencils, sort mail, and operate the new duplicating or copying machines. These machines have eliminated much copying by typewriter in many offices.

## Stenographers

Stenographers are required to have skill in typing, and in taking dictation either by shorthand or by listening to dictaphone records. In many offices dictation is frequently put on records which the stenographer then plays on a machine for transcription. When this process becomes a full-time position, the worker may be called a "transcribing machine operator."

The precise duties of stenographers vary from office to office. This is especially true of religious organizations, which have a history of relatively informal or unstandardized organization. Some stenographers take dictation not from one but from two or more persons. Duties other than typing and transcribing may include compilation of papers and reports, answering the telephone, handling inquiries by writing letters, and almost any other office function.

A small proportion of stenographers in religious organizations handle relatively technical materials, such as those having to do with real estate, investments, and legal matters. A still smaller proportion may be expected to know one or more foreign languages.

Stenographers are sometimes classified as junior, senior, or technical.

For personal and educational qualifications see the introductory paragraphs above.

## Secretaries

While a small proportion of secretaries do not have to take dictation, the large majority of them are expected to do some stenographic work, even typing, and a variety of other office duties. The extent of responsibility depends largely on the policies and practices of the employing organization, or of the executive or executives to whom she is assigned. It seems to be increasingly the custom for a secretary to work for more than one person, at least for a short time. Persons known as private secretaries usually work entirely with one executive or professional person, and they generally have the more responsible or varied or confidential assignments.

Secretaries may have authority to make appointments for their executives, and to handle correspondence in their absence. They may be asked to write original letters for their own or their employer's signature; to schedule and arrange for various conferences, consultations, conventions, and other types of gatherings frequently attended by "religious experts in meetingsmanship"; to secure and present information required for meetings; to travel to meetings and work during them for more than seven or eight hours a day; to provide for the permanent care of important records.

One large religious organization classifies its secretaries into four grades, named simply one to four, with the fourth grade having the most difficult duties and also the highest salary.

For personal and educational requirements see the materials above under Office Positions.

## Bookkeepers

Religious organizations, like others, require records of their financial affairs and related transactions. Local churches often employ clerks or bookkeepers, mostly on a part-time basis, while the large majority of local congregations rely on the work of volunteers for the duties of financial secretaries, clerks, and treasurers. Denominational offices and boards, councils of churches, and the various church-related institutions employ full-time bookkeepers.

In the most general terms, the function of the bookkeeper is the maintenance of financial records. As for specific details, the bookkeepers record daily transactions on accounting forms, including journals and ledgers. At regular intervals, probably monthly, they prepare summaries or formal statements for their employers. This will include the amount of money received and that paid out, the sources of the receipts and the various types of expenses, the amounts owed to the organization by consumers or users, and the amount the organization owes to others. Annual statements are prepared on the same basis, usually for publication and distribution not only to employers but also to members of boards or committees or the interested public.

In the smaller religious organizations, as in small business, there may be only one general bookkeeper. This person is required to perform all of the functions involved in keeping "a complete set of books." Most of these bookkeepers do their work by hand, and may even keep their records in longhand, even though they use adding machines or other simple office machines, and do a small amount of typing of statements. A general bookkeeper may also be called upon to do filing or other office work, such as answering the telephone, mailing of summaries and statements, etc.

In the larger offices, one finds bookkeeping departments in which a number of employees work under supervision, usually by an accountant (which see). In these offices each worker is responsible for only one or two of the numerous duties of the general bookkeeper. Some of these employees are classified as accounting clerks, while others, in the highly mechanized offices, are called bookkeeping-machine operators.

Beginners in the mechanized offices may be assigned the more routine tasks of record-keeping, including the use of an adding machine. The more experienced operate the various and complex business machines.

About three-fourths of all bookkeeping jobs are held by women.

For bookkeeping jobs, one should have more than average knowledge of arithmetic and aptitude for working with figures. Manual dexterity and good coordination of movements of hand and eye are also necessary. For the general personal and educational qualifications, see Office Positions, above.

## Office-machine Operators

The types of machines now used in modern offices are so numerous that it is difficult to find even a majority of them listed in one place. In the offices of religious organizations, these machines are probably being used in increasing numbers, but they do not use the extremely expensive kinds that the largest of corporations now have.

There are, for example, machines that open letters, and even classify them into categories. There are bookkeeping machines and billing machines. There are machines used largely by statisticians and their clerks. For operation of many of these, special training is needed before taking the job; for others training on the job or learning by actual experience is adequate.

In general, office-machine operators are trained personnel who can use high speed equipment accurately. They are required to use the keyboards of the machines by the touch system used by the trained typist.

Among the specialties in this field are:

Billing-machine operators who use equipment for preparation of statements for purchasers. These machines are used not only for adding and printing of totals, but also for figuring of discounts, etc.

Calculating-machine operators who use special equipment for preparing payrolls and related statistical work. These calculating machines are more complex than the ordinary adding machine and

129

may be used to find the square root or other equally difficult processes.

Mail preparation and mail-handling machine operators, who run the special automatic equipment that processes mail coming in and that going out.

Addressing-machine operators who put stencils or plates into a machine that completes the entire mail-addressing process.

Duplicating-machine operators who operate devices that produce a given number of copies from a master copy.

Operators of tabulating machines who operate equipment designed to handle large amounts of statistical work.

Most office-machine operators are women. Finger dexterity, good vision, good coordination of eye and hand, knowledge of mathematics are all important. For the general personal and educational qualifications see the notes above under Office Positions.

### Electronic Computer Operators

The use of electronic computers is rapidly expanding. Because they are expensive they are rented or purchased only by large religious organizations and church-related institutions, usually located in metropolitan areas. Most computers are used to handle large quantities of office records, to maintain inventories and related information, to speed the more technical research work.

The use of electronic computers to make up payrolls or related data requires trained operators. In the larger offices several types of equipment are needed. Thus the number and kinds of workers depend upon the size of the operation and the kind of work to be done. There are computers that are made in the size of ordinary office desks, while others fill a large room.

The input of a computer consists of data to be processed and the instructions, which are prepared by executives or specialists known as programmers (which see). It is they who inform the machine what is to be done and how.

In some computer systems, punched cards or tapes that are made on auxiliary equipment are required. The high-speed systems

130

use magnetic tapes. When the work is of the most complex nature, the auxiliary machines are run by persons called peripheral equipment operators. These operators, however, should have a general knowledge of the entire computer system being used. The functions of the peripheral operators include the conversion or transfer of data from cards to magnetic tapes, or from paper tapes to magnetic tapes.

When the figures or other data have been converted to the form required by the computer, they are ready for what is called "the run." This is the responsibility of the computer operator or the console operator. The operator must first understand the instructions prepared by the programmer or the executive in charge. Then the operator makes use of the control switches that manipulate panel lights which must be observed during the operation. If the lights signal an error, the operator must at once try to locate the source of the trouble. Sometimes a console operator also supervises the operator or operators of the auxiliary equipment.

In order to enable the layman to read or understand the output of a computer, it must be translated from the language of the machine to words and numbers of ordinary language. In the large and complex systems this may be done by machines called "printers" or other machines which are connected with the computer and run by the console operator or assistant.

Because the output must usually be stored for future use, the vocation of "tape librarian" has evolved. Sometimes this is a full-time position, but this work may also be handled by a console operator or a peripheral equipment operator.

Since the operation of computers is a relatively new vocation, employers often finance the training opportunities for persons already in the organization. Training may be had from manufacturers of equipment or by educational institutions that have the necessary resources to organize and offer the courses.

At least a high-school education is required for persons entering the field, but college training or work experience may be required for the most difficult duties, for example those of console operator. Special tests are often given to determine the person's aptitude for this work. Work experience and in-service training enable some console operators to advance to the position of programmer (which see).

For the general personal qualifications see the introductory notes under Office Positions, above.

OTHER INFORMATION. For additional information communicate with the Association for Computing Machinery, 211 East 43rd St., New York, N.Y. 10017.

## Programmers

The vocation of programmer is as recent as the development of the electronic computers. In vocational counseling circles, the term programmer refers to the guidance and control of electronic equipment and not to supervision or administration of the many programs of religious bodies and church-related institutions. Computers must have expert instructions with respect to what they are to do. Those who prepare the instructions are called programmers.

A computer is an unusual machine. It makes mathematical calculations at fantastic rates and also has a capacity, called a "memory," by which data may be stored and used again later. Because of their great speed and other characteristics, computers can perform great amounts of work that would take long periods of time if done by hand. Computers not only handle such prosaic matters as payrolls; they have been used to compile published concordances of the Bible.

The problem to be handled by a computer must first of all be defined and analyzed with great care and skill, in order that specific plans may be made for processing data adequately. This preliminary definition and analysis may be made by the professional specialist or executive, and is also at times done by the programmer.

When the plans have been completed, the programmer is ready to write out the details of the instructions for the machine. These will vary in accordance with the type of computer and the nature of the problem. Thus the instructions for making out a payroll will differ considerably from those for making a concordance of the Bible.

No matter what the problem, the programmer must usually confer systematically with the professional expert or executive who has the special knowledge of the subject matter. When this has been done, the programmer makes a diagram, or a flow chart, which indicates the order in which the computer shall do each operation. He also prepares detailed instructions, called routines, for every operation. The routines are stated in terms of a code or the language to which a computer will respond. He should also make a record of the reasoning followed in developing every routine. He must also prepare a set of instructions for the console operator (see Electronic Computer Operators).

Usually the programmer makes a trial run in order to test his instructions. This is done in cooperation with the console operator. The trial run may even be used to test some portion of a solution that can be worked by other means.

The programming process may take only a few hours, or a year, or longer.

Many programmers secure their jobs because they are familiar with the problems to be programmed, or because they have shown some aptitude for the work. They may then learn the specific techniques in special courses available.

Courses in programming techniques are being offered in a small but increasing number of colleges and universities. A few large city high schools are also offering courses. A course in high school or college often needs to be supplemented by some kind of on-the-job training.

Some employers who use computers only for business records prefer to hire people who have a knowledge of bookkeeping and accounting. These place less emphasis on formal schooling than those who use computers for technical or scientific work. The latter want college graduates with a Bachelor's degree or even with graduate study.

In this vocation, reasoning ability, patience, persistence, and accuracy are required. Other qualifications are skill in expression both oral and written, imagination, and ingenuity. For general personal qualifications see the introductory notes above under Office Positions.

OTHER INFORMATION. For additional information communicate with the Association for Computing Machinery, 211 East 43rd St., New York, N.Y. 10017.

## PERSONNEL WORKERS

Personnel workers are employed full time in the larger religious organizations and church-related institutions of education, health, and social welfare.

Personnel workers assist their employers in finding employees and in assigning and reassigning them to work for which they are best fitted and which they can do most effectively. They thus develop and administer recruiting programs, interview job applicants, and make recommendations regarding their selection. They give tests to applicants and evaluate the results. They keep personnel records and at intervals prepare reports based on these records. They classify jobs on the basis of systematic descriptions. They may deal with matters of discipline, if authorized by the general executives of the organization. They plan and administer salary scales and ranges for the various positions in the organization. They administer health insurance plans in effect and recommend changes in them. They carry on educational work among employees with respect to employment standards, provisions, and benefits. In this connection they prepare manuals or similar documents for distribution to employees. They do some counseling with employees, both on personal and organizational issues and problems. They administer retirement systems.

Most of the functions of personnel workers involve contacts with people, both within and without an organization. In the largest of personnel offices a few people may deal only with records and reports and may thus not have frequent contacts with people.

PERSONAL QUALIFICATIONS. In personnel work the emphasis

is distinctly on the personal. The very name implies it. Thus one needs skill and desire to work directly with people all day long. In addition, ability to see with perspective both the employee and the employer positions in an organization; a relish for detail; aptness in expression both in speech and writing are all assets. For the general personal qualifications, see the notes above under Office Positions.

EDUCATION AND TRAINING. Education at a four-year college is increasingly being recommended and required for personnel work, even though some in the field have not had it. Also, some organizations prefer to transfer employees from other departments for personnel work.

College study recommended includes courses in personnel management, business administration, applied psychology, statistics, labor economics, political science, sociology, English, and public speaking. Some large employers prefer graduates who have majored in personnel management or administration, while others ask for persons with a broad background of study in business administration. Still others recommend general liberal-arts study as the most desirable education.

In some instances, for those who expect to do testing or counseling, courses in psychology are especially recommended. A college major in psychology, or even graduate study, would be greater assets for this special work. Courses in law and accounting will be useful for those who will be dealing largely with salaries, fringe benefits, and retirement plans.

WHAT DO THEY DO? In the smaller offices, one person may be expected to do as many as possible of the duties described above. Even a beginner in such an office may have to deal with the many functions as best he can.

In the larger personnel offices, college graduates may be employed in the "junior" positions. They thus acquire experience or take additional training, and are advanced as opportunties arise. In this process they learn about their employer's policies, programs, and other operations. In much the same manner young college graduates are employed as assistants to personnel workers with special knowledge. After training in this manner, they may later secure promotions.

Executive positions go to people with experience and training.

OTHER INFORMATION. For general information on personnel work as a career communicate with the American Society for Personnel Administration, Kellogg Center, East Lansing, Mich.

# PHYSICAL THERAPISTS

Most physical therapists are employed in the hospitals of the nation. About half of those in hospital employment are in private, non-profit institutions, including those that are church-related. A large proportion of physical therapists are women.

Physical therapists, sometimes called physiotherapists, work under the direction of physicians, helping persons with muscle, nerve, joint, bone, and other diseases to overcome their disabilities.

Physical therapists are trained to treat patients with all kinds of disabilities, but this profession, like so many others, is becoming specialized. Thus there are therapists who work only with children, or only with persons with arthritis, or only with those with muscular dystrophy.

PERSONAL QUALIFICATIONS. Because of the nature of their work, physical therapists should have emotional stability, good manual dexterity, and an authentic wish to help people by working directly with them. They are called upon to demonstrate patience, imagination, observation, and both a sympathetic and objective attitude toward persons with disabilities. They must be able to express themselves clearly in spoken English, to have ability to organize both materials and time. They need skill in interviewing relatives, parents, and the people being treated. For general personal qualifications expected in church-related institutions, see the notes under Nurses and Physicians.

EDUCATION AND TRAINING. For professional education in the field, attendance at one of the more than 40 schools approved by the American Medical Association and the American Physical Therapy Association is recommended. Most of these schools are

136

affiliated with the larger universities. A majority of the remainder are operated by hospitals that have university connections.

Half of these schools offer four-year programs of study leading to a Bachelor's degree. The schools are open to high-school graduates, and also to college students who have completed specified courses in science. A college student entering a school of physical therapy can often earn a Bachelor's degree there in less than the full four years of study.

Most of the schools offer, in addition to a Bachelor's degree, one- or two-year courses, which lead to a certificate in physical therapy. The usual requirement for entrance to these courses is a Bachelor's degree, including instruction in biological, physical, and social science.

The curricula of approved schools that offer a Bachelor's degree include courses in anatomy, physiology, pathology, clinical medicine, psychology, and the techniques of electro-therapy, radiation, hydrotherapy, massage, and exercise. Students must also acquire experience, under supervision, in the care of patients in a hospital.

Numerous scholarships are available for study in the field.

Graduation from an A.M.A. approved school is required for membership in the American Physical Therapy Association, see address below, and for registration by the Association. A degree from an approved school is usually essential for entering the profession and may be necessary for securing a license or registration by some state boards. A large majority of the states now require licensing or registration of physical therapists. Some large hospitals will consider applications for employment only from those who are graduates of A.M.A. approved schools.

Advanced programs of study are also available, and a few universities offer courses leading to a Master's degree. Graduate education, plus experience, qualifies persons for supervisory, executive, and teaching positions.

WHAT DO THEY DO? Physical therapists, under physicians' instruction, treat disabilities by means of one or more of the following: physical exercise, mechanical equipment, and application of light, heat, massage, water, or electricity.

They obtain the information they need for development of treatment programs by tests of nerves and muscles, They keep records of results of processes of treatment. They discuss patients' problems, and assist them in accepting and understanding a handicap. They often teach patients how to use braces, crutches, and artificial hands or legs. They also teach patients and members of their families how to continue treatments in their homes after they leave a hospital.

They cooperate with other members of the health service professions, and attend conferences conducted by physicians.

Experienced therapists become teachers of physical-therapy students, of classes in related professions, of assistants in physical therapy, and orderlies. They may also advance to supervisory and administrative positions.

OTHER INFORMATION. The Woman's Bureau, U.S. Department of Labor, Washington, D.C. 20210, publishes information on the outlook for women as physical therapists.

General information on the profession may be had from the American Physical Therapy Association, 1790 Broadway, New York, N.Y. 10019.

## PHYSICIANS

Of some 250,000 physicians in the U.S., most are in private practice either as general practitioners or as specialists. Out of some 34,000 physicians who are residents or interns in hospitals, a considerable portion are employed in Protestant church-related hospitals. Also, of some 10,000 others holding regular positions on hospital staffs, many are in the Protestant, church-related institutions. About 6 per cent of all physicians are women.

The maintenance of hospitals was from early years a function of some Protestant churches of Europe, and this tradition was brought to the U.S. and put into practice. Thus church-related hospitals not only employ physicians but also permit others to use their facilities as part of their private practice.

The practice of medicine in its various forms is now a "high-demand" vocation. But it is comparatively very costly to secure a medical education.

PERSONAL QUALIFICATIONS. Physicians diagnose and treat diseases and injuries. They are also increasingly concerned with prevention and rehabilitation. Among the personal qualifications frequently mentioned are interest in science, devotion to hard and long study, above-average intelligence, and a strong desire to aid in meeting the needs of people. But these are not all. A physician deals with terrible emergencies in human life. He aids in the process of birth and treats people facing death. Thus he should possess a high degree of emotional stability, so that he can make good decisions in difficult situations. Sometimes his successes are dramatic; at other times he works with varieties of unspeakable tragedies. Thus the churches ask him to be committed to the values of religion as he constantly meets people. There is opinion, obviously not shared by all physicians, that cooperation between physician and trained minister aids in healing and prevention, and is to be encouraged.

EDUCATION AND TRAINING. Prior to applying for admission to a medical school, a student is usually required to have completed at least three years of undergraduate college study. Some medical schools require four years. Whether required to do so or not, about 80 per cent of students entering medical schools have completed four years of college. A few medical schools deliberately choose for admission carefully selected students who have completed only two or three years of college. These students are then able to earn their Bachelor's degree while in medical school.

The type of pre-medical study is rather rigidly defined by the medical schools. It must include courses in chemistry, both organic and inorganic, biology, physics, and English, in an accredited college. The study of mathematics, social science, and the humanities is also encouraged. Medical schools also judge candidates for admission by evidence of personality development, student leadership, etc. Frequently an applicant is required to have an interview with an officer of the school before admission is granted. Many

139

state-supported medical schools give preference to residents of their own states and of nearby states.

Every year many more young people apply for admission to the nation's medical schools than can be accepted. Most of the 86 medical schools require four years of full-time study; others offer basic courses for two years of study, after which transfer is made to a four-year school. After four years at medical school, the degree of M.D. (Doctor of Medicine) is awarded on successful completion of the courses.

A number of citizens of the U.S. are going abroad to study medicine in schools of other countries. Such persons are required, on completion of their courses and return to the U.S., to pass a special examination given by the Educational Council for Foreign Medical Graduates.

During the first two years at medical school, students spend their time in classrooms and laboratories in study including anatomy, biochemistry, physiology, pharmacology, microbiology, and pathology. During the next two years students usually study in hospitals, where, under the supervision of trained physicians, they learn how to make examinations, recognize diseases and injuries, and write case histories. This is followed by a one-year internship in a hospital; most young physicians take an additional year as resident physicians or interns.

Young physicians intending to become specialists in one of the 32 recognized medical fields, must spend from two to four years in advanced hospital training as residents, plus two years of practice as a specialist. Then they may qualify for the specialty board examinations. If they complete these satisfactorily, they are recognized as specialists.

LICENSING. All states and the District of Columbia require a license for the practice of medicine. Candidates must be graduates from approved medical schools and pass a licensing examination. In about three-fourths of the states and in D.C., a one-year hospital internship is also prerequisite to licencing. In the states that give a license to practice to an applicant on completion of medical school only, the medical profession nevertheless requires a year of intership for acceptance by the profession. State boards give the licensing examinations. There is also a National Board of Medical Examiners that gives an examination acceptable by most states. A physician licensed in one state can usually without difficulty also secure a license in another state, without additional examination. However, this reciprocity or courtesy is not exercised by all states.

SPECIAL FIELDS. There is a marked trend toward specialization in medicine. Among the 32 recognized fields of specialization are surgery, internal medicine, pediatrics (care of children), pathology, obstetrics, gynecology, psychiatry, radiology, ophthalmology (care of the eye), and otolaryngology (care of eye, ear, nose, and throat).

OTHER INFORMATION. Women are generally accepted by medical schools and have opportunities to become both general practitioners and specialists.

Doctors tend to work long and irregular hours, particularly those numerous persons in the profession who are general practitioners. Many doctors work until they are far beyond the customary retirement age of 65. Physicians on salary work shorter hours and more regularly than general practitioners, and are also reported to have somewhat lower incomes. Specialists tend to earn more than general practitioners.

For service as interns and residents in hospitals, board, room and other maintenance are generally provided, along with the modest cash stipend.

Earnings of physicians vary by size of community, by region, by years of experience, by training and skill. Established physicians are, however, reported to be among the best paid of professional people in the U.S.

For general information on pre-medical education, medicine as a career, and lists of approved medical schools, communicate with the Council on Medical Education and Hospitals, American Medical Association, 535 N. Dearborn St., Chicago, Ill. 60610; or with the Association of American Medical Colleges, 2530 Ridge Ave., Evanston, Ill.

## PRINTERS AND RELATED WORKERS

A few of the larger religious publishing houses, and other boards and agencies, maintain their own printing plants and thus employ persons in the printing vocations.

Printing is usually done in three stages: typesetting, plate-making, and press work. Binding may be done in a department of a printing plant, or may be arranged under contract with plants that specialize in the process. In years past there were many printers who could perform every one of the printing processes. This was usually the situation in the smaller plants. Now there is generally division of labor, and printing craftsmen usually specialize, even at the beginning of their training.

In the processes requiring the greatest skills, most of the workers are men. A number of the less-skilled jobs have been held by women, for example in binderies. However, technological advances have made it possible to bind many books by complex high-speed machines that have replaced many of the less skilled workers. Technological changes have also greatly affected composition and plate-making. Among these are developments in photo-composition, in cold-type composition, and in the wide use of electronic devices and controls in photo-engraving and printing. Thus the craftsmen in the printing trades are continually being challenged and affected by what is commonly called automation.

Although printing jobs are found all around the nation, those in the church-related organizations are probably mainly in the larger cities and metropolitan areas.

PERSONAL QUALIFICATIONS. Among the personal qualifications desired in the printing crafts are good eyesight, better than average physical stamina, high manual dexterity, speed with accuracy, alertness, ability to cooperate with others. An interest in art is an asset in some jobs. Employers may require applicants to take aptitude tests, which are given in the local offices of the U.S. Employment Service. For the general personal qualifications expected by religious organizations, see the notes under Office Positions.

142

EDUCATION AND TRAINING. The usual way to enter the *skilled* printing vocations is still by apprenticeship. It is generally the only way in a unionized shop, and some religious organizations have contracts with unions. Apprenticeship may last from four to six years. Sometimes one may acquire experience in a small "letter-service" shop.

Several thousand high schools, vocational schools, technical institutes, and colleges give courses in printing. High-school study will be of help to a person applying for apprenticeship. Apprentices are also sometimes chosen from among the unskilled workers who are employed in printing plants, if they demonstrate an interest in a craft.

WHAT DO THEY DO? The printing shops of religious agencies do work comparable with that of commercial or job printing plants. They produce letterheads, leaflets, pamphlets, periodicals, books, and advertising matter. Much of the total volume in these plants is in the form of materials for use in religious education, not only in Sunday schools, but also in vacation and weekday classes and courses.

The method of printing generally used is also the most common form found elsewhere—letter press or relief printing. Most periodicals and books in the church-related plants are produced by this method. Newer methods coming rapidly into use include lithography, photo-offset, and screen printing.

The largest group of craftsmen employed in plants of all types throughout the nation are those who work in composing rooms. These include hand compositors, typesetting machine operators, imposers, and proofreaders. Other large groups are the letter pressmen and book binders. Printing plants also employ stenographers and secretaries, bookkeepers and accountants (all of which see). They also obviously need managers (see Business Administrators).

OTHER INFORMATION. Further information may be had from officers of publishing agencies of denominations having printing plants; and on the industry in general from Printing Industry of America, 20 Chevy Chase Circle, N.W., Washington, D.C. 20015

# PSYCHOLOGISTS

Psychologists are employed in considerable numbers as teachers in church-related schools and colleges, and as counselors in hospitals, social-welfare agencies, and in the newly organized special counseling centers which some local churches have established or with which they are cooperating. Because of the expected rapid increases in total college enrollment, employment opportunities in colleges are expected to be relatively numerous. Also, the local counseling centers of churches are apparently being established in increasing numbers.

Psychology is a discipline with many specialized branches. Thus psychologists usually decide rather early in their study or training to specialize, recognizing that the various branches are related to one another. Psychologists study human behavior. Many of them also try to assist people readjusting or re-educating their emotional attitudes and behavior. Largest in this latter group are the "clinical psychologists." They work mainly with troubled or disturbed people and counsel with them.

Psychologists are also employed as teachers in departments of psychology in colleges (see Psychology in the section on Teaching). This teaching is also becoming specialized, and may include courses labeled child psychology, educational psychology, etc.

EDUCATION AND TRAINING. It appears established that a Master's degree with a major in psychology is the minimum educational requirement for professional employment. Those with a Bachelor's degree and a major in psychology may sometimes secure the more elementary positions related to psychology or those in which some knowledge of psychology is valuable. Increasingly, too, the Ph.D. degree is necessary for promotion or assumption of the more difficult tasks of psychologists. Those with this degree can qualify for the higher level positions in education, research, or counseling.

A Master's degree enables people to start teaching in a college, or assist in counseling students. In secondary and elementary schools they may secure positions as counselors or psychologists. It also enables a person to secure a position in conducting and interpreting tests, in statistical work, in assisting in experiments, and in performance of elementary administrative functions. At least one year of full-time study beyond the Bachelor's degree is ordinarily necessary to secure the Master's. However, it is reported that many students of psychology take more than a year of graduate work. In some instances five or six years of graduate study may be necessary to secure a Ph.D.

For clinical or counseling work a year of supervised experience or of an internship may also be required for the Ph.D.

In some universities a major in psychology during undergraduate study is required for admission to graduate study. In others, broad cultural study, including psychology, is regarded as desirable.

Many scholarships, fellowships, and part-time positions are available in this field.

WHAT DO THEY DO? There are several ways by which psychologists secure information and insights with respect to the traits, capacities, assets, and problems of people. They may systematically interview and observe persons. They may make use of various tests or rating scales, or may devise these themselves. They may make surveys in order to learn attitudes and opinions, either by oral interviews or mailed questionnaires. They may work with groups as well as with individuals. Some psychologists do research in which the most advanced statistical methods are necessary.

For the general personal qualifications in church-related work see Teaching in Colleges and Universities and Teaching in Secondary Schools.

OTHER INFORMATION. Most psychologists are employed in the larger cities and university centers. Many positions in personnel offices are filled by persons with training or experience in psychology.

For general information and career opportunities and a list of universities with approved doctoral programs in clinical work and counseling communicate with the American Psychological Association, 1333 16th St., N.W., Washington, D.C. 20036.

## PUBLIC RELATIONS WORKERS

Public relations is a vocation that has expanded phenomenally in church and other circles since World War II. In local churches, public relations is usually the part-time responsibility of a minister, or the incidental work of volunteer officers of organizations within the churches. In denominational offices, and in those of specialized boards, public relations is becoming a full-time function of one or more persons. Both men and women go into public relations.

A generation ago, the tendency was to label this function as "publicity," and the larger church organizations began to employ workers to devote themselves to publicizing—in various media—the programs and, indeed, the officers, including their speeches, travels, and activities. Church officials vary greatly in their attitudes toward publicity for themselves. Some have never had enough, even though their remarks are relatively widely quoted. Others are more modest in their aims and motives.

Public relations still goes sometimes under the label of publicity. Others use the term communication, interpretation, or even information. Journalists often shift from journalism into public relations, and vice versa.

The function of public relations workers is briefly defined as that of developing and maintaining public opinion favorable to the organization, its officers, its publications, its pronouncements, etc. In order to do this, the workers must study the various media that they wish to use, and also know the opinions of officers and employees, as well as the nature of their programs. They are often called upon to conduct activities directly or indirectly related to the familiar task of raising money. Indeed, in some religious organizations, public relations is narrowly viewed as something to help raise the budget or to avoid a deficit, while in others a much broader view is taken of the vocation. Public relations workers are also expected to know something about the "unreached" or those not contributing. In denominational boards they may be expected to enliven the interest of local churches in the general or national programs of the organization.

146

In church circles, public relations workers may concentrate on higher education, or hospitals, or relief abroad, or missions; or may be responsible for interpreting specialized programs, or drives for money.

PERSONAL QUALIFICATIONS. In a relatively new vocation, the personal qualifications are not yet well defined. Many presently in this field have come from other jobs, e.g., the ministry, newspaper reporting, education, and many others. A wish to write and personal interest in the skill of writing are essentials. A noted writer, E. B. White, says that the personality of the writer determines his style of writing. His personality determines whether he should go into writing in public relations or writing in technical research. The two abilities are seldom found in any one person. A wish to study the trends and cross currents of public opinion in a period of rapid change also is regarded as desirable. Some church agencies require an attitude of "salesmanship" among their public relations; others take a somewhat broad educational view, wishing to teach people about the valuable services of the organization.

This leads into considerations of personal dilemmas or conflicts. If one wishes to "sell" a program, he will be more satisfied with his job if he is genuinely convinced of its value, rather than having only an official or routine interest. Mechanical use of techniques can only be deadly—or dead. A further dilemma often comes in the choice of materials or ideas to publicize. Does one indicate that the employer's program is without flaw? Or, does one go on to admit at times that the organization can probably do some things well, and others not well, or not at all? Does one act as if his employer should never be adversely criticized? Does one ever circulate unfavorable opinion or trends? How shall the public relations worker develop an authentic, and to him, ethical type of public relations? What are good means toward good ends?

EDUCATION AND TRAINING. A Bachelor's degree is usually recommended for full-time work in this vocation. Should this be a degree with a major in public relations or journalism, as offered only in the larger colleges, or one with broad liberal arts study? Employees and employers differ on this point. Some employers seem to prefer the Bachelor's degree with a major in English, expecting that the young practitioner will acquire training by doing his tasks.

Study of psychology, economics, sociology, political science, business administration, public speaking, are recommended in college, in addition to English or special courses for writers.

Study of radio and TV is advised, in addition to that of magazines and newspapers. (See Radio and TV Broadcasters.)

Extracurricular volunteer activities in writing, speaking, and studying public opinion may provide valuable experience for students. Part-time and summer jobs in the field are advised.

Summer and evening courses offer opportunities for pursuing graduate study or continuing education.

WHAT DO THEY DO? The functions vary from routine filing and classification of previously issued materials to administration of relatively large departments. Administrative jobs are still available only to a few, however. (See separate articles on Journalists, and Radio and TV Broadcasters.)

The usual duties consist of disseminating information about the employing organization's activities, programs, and officers to magazines, newspapers, radio and TV stations, public meetings, etc.

This involves planning and timing a particular item for a particular medium or media. It involves seeking knowledge of the people and organizations that operate the media.

Often the public relations worker emphasizes the "human interest" aspect, or makes use, if possible, of an already prominent name. Often the task consists of reporting a public meeting held by the organization or one in which an official speaks or has other responsibilities. Sometimes an officer's comments on big news is disseminated; or a copy of a letter of public interest by an officer is released to appropriate media.

Cooperation with a somewhat diverse "religious press," meaning religious magazines, mainly monthlies, is usually required.

Public relations work for church-related colleges and social-welfare agencies, with some of the methods here noted, is also a rapidly developing vocation.

OTHER INFORMATION. Further information may be had from officers of the Religious Public Relations Council, 475 Riverside Drive, New York, N.Y. 10027, an association of individuals, engaged in public relations and closely related fields in religious organizations. Also, from public relations workers in the larger denominational agencies, interdenominational organizations, and church-related colleges and other institutions. For general information, consult the publications of the Public Relations Society of America, 375 Park Ave., New York, N.Y. 10022.

## PUBLISHING WORKERS

Publishing is one of the main activities of religious bodies, especially of the large ones. The American Book Publishers Council, 58 W. 40th St., New York, N.Y. 10018, has compiled figures on the distribution of religious books, indicating that the number of copies of religious books sold, increased from 40,140,000 in 1956 to 50,084,000 in 1961. In terms of dollars, the sales of religious books increased from $35,202,000 in 1956 to $43,210,000 in 1961.

About 1,400 religious periodicals in the U.S. are listed in the Directory published annually by N.W. Ayer and Son, Philadelphia, and this list does not include all of them in the nation.

Publishing houses may be roughly grouped as follows:

1. Denominational publishers who bring out literature for use in religious education, including the Sunday and Sabbath schools, and weekday and informal religious education.

2. Denominational publishers who produce both religious education materials for use in the schools, and religious books of general interest.

3. Denominational publishers who concentrate on books for both adults and children.

4. Independent publishers of religious works, and religious book departments of the well-known commercial book houses.

Publishing houses employ many people who have been trained

149

for the following vocations, all of which are discussed elsewhere in this book under these headings:

Accountants and Bookkeepers;
Bookstore Managers;
Business Administrators or Managers;
Commercial Artists;
Journalists, including both writers and editors;
Office Workers;
Printers and Related Workers;
Public Relations Workers;
Religious Education specialists.

## RADIO AND TV BROADCASTERS

This relatively new and very large field has not only been attractive to many young people—it has also been regarded as one that is exceptionally exciting. Persons are employed for work in radio and TV by denominations, boards of denominations, councils of churches, social welfare agencies, and church-related colleges. Because relatively few of these church bodies own and operate stations of their own, they generally employ people who prepare and produce programs to be broadcast by the various stations and networks. Music is an important part of all radio and TV broadcasting, and also in the programs sponsored by the religious organizations. Both full-time and part-time employment is available, for both trained men and women. Ministers of local churches are often invited to speak on local radio stations. Sometimes short dramatic productions of local churches, or forums and discussions, may be granted radio time.

Religious programs to be broadcast fall into two main groups: Those accepted for free time as part of the "public service" function that radio and TV stations are required by law to provide for; those for which individuals or church agencies or committees pay for at the regular rates for time. On the latter, considerable direct solicitation of contributions for programs or causes takes place; on the former it usually does not.

150

PERSONAL QUALIFICATIONS. For the preparation and production of religious programs, or those of religious interest, the general personal qualifications are much the same as those for journalists and public relations workers (which see). Knowledge and interest in everything having to do with communication are essential—writing, drama, music. Ability to achieve and maintain cooperation with other people, mature judgment of persons and issues, interest in church history and current religious programs and events, an inclination to travel—these are all assets. A programmer is one who must enlist the talents of many others—sometimes for pay, at other times in a volunteer capacity.

EDUCATION AND TRAINING. For work in programming of radio and TV in religion, a college education is preferred. Theological education is also sometimes an asset. Women generally work on programs for children in the field of religious education.

Majors or specialized study of writing, dramatics, and music are desirable. Knowledge of make-up, design, and even "sound effects" may be of additional help.

Short and intensive courses in use of radio and TV are arranged from time to time by denominations, colleges, theological seminaries, and councils of churches. Summer courses are also available.

Because this is a new field of communication of religion, many have learned by doing, after having had experience in the pastorate, religious education, journalism, or public relations.

WHAT DO THEY DO? Programmers plan, prepare, and produce radio and TV programs. In the smaller organizations, the work is handled by one person, who performs as many functions as he can. In the larger organizations the work becomes specialized.

Programs may include planning and preparing for broadcasting:

A conventional local church worship service, either "live" or by recording in advance. This is still a widely used type of program, the extent of which depends on how well the minister conducting is known, or how the type of service appeals.

Early morning, or other broadcast, of brief devotional periods, conducted by a minister, or by a number of ministers, in sequence.

Readings from the Bible, either at one sitting, or in a series, by a minister or a lay reader.

Reports of conferences or conventions, in the form of several speeches or of panel discussions.

A special musical program.

A special dramatic program.

Recognition of significant anniversaries of local churches and state, national, and international bodies.

Reports of religious news.

Discussions of warm issues in the relation of the churches to social needs, or legislation, or public affairs.

Recognition of cooperation among the historically separated religious bodies.

The duties may include the employment of free-lance writers, musicians, and others.

Even when free time is available, there are expenses for a religious organization connected with broadcasting. Thus programmers administer budgets, supervise secretaries and other office workers, and maintain many contacts with commercial stations.

OTHER INFORMATION. Further information may be had from denominations and councils of churches with radio and TV departments.

## RELIEF AND REHABILITATION WORKERS ABROAD

Large organizations within Protestantism administer programs of relief to needy persons abroad, and, when there are opportunities, projects in self-help that lead to rehabilitation and reconstruction. These church agencies have been responsible for aiding numerous refugees to resettle in countries where they have become self-supporting, and have given advice and assistance to refugees who still must remain in camps or other such centers.

These organizations are a part of the response of the churches to sufferings caused by the upheavals accompanying World War II. Most of the agencies were formed during the last war, although a few continued to operate after their establishment in earlier years. Some of the relief agencies do work both here and abroad, but most are responsible for assistance to people in other nations.

These organizations distribute food, clothing, medicines, vitamins, and various kinds of related supplies, including hospital equipment, books, plows, tools. Most of the food now distributed by the church agencies comes from the surpluses held by the government of the U.S., which through its Food For Peace program not only contributes the food but also pays ocean freight. Many of the governments of the receiving nations pay inland transportation. The church relief agencies work with national committees and agencies in distribution of this food, which must be given, by government contract, without discrimination because of race, creed, or color. The Protestant agencies cooperate with Roman Catholic and Jewish agencies in their work both here and abroad. These agencies in the U.S. are generally administered separately from boards of foreign missions in the U.S., and in distribution abroad.

The Mennonites, Friends, Brethren and others have long traditions of giving aid at times of disaster in the U.S., and abroad. In the U.S. they also carry on projects to stimulate self-help among the poor or otherwise handicapped.

PERSONAL QUALIFICATIONS. The requirements for relief work are special, and often difficult to attain. The work is only for the physically rugged, the patient, and the tough-minded. Also necessary are compassion, perspective, and high standards of personal conduct. Usually some experience in the U.S. in educational or religious organizations—not always in relief work—is necessary before appointment to responsible positions abroad. One must know how to negotiate, and to go on in spite of the heartaches that are inevitable in dealing with great need and often inadequate supplies. When there are not enough vitamins for everybody, for example—to whom shall they be given?

Some personal dilemmas arise from the relation of the relief, rehabilitation, and reconstruction work to that of the foreign mission agencies. A blunt way of putting one of the issues is this: Does one give food to suffering people for the purpose of securing conversions? Has rice been given to people in order to make Christians out of them? The term "rice Christians" is well-known. The prevailing opinion among church officials is that relief work is an aspect of the historic charity of the churches, and that one should not require creedal tests or results as a direct result of the charity. And relief work with compassion and understanding is itself a Christian witness.

EDUCATION AND TRAINING. No specified education or training is generally required to do relief work abroad. A college education is usually expected, but not absolutely necessary.

One thing is certain: One does not need to be an ordained minister to do relief work abroad. Also recognized is the fact that ordained ministers can do well in the enterprise if they have ability to organize, negotiate, and interpret.

Relief agencies generally give short intensive instruction to workers going abroad for the first time. This is usually done at their headquarters in the U.S. Some agencies send young people abroad as teachers for short periods.

Young people can test their aptitude for relief work abroad by joining in one of the various work camps, conducted by interdenominational and denominational agencies. Usually a team goes to a village abroad for a specified period and constructs needed community facilities, conducts recreation and informal discussion, and tries to leave tangible and intangible results in the form of self-help or local cooperative activity. The young people in the work camps are required to pay a fixed sum for their maintenance and supervision. Sometimes a young people's group will raise money in order to send an officer, or one whom they elect, for the work camp experience.

Work camps are also conducted in the U.S. in isolated or badly depressed areas. Summer work in the Migrant Ministry (which see), would also be helpful.

Overseas relief agencies in the U.S. employ people at headquarters and in the field. These people are office workers, journalists, public relations workers, and executives.

Young persons beginning their relief work may secure office

jobs, or work as journalists, in public relations, or assisting in money-raising campaigns. Executive jobs are filled by people with experience in relief or related work.

OTHER INFORMATION. Further information may be had from the following organizations, which, among others, have had broad experience in the field:

Church World Service, National Council of Churches, 475 Riverside Drive, New York, N.Y. 10027.

Lutheran World Relief, 50 Madison Ave., New York, N.Y. 10010.

CROP (Christian Rural Overseas Program), 117 W. Lexington Ave., Elkhart, Ind.

Heifer Project, North Manchester, Ind.

Mennonite Central Committee, 21 S. 12th St., Akron, Pa.

Brethren Service Committee, Elgin, Ill.

American Friends Service Committee, 15th and Race Sts., Philadelphia, Pa. 19102. (Work Camps in U.S. and abroad and general activities.)

National Student Christian Federation, 475 Riverside Drive, New York, N.Y. 10027. (Voluntary service projects, including work camps abroad.)

International Christian Youth Exchange, 475 Riverside Drive, New York, N.Y. 10027.

International Voluntary Services, 1903 N St., N.W., Washington, D.C. 20036. (This private organization recruits personnel for projects that it administers by contract with government agencies. It also counsels with interested individuals.)

(A number of denominations not mentioned here have relief agencies, of which their own pastors have knowledge.)

# RELIGIOUS EDUCATION

## Directors or Ministers of Religious Education

There are many full-time professionals employed in local churches as directors or ministers of religious education or of

Christian education. Both men and women are in this profession, also both ordained and unordained persons. This position evolved out of the teaching ministry of the churches. In general, the larger urban and suburban churches employ full-time directors or ministers of religious education.

In some local church situations the director of religious education is called upon to combine his distinctly educational duties with responsibilities such as those of assistant pastor, musician, secretary, or recreation worker. This may be necessary in some churches, but it is often unsatisfactory.

A person considering this vocation should first of all examine himself, officials of one denomination suggest, in terms of such questions as: "Do you have strong convictions; a clear life purpose; a sacrificial spirit; love for God, for man, for the church; a desire to find out where and how you can serve God? Are you physically sound, emotionally stable, intellectually alert, socially sensitive, religiously literate, spiritually impelled?"

PERSONAL QUALIFICATIONS. As for personal qualifications, of first importance in this profession is religious experience. Each person will know best how to express this or to judge its significance. A person who has participated in the church and religious education, who has endeavored to grow in Christian experience, will realize how important this is and how practical and tangible it is in church-related careers. For other personal matters, one experienced writer puts "love for people and ability to work with them" at the top of a list. Along with this talent come others, including disciplined work habits, systematic study, sense of mission, skill in communication, a sense of humor, and attractive personal appearance. A director of religious education is in a Christian ministry just as the missionary sent to Africa or the pastor of the local church.

EDUCATION AND TRAINING. Generally recommended for this vocation are four years in a liberal arts institution, plus one or more years of graduate study leading to the degree of Master of Arts, or Master of Religious Education, or Bachelor of Divinity. One must know the Bible, church history, and methods of edu-

156

cation and communication. There should also be practical experience in teaching in Sunday or Sabbath Schools and some supervised field work.

TYPICAL DUTIES AND RESPONSIBILITIES. These are sometimes summed up in a grand generalization as follows: Supervision of the whole Christian education program of the local church. This is usually quickly elaborated to include such as the following: The director works with a committee or board or commission on Christian education in the local church; cooperates with the pastor, the lay superintendent of the Sunday school, and other officers of the church; promotes special aspects of the religious education program, e.g., weekday classes, vacation schools, camps, nursery schools, etc.; calls on church members and officers concerning the Christian education program; serves as a leader of, and/or promotes, participation in conferences, leadership training institutes, etc.; develops parent education as may be needed in the local church; makes plans for securing adequate equipment and materials for religious education; interprets the Christian education program to the entire church and organizations within the church; encourages formulation and adoption of systematic policies and standards of the local Christian education program, including the curriculum.

Decisions with respect to employment of directors of religious education are made in the local church. Many denominational boards of education receive, file, and process data on qualifications and experience of applicants, and transmit this information, on request, to local church officers, but they do not make selections or appointments. There is also no interdenominational placement service for directors of religious education. Local councils of churches often have information about positions in local churches.

ASSISTANT IN CHRISTIAN EDUCATION. As noted above, the title of director or minister of religious education is normally given to persons who have a graduate or professional degree in addition to a Bachelor's. There are also "assistants in Christian education." This title is generally given to a person employed for Christian education in the local church who has a Bachelor's degree or who is engaged in study leading to a Bachelor's degree. Such persons have considerably less professional education than those with graduate study, and are called upon to assume fewer of the typical duties summarized above.

FOR FURTHER INFORMATION. An interested person seeking more detailed information should consult with an experienced director of religious education, a pastor in a church employing a director, an executive secretary of a council of churches, or an officer of a national denominational board of Christian education with professional responsibility for this field. General information on the profession may be had from the Division of Christian Education of the National Council of Churches.

There is an American Association of Schools of Religious Education, with offices at California Bapist Theological Seminary, Covina, Calif., which publishes a list of accredited and "associate" schools.

## Weekday Religious Educators

In many communities there are weekday classes in religion, taught by paid teachers, meeting on time "released" by public schools for the purpose. This Protestant religious education is usually arranged by cooperation among the local churches interested. It may be administered by an organization formed for the purpose or by the local council of churches or by a unit or committee of a council. The pupils are from elementary and/or high-school grades. The curriculum is determined locally. Employment is usually for the same number of months as the public school operates.

EXPERIENCE. Some experience in teaching or in group leadership of children is necessary before applying. This may be in the form of teaching in Sunday school classes, vacation schools, summer camps, or practice teaching in a summer school. The more experience, the better.

Experience in teaching public school is also a good qualification, because there the guidance of boys and girls is stressed. In religious education, additional emphasis is put on the development

158

of Christian attitudes, actions, and spirit, as well as on facts and skills.

TRAINING. Formal training that is helpful includes, for beginners, a Bachelor's degree, with a major in religious education. Study should include courses in the Bible, religion, educational psychology, and teaching methods. "Continuing education" in summer schools, conferences, personal reading, observation of classes, always help.

OPPORTUNITIES. Weekday religious education presents opportunities to encourage interdenominational cooperation in a community. Throughout the nation the program is one of the well-known expressions of Protestant cooperation.

Classes are usually small, and one has the opportunity to work closely with children, to encourage their growth, and to have their companionship in one's own religious growth.

The work offers opportunities for friendships with other teachers. Several states now have weekday teachers' organizations with annual meetings.

Experience indicates that some people who have taught in public school have turned to the personal opportunities in weekday religious education, especially in terms of the variety of interesting activities. These include Bible study, worship, dramatics, music, art work, picture study, all centering on religion as the force most vital in a person's life.

OTHER INFORMATION. For positions open inquire of the council of churches in or near your community.

Salaries are reported often to be comparable with those of public-school teachers of similar training and experience. The sponsoring organizations are also reported often to offer Social Security coverage and funds for travel to professional conferences.

For general information and literature write to your denominational board of education or to the Division of Christian Education of the National Council of Churches, 475 Riverside Drive, New York, N.Y. 10027.

Decisions with respect to employment are made by the local organizations or committees in charge of the cooperative program.

## Directors of Adult Education

A specialty within religious education is adult education. People who can give most or much of their time to adult education are employed in the larger local churches and in state and national church boards of education. In the church boards, educators emphasize the promotion and improvement of adult education, and are probably best called administrators of programs. In the local churches they organize and arrange courses or forums for adults, enlist people for these events, and advise with respect to local programs, personal resources, and curricula.

PERSONAL QUALIFICATIONS. These are generally the same as for Directors of Religious Education (which see). But work with adults differs considerably from work with children. The discovery of interests, insights into peculiarly adult personal problems, awareness of issues being considered by adults in a workaday world and their relation to religion—all these are expected of the person working with adults. Adult programs may be arranged within the Sunday school or outside of it. These require special skills and good judgment.

Adults have been called "short termers" in adult education. Some adults reveal antipathy toward formal study or education. One educator in a large growing parish found as a result of his inquiries among adults that they did not wish to join a study club (one said he would not wish to be found studying). They also did not wish to pledge themselves to take a systematic course, and did not enthuse over an "educational" program. The educator then invited a large number of adults to a simple Sunday evening meal for fellowship, at which a number of programs would be tried. They came with relish, and also liked the "programs" that were put on. They were on topics handled by lay people. They were also the same programs recommended by that denomination for religious adult programs. In the end the group enjoyed a religious adult study program—without that label!

EDUCATION AND TRAINING. The general recommendations are the same as for a Director of Religious Education (which see). Repeating briefly, a Bachelor's degree with courses in education

160

for beginning; a Master's degree, for more thorough work, with a major in religious education, or education. Personal study, summer and evening courses, are valuable for adding to formal study and for continuing education. Attendance at some of the numerous church conferences should bring new orientation and resources.

WHAT DO THEY DO? They study the ways and means whereby adults can fruitfully study, and then administer programs, or organize and offer courses, for adults.

In the large local churches they may have charge of an adult group that meets in the Sunday school, and often special study or discussion groups during Lent or at other times.

One denomination has listed ten areas for study by adults (noting that young peoples' groups or organizations might also take up the same materials).

1. The Bible. This may take the form of a series of sessions on the Psalms, or the Gospel According to John, or some of the evident groupings of books of the Bible, e.g., the prophets, or the epistles.

2. Comparative religions. This could consist of a review of all the religions commonly called "world religions," or be limited to those found in large numbers in the U.S.

3. History of religion, or history of the Christian Church.

4. Religion and art.

5. Religion and ethics in relation to personal problems.

6. Religion and social justice.

7. Modern theologies; or, philosophies; or, psychologies.

8. Biographies.

9. Practical personal adjustments.

10. A project in discovery of the community about the church.

OTHER INFORMATION. Resources may be had from the denominational educational boards employing specialists in adult education; from the Department of Adult Work, National Council of Churches, 475 Riverside Drive, New York, N.Y. 10027; and on broad aspects of adult education from the publications of the Adult Education Association of the U.S.A., 743 N. Wabash Ave., Chicago, Ill. 60611.

161

## Directors of Youth Work

In the largest of local churches are a number of full-time positions for religious educators who specialize in work with youth. This position may also be combined with other functions, such as Director of Religious Education.

The director of youth work is appointed to guide and supervise the education, worship, and recreation offered by the church to youth. Men and women are employed for this position. Both ordained and unordained persons are eligible.

The usual training recommended is four years at college, plus graduate work in religious education or theology. Obviously courses in psychology, social science, and methods and materials of religious education, worship, and recreation are helpful.

What is said above under Directors of Religious Education generally applies also to prospective Directors of Youth Work.

## Directors of Children's Work

In the largest churches there are full-time positions for religious educators with the title of Directors of Children's Work. The position may also be combined with another, for example, that of Director of Religious Education. Usually women are engaged for this position. Both ordained and unordained women may be considered for the position.

The director of children's work supervises and guides the activities of children offered by churches in clubs, classes, and personal consultations with children and parents.

The training generally recommended is four years of college plus graduate work in religious education or in theology. Courses in child psychology, in methods of teaching and leading children, and in social sciences are desirable.

The article above under Directors of Religious Education applies also to this vocation.

# RESEARCH WORKERS

Research workers are employed full-time in relatively small but increasing numbers by church-related colleges, theological seminaries, denominational boards, and by local, state, national, and international councils of churches. In the state and local councils they generally work on matters related to local church extension and cooperation. In the national boards, the research is again largely oriented to church extension; large national agencies also employ people for both routine and more advanced statistical work as part of their keeping of records of the statistical reports made by the local congregations. However, in the smaller bodies, the ordinary statistical work is done part-time by busy pastors, professors in seminaries, or officials of general or national church organizations. In the national and international councils of churches the work is more specialized and may include projects in religious education, psychology, home and foreign missions, international relief, refugee problems, statistics, communication and administration and organization. This work is done by both men and women, by ordained and unordained persons.

PERSONAL QUALIFICATIONS. A person with religious interests and a desire to do research needs certain personal qualifications. He needs first of all a high degree of perspective with respect to the institutions of religion. He is required to appraise and evaluate numerical information or other data. The very function of appraisal requires certain personality traits. Is one willing to look at decline and fall, as well as growth and rise, in religious institutions? Is one able to see what the churches do badly as well as what they do well? Can one look fully at what churches plainly cannot do as well as what they can do?

EDUCATION AND TRAINING. A Bachelor's degree with a major in social science is usually regarded as desirable now, although not all persons currently engaged in research pursued such study. A person intending to specialize in, say, psychology, would arrange his major accordingly. But a person with a Bachelor's degree can secure only the more elementary jobs in research.

163

Beyond the Bachelor's, a Master's degree is regarded as essential for beginning in the more responsible positions in research. Others take seminary training for the B.D. and major in subjects such as church and community, sociology of religion, psychology of religion, church history, and related subjects.

For the more advanced positions in supervision and administration of research the Ph.D. is now customary.

TYPES OF EMPLOYMENT. The types of employment have already been generally described in the introductory notes above. Following are only brief amplifications.

Statistical clerks. These are employed in considerable numbers for the more elementary or routine functions, no matter what the subject matter. A Bachelor's degree is desirable.

Assistants to directors. These persons are required to have academic training, preferably a Master's degree or study leading to it. They aid in formulation of projects or designs, and carry out the specific methods required in a research project.

Directors of research projects. These people are expected to have advanced academic training or experience and to be able both to design and direct research. This may include the supervision of assistants; relationships with administrators or "clients" wishing the research done. The responsibility includes knowledge of the varied methods that may be used in research projects.

Interpretation of research. This is a relatively new and developing field. These persons study, digest, and interpret the findings of the relatively technical research workers.

OTHER INFORMATION. Research in religion is a relatively new discipline. Its development is recorded to some extent in the Journal of the Religious Research Association, Box 228, Cathedral Station, New York, N.Y. 10025, and in the discussions at the regional and national meetings held by the Association. Qualified persons may join the Association.

Also inquire of denominational boards and state and local councils of churches in your locality; and of the Department of Research and Survey, National Council of Churches, 475 Riverside Drive, New York, N.Y. 10027.

# SOCIAL WORKERS

Many social workers are employed in Protestant church-related social welfare agencies, broadly defined. They are in organizations serving children, community centers, neighborhood houses, settlements, hospitals, clinics, nursing homes, homes for the aged, and other organizations. In these church-related institutions and agencies, social work is an indispensable function in ministering to people in need.

Social work is a profession that traditionally has served the handicapped, the neglected, the poor, the delinquent, the ill, etc. It has to do with service to people of all ages. The profession now sometimes serves the wealthy and the middle classes, although ordinarily it has to do with aid to those with relatively low income. It serves the well, as well as the ill, those disturbed and those not disturbed. It emphasizes prevention, as well as care and cure. It has to do with community organization, social action, legislation, as well as work with families and individuals.

Social work is a relatively new profession, when compared with law, medicine, or clergy. Informal social work has gone on for a long time, but professional standards have been developed mainly during the past fifty years. Also, as in all professions, there have been trends toward specialization, requiring special preparation. About 60 per cent of all social workers are women.

EDUCATION AND TRAINING. In order to be admitted either to simple jobs in social work, or to a professional school of social work, a Bachelor's degree in a liberal arts college is desirable. In addition, there should be a major in social science or related fields, or at least a knowledge of some social science literature. Many colleges offer courses in undergraduate study that introduce social work, or the field of social welfare, or the field of child welfare. Such courses serve one well in entering a school of professional social work or when starting out in agencies. Some agencies employing persons with a Bachelor's degree will encourage further study and professional training by systematic leaves of absence and financial assistance.

For more advanced professional assignments, a Master's degree in a two-year school of social work is desirable, and often essential. This is particularly true of qualification for supervisory or administrative positions. In some church-related agencies, a Bachelor of Divinity degree also is called for in administrative posts. An increasing number of persons with the B.D. also take a Master's degree in social work in order to do full-time social work. There are about 56 accredited schools of social work. A few theological seminaries offer courses of social work. Some theological seminaries offer courses that combine social work and basic courses in theology and religion.

Students in high school who intend to follow a career in social work will do well to seek volunteer work with social agencies, or part-time paid jobs, or summer jobs. Information about them can usually be secured through local social welfare agencies, councils of churches, etc. Thus one can secure a practical introduction to the difficult situations with which social workers often deal. There are those who find social work depressing, while others find it inspiring. Under present conditions, it is seldom possible to enter social work formally without at least a Bachelor's degree.

PERSONAL QUALIFICATIONS. In general, the person entering church-related social work should be convinced that he has a genuine human interest in people and in working with people; in democratic processes of organization; in his ability to apply his values and knowledge in the solution of individual and social problems. Social work in a church-related agency is more than a job. It requires combinations of art, science, religion, disciplined study and work, initiative, capacity to plan, and perseverance in the face of seemingly insoluble problems.

WHAT DO SOCIAL WORKERS DO? Caseworkers. About half of the social workers in the nation can be classified as caseworkers, persons working directly with families or individuals. They serve people affected by various adverse conditions or problems such as sickness, low income, insecurity, inadequate management of resources, difficulties in personal relationships. Caseworkers make careful studies of the situations of those they serve by means of thorough interviews. Interviewing is one of the more important methods in the whole process. After study through interviews, caseworkers endeavor to achieve constructive changes that will help the person or family with whom they are working. This may involve efforts to restore reasonable family cooperation or the changing of interpersonal attitudes and feelings. Again, it may include arrangement of financial assistance, institutional care, vocational guidance, medical or other health services. The caseworker works with his clients in their homes, or in church-related hospitals, clinics, children's agencies, and institutions for the aged, etc.

Medical social workers. These people are employed in church-related hospitals, and other health centers and agencies. They function in cooperation with physicians, nurses, and therapists. Their primary job is to help those with the special problems that result from illness, convalescence, recovery, and rehabilitation. A special group in this field are psychiatric social workers.

Group workers. Church-related organizations employ many of these professional persons. They work in settlement houses, recreation agencies, day-care centers. (See also Y.M.C.A. and Y.W.C.A.). As their name implies, group workers help people by means of group experience, usually in relatively small groups. The activities are recreational, social, educational, religious. Informality is generally stressed in their relationship with those they are helping. Social group workers plan these activities, enlist the participation of members, train volunteer leaders, supervise volunteers, etc. In the more advanced positions, experienced workers administer departments or agencies that do group work.

Community organization workers. This is one field of social work in which the majority of social workers are men. They often work in local councils of churches and plan welfare, health and recreation services; also to some extent, race relations and human relations programs. They may arrange conferences and other gatherings to assist in planning for meeting community needs. They may also assist in fund raising, necessary in church-related

167

as in other voluntary agencies. (See also Y.M.C.A. and Y.W.C.A.)

Other social workers. There are a number of other specialties in social work, not employed by church-related agencies, such as numerous public assistance workers, public school social workers (also called visiting teachers), social workers in parole, probation, and rehabilitation services.

Experienced persons with graduate degrees often have opportunities to teach in schools of social work.

OTHER INFORMATION. Decisions with respect to employment are usually made by local agencies. Some denominational agencies of social welfare give advice and information to young persons considering this field. Local councils of churches may have information.

Salaries of workers vary greatly among church-related agencies, but often compare favorably with those generally paid by public or private agencies. Social Security coverage is generally available, also systematic vacation schedules. Efforts are constantly being made to have employment standards in church-related agencies equal to others.

Information on scholarships available and on accredited schools of social work may be had from the National Conference on Social Welfare, 345 East 46th St., New York, N.Y. 10017.

On social work in church-related agencies in general, communicate with the Department of Social Welfare, National Council of Churches, 475 Riverside Drive, New York, N.Y. 10027.

## STATISTICIANS

Statisticians are employed in the larger church-related educational institutions to teach in social science or natural science departments. They are also engaged in two ways by denominations and their boards and agencies. First, the over 250 denominations (apparently with one exception) have officers traditionally named statisticians. These officers are usually not professionally trained statisticians, but persons who gather, summarize, and report the figures that local churches file at annual or other intervals with

168

their national offices. Second, in denominational boards and other agencies, statisticians are employed by the research or study departments. (See Research Workers.)

Statistical methods are increasingly used in many ways, as knowledge expands—or explodes. Statisticians use methods approved in the profession to gather, summarize, analyze, and interpret data in numerical form. These data may be used to understand the past and the present—they are also at times the basis for "projections" which are becoming important to some administrators in a period of rapid change.

Statistics is both a separate discipline and a tool of many other professions or vocations. Thus a person who is expert in statistics and specially interested in developing new methods may have the title of mathematician (see Teaching Mathematics). One who works altogether on data in economics, may be regarded as an economist, and may teach in a college department of economics. It is often difficult to distinguish between statisticians and specialists in other subject matter fields.

Statistics is also becoming a highly specialized field. Some statisticians spend a good deal of time in the field gathering their data, while others concentrate on analyzing what others have assembled. Some plan experiments or surveys that they—or others —may carry out. Some become specialists in preparing instruments for personal interviews or for the mailed questionnaire method. Some give all their time to supervising clerks or computer operators. In all statistical work, the use of high speed computers is increasing. (See Electronic Computer Operators under Office Positions.)

EDUCATION AND TRAINING. Generally a beginner in the field must have a Bachelor's degree with a major in mathematics or in a social science, such as sociology or economics. For college teaching and for many other positions, a Master's degree in statistics or mathematics is necessary. Graduate study has become generally necessary for advancement in the field. The Ph.D. is not only an asset but also usually a requirement for the high-ranking positions either in college departments or elsewhere.

People intending to become statisticians should plan their

college courses, so as to include algebra, plane trigonometry, analytical geometry, differential and integral calculus, and specific courses in statistical methods. The more advanced courses in mathematics and statistical theory are necessary for some of the highly specialized jobs. Likewise, if one wishes to do statistical work in economics, or another social science, one must also include study in this specific discipline. Knowledge of electronic equipment is increasingly recommended.

PERSONAL QUALIFICATIONS. The personal qualifications obviously differ from those who wish to do counseling or personnel work. One usually need not work directly with many people—one must enjoy working with numerical data and have a strong interest in mathematics.

However, those interested in the practical application of statistical data to, let us say, health or social welfare, find themselves in positions with many public contacts.

Teachers of statistics in church-related colleges face the same personal opportunities, issues and dilemmas as those who teach sociology, history, or economics. For general personal qualifications, see the notes herein under these vocations.

WHAT DO THEY DO? Persons with a Bachelor's degree and no practical experience are usually assigned to the more routine tasks in statistics in college departments or elsewhere in research. In the colleges, teaching and research are frequently combined, or alternated. Young beginners may be given research work at first, with later opportunities to teach—if they acquire a graduate degree.

Applicants will in all probability be asked to demonstrate their knowledge of modern electronic equipment and its use.

OTHER INFORMATION. For more information on statistics as a career, communicate with the American Statistical Association, 810 18th St., N.W., Washington, D.C. 20036.


## TEACHING IN MISSION SCHOOLS IN THE U.S.

Mission schools under the sponsorship of national boards of home missions have been organized and are maintained in many special situations. In general the schools are among Negroes, American Indians, young people in low-income families of isolated areas, and children from homes where normal family life has broken down. The boards endeavor to furnish a good education in a setting that seeks Christian commitment from the pupils.

Mission schools thus offer opportunities for service to qualified teachers who wish not only to teach but to express their Christian faith through their teaching. (See Teaching in Elementary Schools and Teaching in Secondary Schools.)

PERSONAL QUALIFICATIONS. Teachers in mission schools do not limit their responsibilities to the classroom. They are interested in relating formal instruction to personality development, and, more specifically, to Christian motivation and character. They are asked to stimulate religious growth and maturity in their pupils. It is surely a full life that is offered, and one with special rewards.

EDUCATION AND TRAINING. Those wishing to teach at the elementary level should have a Bachelor's degree with a major from a college or university. Those who desire to teach high-school classes should have a Bachelor's or Master's degree in the subject or subjects which they wish to teach.

Students should arrange courses of study so that they may qualify for full-state certification for either elementary or secondary teaching. Most states now require at least a semester's study after completion of a four-year college course.

In college there should be participation in various school activities and thus preparation to lead in extracurricular activity in a mission school, including arts, crafts, music, drama, athletics, etc.

WHAT DO THEY DO? They teach either elementary or secondary classes—and also help develop chapel or auditorium programs, counsel with individuals and groups, lead hobby clubs or groups, and recreational events.

Because mission schools are relatively small, teachers of secondary-school subjects are sometimes called upon to teach more than one subject.

"I'm really having an experience teaching history and physical education!" one young teacher writes. She notes the "atmosphere" of the school, and its useful purpose in providing an adequate education for boys and girls who would otherwise not have it. There were 118 girls in the school. Classes began at the fifth grade and continued through high school. The glee club presented six special programs at Christmas time. This teacher worked with the director of religious education in putting on a drama.

OTHER INFORMATION. Additional information may be had from offices of missionary personnel of denominational boards of home missions. These may gather personnel information for consideration by boards of schools.

## TEACHING IN HOMES FOR CHILDREN

Home missions boards and church-related social welfare organizations maintain a number of institutions for children, in which elementary education is systematically carried on, and considerable counseling is necessary. (See Social Workers and Teaching in Elementary Schools.)

The children in these institutions come from families in which the parents, for various reasons, do not have the personal resources or the understanding to aid their children toward mature living. They are thus unfortunate, handicapped, or neglected children who, for a time at least, need institutional care and services.

The home missions and other church agencies arrange their institutions for the purpose of guiding children and releasing their potential assets. They offer education and loving, mature care so that the individuals in the institutions will be able to develop, so far as possible, in the way they should in a successful, responsible family situation.

PERSONAL QUALIFICATIONS. Every year there are openings in these institutions, and some boards report "many demands for increased services." In order to meet the needs for services for children, the boards wish to interest young people who are both well-trained, and who have sympathetic human understanding and a desire to make creative use of the individual and community resources. Those who work with children in these institutions must have special talents for work with individuals, and for helping children to help themselves.

EDUCATION AND TRAINING. A person with a Bachelor's degree with a major in elementary education is usually well prepared in this field, particularly if study has included child psychology, sociology, and child care. Informal preparation that helps includes experience as a teacher in Sunday schools, as a leader in vacation church schools, and related work with children. Persons who have studied "group work" as part of their training for social work may also be qualified. In state supervised private schools, a teaching certificate is necessary; most states require an additional semester's study after the B.A. has been granted.

WHAT DO THEY DO? The workers teach elementary school subjects, and supervise many recreational and social events. Many contacts with children are involved, probably many more than teaching in elementary schools generally.

One worker reports that her experience in these institutions has made her convinced that "no matter how small your talent is, it can always be used." For example, she went one Monday morning and bought yarn and knitting needles, an action that later brought "enormous dividends." When she returned to her home, she sat on a porch and started knitting. From that moment on numerous girls—and boys—wanted to learn to knit. Soon several of the older girls had learned to knit complete sweaters. The worker regarded this as employing her talent "in God's work," and both pupils and teacher gained joy and insights.

OTHER INFORMATION. Decisions with respect to employment are made by local boards, but personnel information is gathered by national boards.

Further information can be had from administrators of child-care institutions, or from offices of missionary personnel in a number of national home-missions boards.

173

## TEACHING IN ELEMENTARY SCHOOLS

A GENERAL INTRODUCTION. Teaching in elementary schools, here defined to include nursery schools and kindergartens, is throughout the nation one of the largest of fields for professional employment of women. It is also one that men are entering in growing numbers. Elementary school includes grades 1 to 6 or 1 to 8, depending upon the organization of the school system.

There are church-related schools of all three types—nursery, kindergarten, and grades 1-6 and 1-8. During the past two decades church buildings have been found to be good places for housing the new nursery schools or kindergartens necessary for mothers who work or study. Some of these schools are only housed in church buildings and the relationship to the church is of slight significance. In others church people have recognized the need and have organized such schools, in part, for the purpose of providing some formal religious exercise and teaching as part of the education.

Nursery schools and kindergartens are frequently organized with teaching programs for half a day only. If the school is large, one group may come for the forenoon and the other in the afternoon. Some schools, however, go on for the entire day with one group, particularly in highly industrialized cities where both parents of many children have jobs.

In both nursery schools and kindergartens the emphasis is on play, music, stories. For the older children, art work and beginning-reading may be included. For both, rest periods and provision of milk are part of the procedure. Teachers keep records and frequently confer with parents after school hours. They are also required constantly to prepare for their regular programs and for special events.

Teachers in the lower elementary grades almost always have one group of pupils during an entire school day. They teach several subjects and are also responsible for supervising play periods on school grounds or in the building. In the larger schools, and in the upper grades, elementary teachers may teach one or two subjects, to different classes. Schools with the resources may also engage part-time teachers of special subjects, such as art or music. Teachers also administer and correct tests, keep records, make reports, correct homework and grade papers, and confer with parents.

PERSONAL QUALIFICATIONS. Love and enjoyment of children are important personal qualifications for teachers in these church-related schools. Others are patience, self-discipline, ability to maintain discipline, and high standards of personal conduct. A liking of arts, literature, history, sciences is an asset. Ability to cooperate with other teachers and with parents is essential.

Church-related schools are organized with a main purpose of giving instruction in religion. Thus it is expected of teachers that they have interest in, and commitment to, religion; and they may also be responsible for religious exercises and formal or informal teaching of religion.

EDUCATION AND TRAINING. Most colleges and universities now offer courses in education that furnish a teacher with the necessary training. Since private schools must meet state standards, a prospective elementary-school teacher in a church-related school should take the necessary training to be able to obtain a certificate.

In many four-year courses leading to a Bachelor's degree, a prospective elementary-school teacher will spend about one-fourth of the time on courses in education. These will include such as methods and materials of instruction, educational testing, the place of the school in society, the learning process, and practice teaching under supervision. Most states require an additional semester of study after graduation.

OTHER INFORMATION. Decisions regarding employment are made by the responsible authorities in the schools.

For information on requirements for obtaining a certificate to teach elementary grades, inquire of your State Department of Education at your state capital.

General information on teaching is published by the U.S. Office of Education, Washington, D.C. 20202; and the National Education Association, 1201 16th St., N.W., Washington, D. C. 20036.

The denominations with the largest number of church-related schools are the Lutheran Church—Missouri Synod, the Seventh-day Adventists, and the Christian Reformed Church.

The National Association of Christian Schools, Box 28, Wheaton, Ill. publishes a list of private Christian schools.

## TEACHING IN SECONDARY SCHOOLS

A GENERAL INTRODUCTION. Secondary schools are organized in two ways in the U.S. They may include grades 7-9, which are called junior high schools, grades 10-12 in senior high schools. In other systems the secondary grades are 9-12. Most church-related schools adopt the latter system. These schools have been established with a purpose of providing instruction in religion.

In secondary schools teachers may teach one or several combinations of subjects. In the larger schools, a teacher may instruct several classes every day in his special subject. In the smaller schools, a teacher may have classes in more than one subject. Combinations often found are English and history; history and social science; mathematics and general science; chemistry and biology; chemistry and general science. Schools that have teachers of home economics, music or art usually do not require them to combine their special subject with another. Religious exercises and instruction may be a full-time or part-time responsibility. A teacher of physical education may also be asked to assume the high-status position of football coach.

Men and women teach in all secondary schools in almost even numbers throughout the nation. There are no separate statistics on Protestant church-related secondary schools, but the breakdown is probably near the national average. Men outnumber women in supervisory and administrative positions in public and private schools of all types and faiths.

Teachers usually have about 20 to 30 hours of classes per week, but their work week is always much longer. They often supervise student activities or publications after school hours. They interview parents and confer with fellow teachers. They prepare for conducting tests, correct papers, tests and homework, keep records, make reports, supervise study rooms, attend or conduct chapel or assembly programs. On a Sunday morning, they may be expected to attend a worship service in a chapel in school or in a local church.

PERSONAL QUALIFICATIONS. Among these are appreciation and understanding of children, devotion to guiding their growth, patience, self-discipline, and high standards of conduct. A wish to take part in social and recreational activities may or may not be expected. Special personal interest in history, art, science, literature is welcomed.

Beyond these, because the schools are church-related it is expected that teachers have both interest in, and commitment to, religion; and some secondary teachers are expected either to conduct religious exercises or to teach formal courses in religion.

EDUCATION AND TRAINING. In every state a certificate is required for public secondary school teaching. And because private schools must meet state standards and are under state supervision it is best that a prospective teacher in a church-related public school take courses preparing for certification.

To qualify for a certificate, a prospective teacher must have a Bachelor's degree, and in most states equivalent of a half year beyond the Bachelor's spent in special courses in education and practice teaching are required. And in a few states, a year of graduate study is necessary before a certificate is issued.

In the many colleges and universities that offer teacher-preparation programs, the prospective secondary-school teacher spends about one-third of the time in education courses and related subjects. This will include practice teaching under supervision, methods and materials of instruction. The rest of the time is given to general or liberal arts subjects, including the subject or subjects that the prospective teacher wishes to teach in a secondary school.

It is ordinarily possible for a teacher who has a certificate in one state to secure one in another state without undue delay. At times temporary certificates are issued until some particular requirements are met.

177

OTHER INFORMATION. See articles below on specific subjects or disciplines. These include many that are taught in both secondary schools and colleges.

Information on requirements for obtaining a teaching certificate in your state may be had from State Department of Education, at the state capital.

General information on teaching as a career is published by the U.S. Office of Education, Washington, D.C. 20202; and the National Education Association, 1201 16th St., N.W., Washington, D.C. 20036.

## TEACHING IN COLLEGES AND UNIVERSITIES

The U.S. has been called a "land of colleges." Most of the early colleges were established by religious bodies with the main purpose of educating men for the ministry. Even later when purposes broadened, many religious bodies and many religious people (humble and great), planted numerous colleges in our land. These were usually liberal arts institutions.

A proportion of these church-originated colleges have long since become altogether independent, maintaining no ties with current religious bodies. Others are often called church-related. This is a term that covers a wide range of relationships. It may include colleges altogether independent of church control which nevertheless have certain ties with a denomination—as in the denominations wholly congregational, that is, with a church government in which there is no authority over that of the local congregation. It may embrace colleges in which there is only a sentimental recollection, at times, of the sacrificial labors of founders. It may include institutions under the full control of religious bodies through their representatives on boards of trustees. Between these extremes are all sorts of arrangements, sometimes by contract, sometimes by informal understandings.

Because of this history, there has always been in the U.S. a good deal of interest in the interconnection of faith and learning. Although it started in colonial days simply by the educating of ministers in college, this interest is now broadly expressed in a widespread concern about the relation of religion and science (a subject absorbing to many scientists as well as to religious leaders), and about the ways whereby attention should be given to religion in the liberal arts colleges and even in the state universities. Most of the state institutions also find it proper, desirable, or necessary to have, or be related to, some formal study of religion as a discipline. Much of the work of the campus ministries, (which see) is conducted on or near the campuses of state universities.

There is a good deal of current writing on faith and learning, as modern authors try their hands at formulating philosophies of education that have been the subjects of giants in the past. For example, John Henry Cardinal Newman wrote on the *Idea of a University Education* about 100 years ago. Recently Elton Trueblood, a Friend, wrote a book on the *Idea of a College* (New York: Harper and Row, 1959) and said he wished his readers to be reminded of what Newman wrote a century earlier.

The diversities of higher education in the U.S. are everywhere evident. They surprise visitors from abroad. Among the recent trends in higher education in general, which affect the church-related colleges to some degree, are these:

The rise of urban universities, which carry on without the beautiful green campuses associated with much college life.

The progressive democratization of higher education.

The recent emphasis on science, which disturbs some of those committed to the humanities and religion.

Discussion of the relative roles of religion and science, with conclusions ranging from renewed conflict between the two to other views looking upon them as complementary, at least, or as "partners."

The rise of specialization, leading into new discussion of the value of general education in relation to specialization and of how this shall be arranged in curricula. Is there such a thing as "fundamental education" for all students?

Assumption of responsibility for adult education by colleges

179

and universities, and requiring special preparation and organization by the colleges making the offerings.

The role of the federal government in higher education, and how it should be exercised. Here a significant factor is the increasing number of large specific grants by federal agencies for research of many kinds, particularly, in physics. Apparently the officials of Protestant churches look with more favor on federal aid for *higher* education than for general federal aid to elementary and high schools.

The rising costs of higher education, and how they shall be met. One response on the part of church boards of higher education is to try to raise large sums for loans and for scholarship aids.

The special problems of liberal arts colleges, among which many are church-related. One issue is this: Have the liberal arts colleges become so subservient to graduate education, that needs of graduate courses and schools are so emphasized as to lead to a "decline of liberal education?" What is the proper role of the Christian churches so as to encourage a free, liberal education, and also allow for systematic consideration of Christian values?

Thus young persons going into college teaching are in the midst of many ferments of discussion of religion. In at least one old eastern Protestant college there are more Roman Catholic students than there are of any one Protestant body, including the body founding the college. What does one do in such a "pluralistic" student body?

How should attention be given to religion in a church-related college? The schools of thought fall into a broad scale:

1. There are those who would have no formal teaching of religion or theology as a separate or distinct discipline, adding that religion should be taken up obviously in courses in ethics, art, history, English, social science, economics, and other studies called the humanities. It should also be considered in relation to science and technology by those who teach these courses. These persons would try to make it crystal clear that the church is not

a college and a college not a church. Thus they would not have the college arrange for formal worship by students but would see to it that students know of the services of churches of the community.

2. At the other end of the scale are those who contend that since a church founded a college, the college exists primarily to serve the church. Thus they would have the college assume responsibility for formal worship by students, for formal study of religion as a discipline, and for enlistment of students for professional and volunteer service of the churches.

3. Between these two come those who occupy somewhat differing middle positions. Some would say, for example, that the religious aspects of all studies should be indicated, but that religion is also a discipline that should be formally taught. (There are said to be over 2,500 teachers of religion and Bible in American colleges and universities, many of these being only on part-time.) Some of these persons favor the offering of courses on the Bible, on church history, on comparative religion, Christian ethics, the relation of churches to community and public affairs issues—including religion and race relations and the development of interdenominational agencies, often called the "ecumenical movement."

One writer says that when all subjects are taught "Christianly," much has been done to relate religion to higher education. Probably most church-related colleges expect of their teachers some interest or participation in church life or organized religion. But this may be variously interpreted or expressed.

College teachers come into contact with young people at a time when their influence on students may be very great. This may be intangible and indirect—and difficult to document. Many have influence on students not noticeable until later years. Sometimes those with the most influence do not consciously plan to have influence but leave such matters to the mysteries of personality and inter-personal relationships.

OTHER INFORMATION. See sections following on specific subjects or disciplines.

Information on higher education in general may be had from

publications of the U.S. Office of Education, Washington, D.C. 20202; and, those of the American Council on Education, 1785 Massachusetts Ave., N.W., Washington, D.C. 20036.

On the relation of religion and education, communicate with the Council of Protestant Colleges and Universities, 1818 R St. N.W. Washington, D.C. 20009; the Commission on Higher Education, National Council of Churches, 475 Riverside Drive, New York, N.Y. 10027; the board of education of your denomination.

## TEACHING OF SPECIFIC SUBJECTS OR DISCIPLINES

### Anthropology

Anthropologists study man in both primitive and modern societies. This includes man's origin, physical characteristics, language, traditions, religion, social life, and his material possessions. There are probably fewer professional anthropologists than there are professionals in any other social science. However, there is probably no social science in which foreign missions' boards, their administrators, and the missionaries overseas have had a greater interest. Many missionaries study anthropology before going to service overseas, and while on furlough. As evidence of this interest, the Missionary Research Library, 3041 Broadway, New York, N.Y. 10027, maintains one of the largest collections of publications in anthropology in the U.S., where it may be consulted by students and missionaries on furlough.

Anthropologists, though few in number, cover a wide subject matter. Most anthropologists concentrate on cultural anthropology, which in turn has two emphases, ethnology and archaeology. A small minority major in physical anthropology, which includes intensive study of anatomy and biology, and measurement of physical differences among the peoples of the earth.

The cultural anthropologists often spend long periods in communities of either primitive tribes or more developed societies, where they learn much about ways of life. They write long notes on language, customs, beliefs, practices, and possessions of people. They often acquire a knowledge of the language of the people among whom they live. Indeed, some anthropologists specialize in linguistics, which is the scientific study of the sounds and structures of languages, and of historical relationships among various languages. In this total process, cultural anthropologists have given much time to the study of religions of people.

Anthropologists are mainly college teachers. In some colleges, teaching of anthropology may have to be combined with teaching of another social science such as sociology or geography. This is particularly true in church-related colleges, many of which are too small to have a full-time anthropologist on the faculty.

PERSONAL QUALIFICATIONS. The general personal qualifications of teachers are the same as for others in church-related colleges. The anthropologist is in a peculiar situation, however, in that he often possesses personal knowledge of ways and languages of people, among whom the churches maintain missions. Church agencies often call upon anthropologists because of their knowledge, particularly of religions in particular countries.

For example, anthropologists have often studied American Indians, among whom three tendencies in religion are reported: 1. Adherence to the traditional tribal religions. 2. Acceptance of the religion of the white man, that is, the missionary evangelist or teacher who works among them. 3. A middle course, which involves a mingling of both. The anthropologist is in a special position to interpret these situations.

EDUCATION AND TRAINING. This is one of the disciplines in which the Ph.D. is usually recommended. People with a Bachelor's degree can obtain temporary positions in which they are usually expected to continue their graduate study. A Master's degree, combined with some experience in field study, may be sufficient for starting in college teaching, but usually graduate work leading to the Ph.D. is required for advancement.

During undergraduate study, courses in linguistics are especially recommended. Students will also do well to have some field experience, which may sometimes be had by accompanying professors on field expeditions.

183

WHAT DO THEY DO? Anthropologists teach college courses ranging from surveys or introductory courses to the more specialized branches of the discipline. Some anthropologists offer courses in race relations, a subject of great interest to many churchmen.

Usually anthropologists use their field notes for preparing doctoral dissertations, and thus have had field experience before acquiring a doctorate. They later endeavor to do field work either in summer, or during semesters when they are relieved of teaching duties.

Anthropologists are sometimes consultants to foreign mission boards and agencies, and write articles and monographs of special interest to church constituencies.

OTHER INFORMATION. Additional information may be had from college teachers of anthropology and administrators of the larger denominational foreign mission boards.

For general data on the discipline, see a booklet, *Anthropology As a Career,* Smithsonian Institute, Washington, D.C. 20560; for development of the profession, see publications of the American Anthropological Association, 1530 P St., N.W., Washington, D.C. 20005.

## Art

Teachers of art are needed in both church-related schools and colleges. In the elementary grades, the teaching is frequently in elementary "arts and crafts." In the smaller schools, this teaching may be combined with that of other subjects, while in the larger ones a full-time teacher may be employed.

The teaching of art has been a rapidly developing field, especially during the past few decades, when it was discovered that most people can paint.

In both secondary schools and colleges the teaching has come to be divided into two fields: the fine arts, and applied or commercial art. In the second field, highly specialized instruction can only be given in the larger institutions. Many women are teachers of art in both schools and colleges.

184

PERSONAL QUALIFICATIONS. Of first importance are a genuine interest in art, initiative in developing artistic talent, imagination, and creative ability. Beyond this there must also be a personal wish to teach. It is one thing to paint a good still-life or a landscape. It is altogether another to teach others. Many very good artists cannot teach others. As in other fields, such as literature, a person can be an excellent teacher without being an excellent performer. A good artist may not be a good teacher. For other general personal qualifications see the notes under Teaching English Literature or those under Commercial Artists.

In the church-related educational institutions, an interest in religious art is a great asset. Probably only in the larger institutions will there be special courses or emphases in religious art. The teacher may or may not make use of religious art in classes. But knowledge of it may be of use in connection with special exhibits or with developing historical perspective among students in classes. Much great religious art of the past was painted not to exhibit artistic skill but rather to instruct people in religion. Modern religious art reveals much of the emotions and attitudes of people today.

EDUCATION AND TRAINING. Prospective teachers must plan to have not only specific courses in art but also courses in education, as may be required for securing certification to teach. In connection with courses in art and education, those in English literature, history, psychology, and social science may be recommended.

A Bachelor's degree with the necessary education courses may qualify a person to teach in elementary and secondary schools. However, most states now require at least a semester's work or equivalent after college graduation before a certificate is issued.

For college teaching a Master's degree is usually essential for beginning, although in schools of fine arts, exceptions may be made for able artists who are also accomplished teachers—without the usual hours or years of academic study.

WHAT DO THEY DO? As has been implied above, teaching in elementary and secondary schools is usually of an introductory or general character. But in large high schools some specialized

185

teaching is done, including an emphasis on applied or commercial art, such as illustrating or lettering.

College and university courses vary greatly, from the more general or introductory content to that requiring highly specialized teaching.

In one middle-sized church-related college the courses offered are as follows, with the less difficult courses listed first, advancing to the more mature offerings:

| | |
|---|---|
| Art History and Appreciation | (2 courses) |
| Drawing and Painting | (2 courses) |
| Advanced Drawing and Painting | (2 courses) |
| Special Drawing and Painting | (2 courses) |

OTHER INFORMATION. See general introductions to Teaching in Elementary, Secondary, and Mission Schools, and to Teaching in Colleges and Universities.

## Biology

The biological sciences have to do with microbes, plants, insects, birds, fish, domestic and wild animals, and human beings—in short with the whole vast realms of living things. These sciences, which are divided into numerous specialties, embrace study of the structure of living organisms, their life processes, and relations between living organisms and their environment. Because of the variety of plants and animals and of their environments, and the complexity of their life processes, specialization became inevitable as knowledge expanded.

There are biologists who spend many years, even all their years, of active work learning as much as can be learned about one plant or animal. A well-known scientist once devoted about twenty years to a study of palms. Others become specialists in life processes and thus study how food is assimilated; or they may study the nervous system, or the effects of diseases on organisms. Still others emphasize the development or evolution of living organisms, heredity, and the many ways by which the many different environments affect plants and animals. These are concerned with changes of climate and radioactivity.

A large proportion of biological scientists are employed by colleges and universities for teaching or research, or both. In church-related colleges as in others, teaching may consist of a general survey of the various fields; or it may be devoted to one specialty. Biological scientists and those who teach biology, have been classified in three broad groups, as follows: 1. Botanists, or plant scientists. 2. Microbiologists who deal with micro-organisms. 3. Zoologists, or animal scientists. Those who, like many college teachers, work broadly in these fields may be called simply biologists.

But specialization has gone on to the creation of numerous fields, including agronomists, anatomists, biochemists, biophysicists, embryologists, entomologists, geneticists, horticulturists, animal husbandry specialists, nutritionists, pathologists, pharmacologists, physiologists, and phytopathologists. Only in the larger church-related colleges, including the medical schools that are part of them, will many of these specialties be taught.

PERSONAL QUALIFICATIONS. The general qualifications of teachers of biology, men and women, in colleges are the same as in other teaching careers. There are certain aspects of this discipline, however, that inevitably raise questions of relationships to religious history and principles. The administrators of the church-related colleges expect their teachers of biology to have an awareness of these problems, and to demonstrate some capacity to deal with them, even though the professional preparation of the biologists may not have included such matters.

The teacher of biology is first of all called upon to be a scientist and educator. Most of the students of courses in biology in the church-related colleges will not become biological scientists, however, and may be expecting of the teacher more than technical knowledge of his field. Thus the teacher of biology is required to give his students thorough knowledge of the findings in this science, an awareness of the principles on which the knowledge is based, and some training in methods of study in this field. Then come relations with other disciplines—religion among them.

What shall be done about the hymn of creation found in Genesis, and the latest thinking on evolution of mankind? In the church-related college, the teacher will find some students with considerable knowledge of the Bible and some awareness of the conflicts between scientists and religious leaders. The biologist chose a science to which inevitably come ideas from what was, and is still, called the queen of the sciences, namely theology. Students may ask concerning the origins and problems of life, and concerning purpose and faith. "The chief end of man is to glorify God," says the famous Westminster (Presbyterian) Catechism.

Should biological scientists and ministers of religion, both deeply involved in consideration of the great issues of life, go their separate ways, or should there be at least "dialogue?" Probably just as one cannot expect most ministers to be also scientists, one cannot expect the biologist in his classroom to be also a specialist in religion. Some biologists declare that there is no relation between science and religion. Some have concluded that there is no evidence of purpose in life. Others declare the evident limitations of science and profess interest in the insights of prophets and poets and in the values of those who minister with compassion to their fellow men. Thus in some circles at least the historic antagonisms have given way to agreements that there is no essential conflict between theories of evolution and their religious beliefs, and that there should be a "partnership" of science and religion.

EDUCATION AND TRAINING. For teaching in high schools see Teaching in Secondary Schools, above.

For college teaching a Master's degree is generally required, and the Ph.D. is necessary for many courses. For elementary assignments in research projects in colleges a Bachelor's degree with a major in biology may suffice. Those who have only a Bachelor's degree will generally be advised to do graduate study if they wish to continue in the field. A knowledge of mathematics and statistics is essential.

Summer schools and special courses offered evenings provide opportunities for graduate work and for continuing education.

Professional journals and meetings of professional organizations are valuable for both students and teacher.

WHAT DO THEY DO? In most of the smaller schools and colleges the teacher will be offering mainly general or introductory courses in biology. In the larger institutions, these will be supplemented by specialized courses. These will be emphasized in pre-medical curricula now offered by many colleges. One of the courses generally offered is in physiology.

Research may be combined with teaching, or a trained person may readily shift from teaching to research, and vice versa. Experienced teachers may become administrators of research. There may also be opportunities for experienced persons to do consulting, writing, testing, and other related activities.

OTHER INFORMATION. For further information consult publications of the American Institute of Biological Sciences, 2000 P St., N.W., Washington, D.C. 20036; and the U.S. Department of Health, Education, and Welfare, Washington, D.C. 20201.

## Counseling

School counselors work with students in planning the courses they should take, the colleges they may apply to for admission, and the work they may wish to do after completion of their schooling. Full-time counselors are usually employed in the larger schools. However, counseling may be combined with other duties, such as teaching social science.

Counselors in elementary schools work with the classroom teachers, aiding them in gaining understanding of pupils and in meeting the specific needs of the individuals who are being taught. They also meet and consult with parents. Among younger children, counseling differs from that of older students. The use of tests and recreation is frequent in the lower grades.

Counselors usually have available for use by older students books on occupations, schools and colleges, and related information.

The number of teachers who counsel is increasing. In a time of rapid social change, and high mobility among the people, the needs of pupils are much greater than in prior, more stable times.

EDUCATION AND TRAINING. Teachers who counsel in state-supervised schools are required to have teaching certificates issued by state departments of education. Because private or church-related schools come under state supervision, it is advisable that prospective counselors take the courses recommended for teacher education in liberal arts colleges and schools of education. Most states require a semester's work beyond the four years. Courses in psychology and sociology are especially recommended.

In some states teaching experience is required for a year before a special certificate in school counseling is issued. Some states also issue counselor certificates only to persons who have a Master's degree or equivalent in counseling education.

In many schools of education and liberal arts colleges, prospective counselors are asked to take specific courses in techniques of counseling and introductions to the sources of materials available.

PERSONAL QUALIFICATIONS. Since counselors are constantly meeting people, it is evident that they must have an aptitude for working with people. It is obviously akin to personnel work, but far different from much statistical work, although counselors are called upon to keep records. Counselors in schools are doing work roughly comparable with that of clinical psychologists. In some places the term guidance is used instead of counseling. Those who guide are in a career that requires the enlistment of the cooperation of students. Ability to listen is important. The communication of information and advice is often best given informally and indirectly. The counselors and guidance teachers are not people who issue orders. They are people who encourage others to make their own decisions.

WHAT DO THEY DO? Personal interviewing is the general basic technique used by counselors. By skillful interviewing, the counselor learns about the students' needs, interests, and abilities, and on this basis plans are worked out with the students. Counselors may meet with groups of students. They may use psychological tests to aid in the total process. Usually the counselor consults school records of academic achievements and those of health or medical conditions. Counselors frequently initiate interviews with parents, or respond to their requests.

Some counselors give special attention to the numerous drop-outs, or prospective drop-outs, who have become the source of many problems in society and the job market.

In junior and senior high-school years, counselors may give advice about courses to be taken and about future college and careers. In elementary grades, the emphasis is more likely to be on personal adjustments, although this is a function at all grades.

Counselors at times offer special films at assembly programs; arrange "career day" programs; arrange visits by students to colleges and visits by representatives of colleges to schools.

OTHER INFORMATION. Information on educational institutions that offer special training in counseling may be had from your state department of education. The U.S. Office of Education, Washington, D.C. 20202, also has information. General information on counseling as a career may be had from the American Personnel and Guidance Association, 1605 New Hampshire Ave., N.W., Washington, D.C. 20009.

*Earth Sciences*

INTRODUCTORY NOTE. Earth sciences, which are being regarded as a group within the natural sciences, are sometimes broadly defined as including geology, geography, geophysics, meteorology, and mineralogy. Of these, geography is taught in church-related secondary schools and colleges, and geology is generally taught in colleges. Therefore these two are described in detail below.

Natural science is the sum of man's knowledge of the physical world and of the plants and animals in it and on it. It originated in the early inquiries of philosophers, such as those of Aristotle, who wrote on both animal life and physics. As knowledge broadened, the natural sciences became separate subjects, and eventually they were divided into various specialties. (See also Physical Sciences, below.) The trend toward great specialization has been accompanied, however, with a recent tendency to study, or at least be familiar with, several disciplines, two of which may be combined into a new specialty—geochemistry, for example. This has brought

191

about recognition of the interdependence of the natural sciences.

Employment of natural scientists has greatly expanded since World War II, and high interest in these sciences is evident in church-related as well as other colleges.

The personal qualifications, issues, and dilemmas of those who teach the earth sciences are in general those for other disciplines. However, these scientist-teachers face some issues peculiar to themselves. The geologist will face problems of value-judgments like those of the teacher of biology (which see). How does the professor who has been trained in modern science teach students who sincerely believe in the historical and scientific accuracy of the Bible, and its verbal inspiration? Much will depend upon the personal attitudes (and not the technical knowledge) of the teacher. Some of these students do not bring such convictions to the attention of the teacher. Others will accept the scientific findings and thus say that they "lose their religion." Others answer as they think the professor wants them to answer or write papers as they think he wants them written, and mechanically pass the course. Others will go through torment, without the aid of a teacher who can interpret the separate ways of knowing in religion and in science, and seek some reconciliation, and also interpret the tentative and limited nature of scientific knowledge. Many scientists say that science cannot by its methods tell what is reality. Many scientists have moved away from mechanistic views of the universe that seemed settled a generation ago. Some scientists now believe there may be a fruitful partnership between science and religion, in spite of past and current conflicts. Scientists also probably agree that they have responsibilities as citizens outside the classroom, for which their technical knowledge provides no—or few—resources.

GEOGRAPHY. Teachers of geography are employed in church-related secondary schools and colleges.

Geographers gather knowledge about the distribution of people and natural resources throughout the earth. They study the physical characteristics of the world, including terrain, minerals, soils, water, vegetation, and climate. They also study the relationships of people to the physical characteristics, such as where people live, why they locate at particular places, and how they earn a living. Thus geography is closely related to the social sciences, especially economics and sociology, which see.

There are four main branches of geography, which at least in the larger institutions are presented in courses for students who may be preparing to teach. These are: Economic geography, which includes mining, agriculture, manufacturing, commerce, and communication. Regional geography, concentrating on the physical, economic, political, and cultural characteristics of one area, which may be a state or a river basin. Physical geography, specializing on the earth's physical characteristics. Cartography, having to do with compilation of data for maps, and their arrangement and construction.

Many geographers do extensive field work or research. Sometimes they use the instruments of surveyors and meteorologists in these studies. Some make or analyze aerial photographs, and prepare statistical and other information to aid in the use and interpretations of such photographs, which are coming to be of wide interest and utility. Summaries of data, in the form of graphs and diagrams, often accompany aerial photographs and maps. Geographers are frequently consulted by regional or community planners, and by specialists in marketing. The interest of geographers in climate may lead to cooperation with meteorologists, who are specialists in another of the earth sciences. Geographers are often consulted by publishers of textbooks and travel information.

A Bachelor's degree with a major in geography is the minimum educational requirement for teaching positions in secondary schools. In college teaching, graduate study is increasingly recommended.

Many colleges offer undergraduate study in geography, and a good proportion of these will give a Bachelor's degree with a major in this subject. Undergraduate study generally provides an introduction to geography and to research methods. It may also include limited field work. There may also be concentrated study on the geography of one area, such as the state in which the college is located. To the geography student it is often recommended that study include many of the following: mathematics, botany, chemistry, physics, geology, economics, sociology, political science, foreign languages.

Master's degrees with majors in geography are not offered in as many colleges as offer the major for the Bachelor's, and still fewer are prepared to grant the Ph.D. in geography. For a Master's and Doctor's degree, laboratory and field work are required, in addition to the usual resident requirements.

Those with Bachelor's degrees who have majored in geography may secure teaching positions in secondary schools; often, such a position means teaching an allied or different subject, especially in the smaller institutions. The teaching here is general or unspecialized, and may emphasize the state in which the school is located.

Those with graduate degrees may teach in colleges; the smaller institutions will give less specialized instruction and field work than the larger.

In one church-related college, which prepares students to teach in secondary schools after receiving a Bachelor's degree, the following courses are offered:

1. A survey of the factors which influence the human utilization of the earth's surface, such as climate, topography, soils, etc. Some time is given a specific region.

2. A study with special emphasis on the state of -----.

In the larger institutions, research may be combined with teaching, or the teacher may give a period of time, such as a semester, to full-time research, when released from teaching.

For more information write to the Association of American Geographers, 1201 16th St. N.W., Washington, D.C. 20009.

GEOLOGY. Geology has been briefly defined as the "science of the earth." This requires immediate elaboration. Geologists are professionally trained people who study the history, structure, and composition of the earth as these are revealed by formations of rock under and above the earth, and also by the fossil remains of animal and vegetable life. They also hunt for valuable fuels and minerals and study the processes that bring about changes in the surface and structure of the earth.

Geologists, no matter what their specialty, spend much of their time in laboratories and in field work, as preparation for teaching, or for research combined with teaching.

Geologists tend to specialize. There are economic geologists, mineralogists, and structural geologists. There are also such combinations as geochemists and geophysicists. Probably in the church-related colleges the highly specialized aspects are given less attention than general knowledge of the field.

A Bachelor's degree with a major in geology has been adequate for starting out in this field. An advanced degree is being increasingly recommended for the better jobs of teaching and research. The Ph.D. is often required for teaching positions in colleges.

Students majoring in geology may be required to do about one-fourth of their study in this discipline in a four-year college course. Study is also recommended in mathematics, other natural sciences, English, economics, and foreign languages. Some colleges giving a major in geology require that half the time be devoted to this subject. In some engineering schools offering undergraduate programs in geology, perhaps 90 per cent of the time must be given to this and related technical subjects.

The student wishing a career in geology is required to have the physical stamina to enable him to do strenuous field work, including camping under primitive conditions, and willingness to travel abroad or great distances in the U.S.

College teachers of geology give courses varying from introductory and general subject matter in the field, to the more specialized branches that are developing. In the church-related colleges, the smaller institutions provide mainly the general, introductory courses, while the larger institutions can offer the specialties. There will also be supervision of laboratory work by students, and, in many instances, supervision of students in field work.

In church-related secondary schools, geology is probably usually taken up as part of more general courses in natural science.

OTHER INFORMATION. For general information on the field as a career, write to or consult with American Geological Institute, 2101 Constitution Ave., N.W. Washington, D.C. 20037.

## Economics

"Every economic problem is also a religious one," is a generalization sometimes heard in circles where people are interested in the relation of economics and religion.

Economics, taught by men and women, mainly men, has been called "the dismal science." Yet students flock to courses in economics for various motives—to help them enter business, to understand economic data and systems, to become successful, to learn ways and means of human betterment, to further personal success, to know how to earn a good income. The large numbers of students alone constitute a responsibility of the teacher of a difficult subject.

Economics is, like many other disciplines, marked by vocal schools of thought. There has been the tradition associated with Adam Smith, who held that beneficent natural forces would turn even selfish activities of men to the common good; indeed that consistently selfish men seeking only their own ends would find that economic law would turn things to the common good. There were soon qualifications among economists who analyzed an economic system to find out that it was more than a mechanical phenomenon, that the institutions of men are influenced by their aims and ends, that a system is to be judged by its results in society. Thus there emerged a school of thought named "welfare economics,"—a social science that explores the ways economic systems advance human welfare, and the ways they do not. This inevitably involves study of value judgments and ethics. This has resulted in a situation in which value judgments are called, by some only, simply "prejudice," while others regard ethical judgments as important facts which the economist must take into account.

Economics, like all sciences, has become highly specialized. There are economists who specialize in economic theory, taxation, manpower, consumption, credit, distribution, corporations, business cycles, or international economic trends and problems, etc.

196

Religious organizations are probably usually indifferent to economic issues and problems. But for a hundred years important personalities and organizations have striven by various means to stimulate interest in understanding of economics and of specific economic reforms. For some decades official agencies of religious bodies have stood for the right of both employers and employees to organize, to establish a minimum wage, and to institute some kind of social insurance. They have contended that religious principles are basic in the building and maintenance of the good society. Probably only minorities in the churches display any effective interest in these matters.

PERSONAL QUALIFICATIONS. The general personal qualifications of a teacher of economics in a church-related college are no different from those of teachers generally. In some respects his task is much like that of the teachers of religion. He needs the ability to handle controversy, because probably the community at large is more interested in the practical aspects of economics—making a living—than in religion. But there are minorities in church circles who would prefer that a teacher of economics favor their special proposals.

Since there is an economic aspect to most legislation, the teacher of economics in a church-related college—as in others—may be asked his opinion with respect to such controversial subjects as general federal aid to the states for secondary and elementary education. Does he, in the classroom, simply assemble economic data on aspects of the question, or does he go on to say where he stands? Or, does he compile the economic data and then be "value-neutral" in the classroom? What constitutes academic freedom?

In church circles, there is a good deal of interest in race relations. During recent years many church officials have acted more specifically than formerly, joining demonstrations and recommending details of proposed legislation. Few economists, it seems, have ever even written on economic aspects of race discrimination. The teacher of economics may be having requests for studies or articles in this field. How shall he respond?

The teacher of economics may be called upon for information

197

on "our system" over and against the "Soviet system." He is thus required to be aware of such matters as the relation of individuals to communities, individuals to the state. Does one teach about communism, or does teaching about communism make the teacher a dangerous man?

The teacher of economics is being called upon for more "interdisciplinary" study than ever before. A professor of marketing who studied mainly economics in college and graduate school remarks that ever since he has been teaching he has been studying psychology.

The teacher of economics is required to be committed to the scholarship of his profession. There is no one way of carrying on that teaching in relation to the values expressed by the chamber of commerce, the local council of churches, or the organizations of church women, church men, and young people. He may decide to be a "value-neutral" teacher when he considers alleged tendencies toward the welfare state, or at times to express choices in terms of what he regards as the human values involved.

EDUCATION AND TRAINING. A Master's degree is probably usually called for in college teaching of economics, and the Ph.D. is increasingly expected either to start certain teaching or soon after beginning. The Ph.D. is asked for teaching of advanced courses or the highly specialized ones.

Courses in research method, and in such related subjects as psychology, sociology, history, political science, and international relations are often recommended.

Summer schools and courses offer opportunities for attaining higher degrees, for exploration of specialties, and for continuing education as may be desired.

Field trips to industries, government offices, etc., often add dimension to the more formal professional education.

Professional journals and professional meetings are good resources for both students and teachers.

WHAT DO THEY DO? Teachers of economics may offer courses ranging from relatively elementary general introductions to the field and to history of economic theory, highly specialized courses in government, finance, research method, the corporation, the labor union. He may, after acquiring experience, conduct seminars in which students make formal contributions for discussion.

He may confer with colleagues in other social sciences. He may be invited to speak from time to time at annual meetings of the Grange, the Chamber of Commerce, or the council of churches. He may be asked to take a special interest in the discussions of young people at a local church. Thus his "extracurricular" opportunities may be numerous, and he may have difficulty in determining the criteria whereby he says "yes" or "no" to an urgent request from the community.

He may be called upon to divide his time between research and teaching, depending upon available funds and arrangements of staff time. He may be asked to give full time to research for a short or long period. He may start his career with research on a particular project and then shift to full-time teaching. He may be asked to be a full-time director of research, after he has acquired the necessary experience.

OTHER INFORMATION. In secondary schools, economics is often taught as part of "social studies"—see Teaching in Secondary Schools.

Further information may be had from the publications of The American Economic Association, Northwestern University, Evanston, Ill.

Consultation with a professor of economics in a college or university is often a good way to secure practical information.

A center of information on the church and economic issues is The Department of the Church and Economic Life, National Council of Churches, 475 Riverside Drive, New York, N.Y. 10027.

The larger denominations have agencies of social action which deal with economic and related issues.

## Education

Numerous church-related colleges, of all sizes, offer courses in education, either in departments or schools of education, for the purpose of preparing teachers. While most of those who take these courses teach in public schools, many go to teaching in the church-related elementary and secondary schools, and those with graduate degrees may do college teaching.

In 1959 there were reported, among Protestant bodies, 1,353 kindergartens, 2,849 elementary schools, and 592 secondary schools, a total of 4,794. In practical terms there are now probably 5,000 of these church-related schools. The number of full-time teachers was not reported in 1959. The enrollments were as follows: 18,058 pupils in kindergartens, 263,839 in elementary schools, and 76,842 in secondary schools, a total of 358,739 persons. The total for kindergarten and elementary schools, which alone were enumerated in two earlier reports, represented rapid increases. In 1937 there were about 2,000 kindergarten and elementary church-related schools with 110,000 pupils; in 1952 there were about 3,000 of these schools with 187,000 pupils. Church-related elementary and secondary schools are reported largely by Lutheran, Reformed, and Seventh-day Adventist bodies. (See *Information Service*, National Council of Churches, January 3, 1959.)

The pressing needs for teachers are stimulating systematic training for them in church-related colleges. Church-related colleges probably concentrate their offerings for professional education of those who wish to teach in the elementary grades and high schools. Generally liberal arts students wishing to major in education are required to make application for admission to these courses in either their freshman or sophomore years.

PERSONAL QUALIFICATIONS. Once a teen-ager tested her sure wish to become a teacher by serving regularly in the nursery arranged of a Sunday morning in a large, well-attended church. Teaching can be a routine job with long vacations, automatic salary increases, encouragement of graduate study, and sometimes fair compensation. It can also be a rewarding experience of those

200

who go forth each morning eagerly to converse with pupils, to stretch their minds and vocabularies, and to endeavor somehow to influence their attitudes toward life.

EDUCATION AND TRAINING. Before admission to major work in education in a liberal arts church-related college, a person may be required to meet certain standards. One medium-sized, rapidly growing church-related liberal arts college in one of the oldest of denominations has this to say about students who wish to prepare for teaching: "They must have a satisfactory record in professional and academic courses previously taken; they must be professionally minded and have a desirable personality; they must have physical fitness and no major speech defect; they must arrange their program to have adequate time for student teaching. A student may be dropped from student teaching at any time, if his or her work is unsatisfactory to those supervising the teaching.

"Student teaching is to the future teacher what internship is to the medical student. It is the student's opportunity to prove himself, to test his ability to put theory into practice, and to successfully demonstrate professional skills in actual school situations.

"The program is planned to give the student teacher experience through directed observation, participation and having complete charge of the class when the student shows ability to assume the responsibilities that are required. College faculty members will guide and aid students in this work through visits and conferences."

Most states now require at least a semester beyond the Bachelor's degree of applicants for teaching certificates. Some educators now recommend five years of study to all beginning teachers, a Bachelor's degree, plus a Master's in a graduate school or a department of education in a college or university.

The Master's degree is generally recommended as a minimum for teachers of education, and the Ed.D. and Ph.D. are also often required.

WHAT DO THEY DO? Teachers of education generally offer resident courses, do some extracurricular educational work in the community, and supervise student teaching.

Teaching, even for students who are only working towards a

Bachelor's degree, is becoming highly specialized. In one church-related liberal arts college, 17 courses, listed below, are offered every year. Education students elect among them during their junior and senior years. The titles are here given to illustrate the range of education courses in a college with a total of about 1,100 students, which, of course, offers many other subjects in the various departments;

Introduction to Teaching
Educational Psychology
Philosophy of Education
Child Development
Health and Physical Education in the Elementary School
Art in the Elementary School
Music in the Elementary School
Teaching of Arithmetic
Teaching of Science and Social Studies
Teaching of Language Arts
Methods of Teaching in Secondary Schools
Audio-Visual Education
Guidance
Observation of Teaching in Secondary Schools
Student Teaching in Primary Grades
Student Teaching in Upper Elementary Grades.

Teaching in education courses may include use of the various tests widely used by educators today.

OTHER INFORMATION. Resources may be had by consulting the publications of the following, or their officers, if possible.

National Association of Christian Schools, Box 28, Wheaton, Ill. This affiliate of the National Association of Evangelicals, issues a periodical, a *Yearbook,* and a list of hundreds of church-related schools.

Denominational boards of education, which have contacts with their own church-related colleges.

Heads of departments of education in church-related colleges.

On teaching as a career, publications of National Education Association, 1201 16th St., N.W., Washington, D.C. 20036.

## English Literature

Just as English literature is a broad world with many shades and accents, so there are varieties of ways of presenting it in the classroom. Literature is always dealing, whether clearly or obscurely, with human aims and problems. Imagery and doctrine, drama and doctrine, are always mingled.

The teacher of a literary work is called upon to identify and to interpret it fully, with all its tradition and relationships. If there is adoration or celebration of life in the work, that must be revealed; if great human conflict is inherent, this should be made clear.

So it is with the authors of the works. There are poets and poets. There are those who enjoy life and those who complain. There are those who convey satire, and others whose language is reverent. Some modern poets seem to have a private language of their own, while others are convinced that they should speak more directly to the reader.

The teacher of literature has an obligation to consider both structure or form and the spirit or fire in a work. Words in isolation are usually of little significance; they acquire significance when they are part of an entity.

The English Bible is frequently taught as literature. Frequently the work studied is the King James Version of 1611. This has been called with much evidence "the noblest monument of English prose." It is still the most widely used Bible in the English-speaking world. Much of it, particularly the New Testament, is based on the work of one man, William Tyndale. The King James Bible has exerted an immeasurable influence on later English prose. There are those who say that the poetic quality of the prose accounts for the way the King James Bible continues to speak to both students of literature and persons committed to religion.

Literature is thus one of the great sources for study of the experience of the human race. Writers have their own way of knowing that experience, which is valid when compared with other ways.

PERSONAL QUALIFICATIONS. The personal predilections of a teacher will determine the way that he will consider the relationship between literature and religion. One way is obviously to consider fully and critically the literary works that are plainly in the Christian tradition, and which are subject to direct Christian comments and interpretation. Or, works with an evident ethical or mystical nature can be explored.

Others will approach the matter less directly. They will say, for example, "Let the poets be the poets," and do not try to cast them into a particular mold in accord with a theology. Let the poets use their imaginations and intuitions to explore the human spirit and adventure. Nothing human is alien to religion. Let the students draw their own conclusions in terms of religion.

Both literary works and expressions of religion make much use of metaphor as a means of exploring the universe, and this is a bond between the two.

The teacher's use of materials is only part of his task. His attitude toward the subject matter in his classes is only a part of his function. His attitude toward the people in his classes, who present to him a wide range of experience and who expect to be exposed to the unique offerings of a college or high school, are also important. One college president says that in his opinion a teacher of literature should not in his classroom treat his students either as animated notebooks or as potential converts. He is not expected to use the usual methods of propaganda or to oversimplify his teaching. He should, says this administrator, try to reveal the richness and complexity of literary art.

EDUCATION AND TRAINING. Persons with an interest in English literature may begin to cultivate it in high school by taking as many courses in English as possible and reading widely and independently.

A Bachelor's degree with a major in English can be secured at a large number of colleges and universities in the U.S. In some states, this will qualify a person to apply for a teaching certificate for work in a high school. However, most states now require of an applicant for a certificate at least a semester's work beyond the Bachelor's degree. A student wishing to teach English literature should endeavor to enter a college offering varied courses. The same general rule applies to graduate study, which is the usual minimum for college teaching.

Carefully selected personal reading, skill in using libraries, attendance at evening and summer courses, are all assets.

Those wishing to teach English literature will also do well to study not only English, but also history, philosophy, classical and modern languages, and social science.

WHAT DO THEY DO? In the smaller colleges, persons entering this profession will probably be asked to teach the elementary or introductory courses, in such as essentials of composition, surveys of English or world literature, and public speaking. The larger the college, the more diversified the offerings. The more advanced and specialized courses may be on the works of Chaucer, Shakespeare, or Milton; or on periods, such as the romantic movement or the Victorian era; or on modern American literature and criticism; or the art of poetry, the art of fiction, history of the theater.

In church-related high schools, the offerings will vary from school to school, but in general the courses will usually be a survey of an introductory nature, with little opportunity for concentration.

OTHER INFORMATION. Decisions with respect to employment are made by the authorized officers of schools and colleges. Teachers of English in high schools and colleges should be good advisers of young people. For general information on the field, communicate with the National Council of Teachers of English, 508 South 6th St., Champaign, Ill.

*Ethics*

Ethics is the discipline in which the moral life of man is studied. It has to do with consideration of the moral standards recognized by groups or cultures. The origins of these standards are often the subject of broad discussion. One perennial issue is the extent to which moral standards are originated and supported by religion and the institutions thereof. What do we owe to the Judeo-Christian teachings for the standards of our society? Does democracy

205

depend upon religion, or is democracy simply something good that is everywhere recognized by both religious persons and those with no professed religion? The changes in moral standards are also frequently considered. In a period of rapid change, traditional standards are often challenged and denied. A clergyman recently remarked that we are in a time of "confusion of values" (standards). Religious organizations have always claimed to know something about "right" relationships among men.

A number of professions have formally adopted codes of ethics. This is true not only of the older professions of law and medicine, but of the newer organizations among teachers. These codes are frequently tested and revised. They are observed and ignored from time to time. Some business organizations have also adopted codes of ethics, bringing evidence to support the ideas of those who say that business management is becoming a profession.

Just as ethics is closely related to religious teachings, so it inevitably involves philosophy. Why is an action right? What is your authority for a particular teaching? Again, what is ethical raises questions with regard to law.

Are we losing our moral heritage, and is our civilization breaking down as a result? Men and women in public life give varying answers to this question. The teacher of ethics will inevitably be dealing with this question, or one closely related.

PERSONAL QUALIFICATIONS. The teacher of ethics is called upon to have the same general personal qualifications of other teachers, and is also expected to have certain special abilities. He is required to be sensitive to the moral standards and all the emotionally charged issues that arise.

He will be called on not only for considerations of personal relations, including all that is involved in the relations of men and men, women and women, men and women. He will also be expected to be aware of moral standards of public life.

He will be dealing with "descriptive" ethics which considers the meaning of words, concepts, and viewpoints. He will also be discussing "normative" ethics which considers what to do, or such related things as "the art of the possible."

He will have in his classroom students committed to "absolutes" —what is right is simply right, here, there, and forever. He will also encounter those who have heard or practiced "relativism" in ethics—that one may well act one way in one situation and another way in other conditions. How does environmental change affect our standards of what to do? How can you know when or how you love your neighbor as yourself?

Ethics is surely one of the "inexact" disciplines. The motives of men seem, in a complex society, to be more and more mixed. Concepts of love, justice, liberty, equality—all general terms, and widely used by people generally—call for definition and elaboration in discussions of ethics.

EDUCATION AND TRAINING. Ethics is probably most systematically taught in separate courses in colleges. Ethics is, of course, taught all the time in elementary and secondary schools, as an aspect of other disciplines, or incidentally in the personal contacts between teacher and pupil. In numerous private schools with an interest in religion, ethics is probably more frequently taught as a discipline than in public schools generally. But public school administrators insist that they have continuing responsibilities for moral education—whether so labeled or not.

For teaching in secondary and elementary schools that are church-related, a Bachelor's degree is often the minimum requirement, but acquisition of a Master's degree is constantly recommended and most states require a semester's study beyond the Bachelor's degree for applicants who wish to acquire teaching certificates.

For teaching in church-related colleges, a Master's is usually sufficient for teaching the simpler courses, but the Ph.D. is increasingly recommended. The Ph.D. may be required for advanced courses or for teaching seminars, or for research.

Summer schools and evening courses offer opportunities for continuous education and graduate study. Numerous church conferences expose a teacher to current opinions within church groups. Protestant bodies are accustomed to passing resolutions and declaring "what is right" on numerous issues.

In this discipline "self-study" by the student and teacher is probably of special significance.

WHAT DO THEY DO? Teachers of ethics in colleges offer courses that may be given in the department of philosophy or the department of religion. The kind of department will usually determine the arrangement. In a department of philosophy there will probably be more time given to philosophical ethics, to the ethical ideas of the various philosophers, and to explanations of such terms as "pragmatism." The significance of "compromise" may receive a philosophical orientation.

In departments of religion, courses may be labeled "Christian ethics," and this determines the perspective. Surely the courses will not be exclusively on Christian concepts, because comparisons with other systems will be taken up. Here there may be some historical study involved—when did church officials begin to teach about a just wage, or a living wage, or a minimum wage? "Compromise" may be considered in the light of the history of religious institutions, or the relation of the individual to the institution. Here social reform and reformers either intrude or are invited in. The whole gamut of the positions of church bodies on social and public affairs may be considered.

Ethics is also taught in theological seminaries, either separately or as a portion of other courses.

Some teachers of ethics have opportunities to do research and to assemble case material based on their research. Some teachers of ethics emphasize discussion of cases in their curricula.

OTHER INFORMATION. Personal consultation with teachers of ethics in departments of religion or of philosophy will be valuable, either in person or by mail inquiry.

A center of ethical studies is maintained by the South Dakota State College, Brookings, S.D., from whose leaders advice and information may be had.

## History

Historians are professionally trained persons who study the records of the past. Most historians teach classes to whom they interpret their knowledge and theses. Sometimes historians are called upon to explain the present, in part at least, by their study of the past. "History always intrudes," a churchman once remarked of current issues, whether we know it or not, like it or not. Historians interpret events, trends, institutions, ideas, people. Some historians rely heavily on their studies of the lives of persons, and certain historians have become excellent biographers.

The oft-remarked trend toward specialization is also noted in this discipline. Some teachers spend all their time on the history of one nation, usually their own, even on one period in their country's history. Lately a number of historians have given special attention to the American Civil War of 1861-65. Another specialty is the history of modern Europe. There are historians of art, of education, and, of course, of churches and religion.

Church-related secondary schools and colleges employ teachers of history in considerable numbers. All theological seminaries have professors of church history. A small number of historians are employed in official depositories of church archives, special denominational historical libraries, and by historical societies of religious bodies. A few are editors and consultants to publishers. Writing is always associated with the discipline of history, no matter what the other functions are.

PERSONAL QUALIFICATIONS. The general personal qualifications of teachers of history are the same as those of other teachers under church-related auspices (see Teaching in Secondary Schools and Teaching in Colleges). But religious organizations have their own special interests in history. In the profession in general there are teachers of history whose main role seems to be that of debunking one that is not viewed with respect by church officials. The teacher of history in church-related institutions is probably expected to have an interest in religion if not the history of religion.

A combination of technical proficiency and a Christian spirit and outlook is expected.

This may lead into personal dilemmas. What, if anything, shall one do in the classroom with an affirmation to this effect: "The aim of history is a divine kingdom of truth and righteousness on this earth"? Or with this: "We must remember that we churchmen do not control history. History is a mystery, and church history is a particular mystery, part of a greater mystery."

Does the teacher of history openly proceed to make a Christian witness in his classroom, or does he conceal such attitudes, or be indifferent to them, or be opposed to their entry into the classroom?

Probably no teacher of history anywhere can completely ignore the role of religion in history, any more than the pastor of a local church can avoid doing some personal counseling. Religion has also had a dual role in history that the teacher cannot avoid: Religion has been a divisive force making for bitter conflict among men; religion has been a healing, conciliating, and integrating influence.

EDUCATION AND TRAINING. For teaching history in secondary schools, a Bachelor's degree with a major in history or education is the minimum requirement, although most states now insist that an applicant for a teaching certificate shall have at least a semester of study beyond the Bachelor's degree. Graduate study is increasingly being recommended.

A Master's degree in history seems to be the minimum education for appointment to a position as instructor, assistant professor, or research assistant in a college or university. However, in many institutions the Ph.D. has become necessary even for those entering on teaching careers. The doctorate is generally required for teaching the more advanced courses, for research, and for executive positions.

WHAT DO THEY DO? Some persons with majors in history secure positions in religious organizations interested in international relations. There they may report on developments and issues, for example those before the United Nations.

In secondary schools, historians usually teach introductory or survey courses, with little specialization. In high schools, history may be combined with social sciences, in courses on social problems.

In the smaller colleges the teaching of history may also be of an introductory or general nature, with little time for major emphasis on one nation, era, or continent. The larger the college, the more specialized are the courses offered.

One church-related coeducational college with about 1,100 students lists the following courses in history:

Survey of Western Civilization
History of the United States
Medieval History of Europe
Renaissance and Reformation
History of England
Modern European History
Constitutional Development of the United States
Constitutional Law
History of Colonial America
American Revolution
Diplomatic History
American Civil War
United States Since 1890
Near Eastern and Greek Cultures
Hellenic Greek and Roman Empires
History of Latin America

OTHER INFORMATION. For further information communicate with the American Historical Association, 400 A St., S.E., Washington, D.C. 20003; administrative officers and teachers of church-related high school and colleges; denominational church history societies.

## Physical Sciences

The physical sciences are often defined as including chemistry, physics, astronomy. Some add mathematics.

In the ancient world, man's scientific knowledge of the physical world and its plants and animals was limited, and was studied by philosophers, for example by Aristotle. In the modern world there has been for some decades a rapid expansion of knowledge of natural science, and specialization has followed. There has been marked specialization within the well-known branches. For example, physicists may now concentrate on nuclear physics or optics. Chemists not only specialize in organic or inorganic chemistry; they may also concentrate on geochemistry or biophysics. More and more the interrelationships of the physical sciences are recognized, and there is much interdisciplinary study.

Within recent years, the significance of the physical sciences for national welfare—including both the defense and the health of the people—has had a high degree of public recognition. Thus employment in all branches has rapidly expanded, especially since World War II. This expansion has gone on in college departments of these sciences. However, one accompanying problem has been the competition between industry and the colleges for personnel. Industry offers jobs at attractive pay to many college teachers, and thus college administrators sometimes have difficulty in finding experienced teachers.

The teacher of physical sciences in church-related institutions confronts the same personal issues and dilemmas as teachers of biology and earth sciences, (which see). Church-related colleges expect the teachers of physical sciences to be competent scientists and educators. Beyond these are matters that involve personal attitudes rather than technical knowledge. One of the main problems is the relation of science and religion. Some teachers and some students ignore or conceal their interest in religion. Everywhere there are students who regard the main teachings of the Bible as in conflict with modern science. The way that the teacher will aid these students will depend on his personality as well as his skill as a teacher. Shall he endeavor to seek earnestly an understanding of the background and opinions of these students? This may involve an interpretation of the limitations of scientific methods and knowledge, and a recognition of other good methods of seeking knowledge. Theology is still named "queen of the sciences," but its methodology is different from that of the chemist or physicist. Does one only point to the "separate realms" of religion and science, or does one note that some scientists and religious leaders believe that there can be a fruitful partnership between science and religion?

CHEMISTRY. Chemistry has been the largest field of employment among the physical sciences. About three-fourths of all chemists are employed in private industry. Of the remainder, considerable numbers are teachers. Chemistry is taught in church-related high schools and colleges.

Most people think of chemists as persons who wear long white coats and spend much of their time in laboratories; this picture is reasonably accurate. Much teaching of chemistry is done in laboratories, and teachers both make tests in laboratories and supervise the tests of students.

There are five main branches of chemistry: Organic, inorganic, physical, analytical, and biochemistry. Then there are subdivisions of these. Organic chemists are the largest group, and they usually deal with the substances of, or derived from, vegetable and animal matter. Inorganic chemists study compounds of other elements, usually minerals and metals. Physical chemists study the relations between chemical and physical properties of both organic and inorganic substances.

No matter what the degree of specialization, all need to know the fundamentals of chemistry. These include knowledge of the composition and properties of substances, and how these can be changed; of the processes whereby substances are obtained from nature and of the methods of producing synthetics; and of the various practical uses of substances.

A Bachelor's degree with a major in chemistry is usually the minimum educational requirement. This often enables one to teach in a high school, but most states now require a semester of study beyond the Bachelor's degree by an applicant for a teaching certificate. Some people with a Bachelor's degree are employed in colleges as research assistants or instructors, usually on condition that they also do graduate work.

Those with a Master's and a Ph.D. are most likely to be employed in colleges for teaching or research. In the highly specialized fields of biochemistry and physical chemistry, the Doctor's degree is required for either research or teaching or both. Study of mathematics is essential, and courses in foreign languages and sciences related to chemistry are recommended.

In secondary schools and the smaller colleges, the courses may deal with introductions to the fundamentals of chemistry, or general chemistry, although anyone teaching the subject may have to be aware of the specialties. In the smaller church-related high schools, the teaching of chemistry may have to be combined with teaching a related science.

In the larger colleges, courses in general chemistry and general laboratory work are supplemented by various and often highly specialized courses, including physical chemistry, advanced analytical chemistry, advanced organic chemistry, and many others. As already indicated, teaching and research are often combined. Sometimes full-time teaching may be followed by full-time research, and vice versa.

Decisions with respect to employment are made by the responsible officers of schools and colleges. For general material on the profession communicate with the American Chemical Society, 1155 16th St., Washington, D.C. 20036.

PHYSICS. Physics is one of the professions that have expanded rapidly, especially since World War II. The popularity of physics has been caused by the discoveries in such fields as nuclear energy, cosmic rays, and electronics, all of which are regarded as important in national defense. The elaborate programs of many departments of physics in colleges has been in large part possible because of grants for research from the federal government.

Physics is the discipline in which energy in all its forms, the structure of matter, and the relations between matter and energy are studied. Physicists endeavor to discover the fundamental laws of nature, and to understand how these laws may be used by man.

Many physicists combine research and teaching. Some of the research is theoretical, and some "experimental." The experimental researchers are often called upon to devise new instruments for their experiments. However, physicists may be interested in both theoretical and experimental research. A large number of physicists conduct applied research.

Modern physics is divided into numerous branches. These include mechanics, heat, light, sound, electricity, magnetism, electronics, atomic and nuclear phenomena, physics of fluids, solid-state physics, classical theoretical physics, or quantum physics. Among the numerous specialties are also plasma physics, and ultrasonics. Still others have developed because of the relationships of physics with other sciences; thus we have geophysics, biophysics, physical chemistry, and astrophysics.

All specialties draw on the same fundamental principles developed in the science; and every specialty is related to other specialties. Further, applied physics is always closely related to engineering.

A Bachelor's degree with a major in physics is the minimum recommended for a start in the profession. This often enables a person to teach physics in a high school, if other requirements are met. Most states now require a semester's study beyond the Bachelor's degree of applicants for teaching certificates. The Bachelor's degree may also enable persons to become research assistants in college departments, where they are also usually advised to do graduate work. The Master's and Doctor's degrees are recommended for college teaching, and many positions are open only to those with a doctorate. Thorough study of mathematics, and strong interest and facility in mathematics, are also essential. (See Mathematics, below)

In church-related high schools and smaller colleges, the instruction may be on elementary or introductory physics, elementary laboratory work, and introduction to the problems of physical science. In the larger institutions, the courses become more specialized, and may include such as optics, electricity and magnetism, thermodynamics, mechanics, electronics, and the numerous other specialties mentioned above. As already said, research and teaching are frequently combined, or are alternated, on a teacher's schedule at colleges and universities.

For general information on the profession, communicate with the American Institute of Physics, 335 East 45th St., New York, N.Y. 10017.

ASTRONOMY. Astronomers study the sun, moon, planets, and stars as the basis for navigation by sea and air, the calendar, and the measurement of time. The data gathered by astronomers are used to test theories of time and space. Astronomy provides a laboratory in which matter and energy may be observed under extreme conditions of density and temperature. Astronomy thus aids in rounding out the knowledge of men about the physical world. Astronomers have contributed to thermonuclear and atomic research by studying the behavior of atoms under the extreme temperatures of the stars. Astronomers also study the size and shape of the earth and the density of its atmosphere.

Modern astronomers use complex instruments, devices, and techniques in making their thorough observations. When they use the telescope, they may often attach specialized devices to facilitate their study. Sometimes astronomers send instruments aloft in balloons and in space vehicles in order to make measurements, although generally they use telescopes that are permanently mounted.

There are a number of branches of this science, including: Astrophysics, in which astronomers study the temperature, luminosity, and chemical composition of heavenly bodies; celestial mechanics, which involves the motions of objects in the solar system, including satellites and guided missiles; radio astronomy, the study of the source and nature of the celestial radio waves; statistical astronomy, in which large numbers of stars are studied in order to determine their properties.

Bachelor's degrees with majors in astronomy are offered by only a small proportion of the nation's colleges.

In high school the student considering astronomy should take a good deal of mathematics and science. Upon graduation from high school, the prospective teacher of astronomy should attend a college or university that offers many courses in mathematics and physics, as well as courses in astronomy. A reading knowledge of at least one foreign language is essential, and courses in chemistry, statistics, and electronics are also recommended.

Most graduate study in astronomy consists of advanced courses in this science, as well as in physics, and mathematics.

Astronomy is a science with a relatively small number of professionally trained persons, and graduate study is very important for those wishing to teach it. Some colleges will appoint only those with a Ph.D. to teaching positions; and the Ph.D. is also essential for most positions in observatories.

Teachers of astronomy are employed in colleges. In colleges where there is not a separate department of astronomy, the astronomy teacher may also be called upon to teach courses in mathematics or physics. It is common for faculty members who give full time to astronomy to combine teaching and research.

Some people with only a Bachelor's degree can obtain positions as research assistants while they continue their graduate study.

MATHEMATICS. Mathematics is a discipline and also a tool for many other kinds of teaching, research, and other activities. It is an old and "basic" field. It is also currently a dynamic and rapidly expanding field.

There are two broad classes of mathematicians: those who major in theoretical or pure mathematics, and those who concentrate on applied mathematics, including mathematical computation.

Theoretical mathematicians are engaged in the logical development of mathematical systems and in the study of relationships among the various mathematical forms. They try to increase their basic knowledge without consideration of how the knowledge will be used in the practical world. However, scientists and engineers interested in applications, make use of what seems to be only abstract knowledge.

Those engaged in applied mathematics develop mathematical techniques and approaches to solve problems in the biological, physical, and social sciences. These mathematicians also need knowledge of the field in which they work.

Lines are not sharply drawn between theoretical and applied

mathematics, and they are usually not neatly separated. Thus theoreticians have learned from those who work on practical problems.

Modern mathematicians tend to make much of modern computing equipment. Some of the work with modern computers can only be done by those with advanced mathematical knowledge, while other kinds of computations may be handled by persons with relatively little technical training.

Among the personal qualifications especially needed by mathematicians are imagination, curiosity, a logical mind, and an unmistakable wish to solve new and difficult problems. Teachers of mathematics are called upon to express themselves clearly to students and others. For general personal qualifications see the introductory notes under Physical Sciences.

A Bachelor's degree with a major in mathematics is the minimum educational requirement for beginning in this field. For positions in colleges a graduate degree is required. Mathematics is taught everywhere in the colleges but facilities vary greatly. If one wishes to specialize in applied mathematics, then it is necessary to try to enter a college with wide offerings. For example, if one wishes to use mathematics in a social science, then one should endeavor to enter a college with strong departments in both mathematics and social science. If one wishes special knowledge of modern electronic computers, one should find out where the relevant courses are offered.

A Bachelor's degree with the required courses in education enables one to begin teaching in high schools. However, in most states some work beyond the Bachelor's degree is required for securing a certificate to teach in high schools. At least an additional semester's work may be necessary.

In the colleges, people with a Bachelor's degree may at times secure positions as research assistants or as instructors, while they pursue graduate study. In the smaller liberal arts church-related colleges, courses may be of a more general nature, but are specialized in the larger institutions. In one medium-sized college, 18 courses in mathematics are offered, beginning with reviews of college algebra, geometry, and trigonometry, going on to advanced courses in these subjects, and offerings in calculus, vector analysis, and theory of equations.

OTHER INFORMATION. For further information communicate with the American Mathematical Society, 190 Hope St., Providence 6, R.I.; or the Mathematical Association of America, University of Buffalo, Buffalo, N.Y.


*Psychology*

Teachers of psychology, both men and women, in church-related colleges are in a rapidly developing field with trends toward numerous specialties and with involvements both in biology and social sciences. There is a section on Psychologists in this volume, but the problems and opportunities of teachers of psychology are now given separate treatment.

The teacher of psychology when in the classroom is both scientist and educator. He may also be a counselor of students. He does this informally outside the classroom, or in systematic interviews. Those who specialize in counseling are called clinical psychologists. The teacher of psychology, whether counselor or not, is inevitably aware of this function of many psychologists. The teacher of psychology in a church-related college may also be called upon to speak at some of the numerous church conferences of both ministers and lay people.

Anyone concerned with the drives, motives, and feelings of people—anxiety, love, hate, and interpersonal conflict, for example —is in the field of psychology. One of the ever present difficulties is the tendency of amateur psychologists to try to deal with these problems and conflicts. The teacher of psychology must be a trained person, studying human behavior in accordance with the scientific standards that are approved in his profession. Study of human behavior and personality may include such matters as faith, doubt, confession, prayer, morality, immortality, mysticism, salvation, etc. The teacher of psychology in his classroom may or may not feel obliged to consider such matters with recognition

219

of the customary presuppositions of the theologian. These presuppositions, however, are part of the data on human experience. Likewise the formulations of experience by philosophers may become relevant data for the psychologist to consider. The teacher of psychology committed to the scientific standards of his profession is, of course, a person with values of his own, in which his students have a great interest, and which he may or may not wish to elaborate on in the classroom. A college is a place of inquiry to a degree not usually found in parishes.

PERSONAL QUALIFICATIONS. Some of these have already been indicated in the paragraphs above. The psychologist is called upon to have historical and experimental perspective. Psychology is not an "exact" science. It is marked by differing schools of thought, and by controversy of both depth and breadth. Thus the teacher of psychology is in the midst of conflicts as difficult and confusing as those of the teacher of economics or religion.

The teacher is also confronted by rapid specialization. It is said that the professional journals in the field of psychology are now so numerous that probably no one person can read them all carefully.

This teacher may be asked to consider modern experimentally derived data on human behavior in relation to much conventional religious teaching and to concepts of students with respect to the Bible. Fortunate, perhaps, is the news that in the past fifteen or twenty years there has been a good deal of cooperation between clergymen and other religious workers on the one hand with psychologists and psychiatrists on the other. It has been said that when Sigmund Freud first used the term "sexual" most churchmen shuddered. That seems to be no longer their general attitude.

EDUCATION AND TRAINING. For teaching in college, a Master's degree with a major in psychology seems essential for beginning. The Ph.D. is increasingly called for in teaching the more advanced classes, research, and counseling when this is a part of a teacher's duties. If counseling is to be done, special training and experience are necessary. For research, graduate courses in statistics are recommended, and courses in biological and social sciences for certain types of projects. Summer schools and special seminars offer opportunities either before teaching or during it. Professional journals publish papers that are helpful, as are meetings of the various professional organizations.

WHAT DO THEY DO? Teachers of psychology offer courses ranging from elementary survey courses, to the highly specialized subject matter of the many branches.

Psychology of religion may be taught either in departments of psychology or of religion, depending upon the situation in a particular institution.

Educational testing may be taught in departments of education or in cooperation with them. These courses are often designed as part of the professional training of prospective teachers in schools and colleges.

Teachers of psychology may give part time or full time to research and experimentation, depending upon the funds available, the teachers' time schedules or their personal inclinations. At the beginning, a teacher may spend full time in research for a few years, then give full time to teaching, and vice versa.

Courses in psychology that emphasize analysis and evaluation of human behavior lead into considerations of motive and thus to philosophy and religion, and counseling. Possibly many teachers of psychology, like ordained ministers, inevitably do some counseling, whether they plan to do so or not. For systematic counseling, the necessary time should be set aside for this purpose.

How does the teacher of psychology deal with historic Christian doctrine? In many instances he will undoubtedly not deal with it at all. He is probably not called upon to be a dogmatic defender of any theology in the classroom, no matter what his personal opinions may be. He as a teacher is called upon to present the findings of his profession. He may also say that science is but one way of knowing, that the insights of poets, saints, sages, philosophers, and theologians are also valid.

But the psychologist who is a Christian has two loyalties—to his profession and to the religious body of which he happens to be a member and to the church at large. He will often deal with cynical and disillusioned students as well as those who are devout. To these all he can witness to his faith by his personality, his intellectual honesty, his search for truth, and his emotional maturity.

A teacher of psychology may also make his findings available to church constituencies by means of publications.

OTHER INFORMATION. For general information on the profession communicate with the American Psychological Association, 1333 16th St., N.W., Washington, D.C. 20036. For information on church-related colleges communicate with your denominational board of higher education; the Council of Protestant Colleges and Universities, 1818 R St., N.W., Washington, D.C. 20009; and the Commission on Higher Education, National Council of Churches, 475 Riverside Drive, New York, N.Y. 10027.

## Religion

The teaching of religion in schools and colleges, both church-related and many others, is now a profession of large numbers of men and women, ordained and unordained, with and without training in theological seminaries. It is a vocation being entered by many students in theological seminaries, who complete their courses and secure the B.D., but who do not go into the parish ministry. The specifications and requirements for such teaching probably vary as much as the institutions of higher learning in the nation.

The teaching of religion, no matter what the institution, is an obvious form of Christian vocation. Historically, it has been marked by several broad trends. For example, there have been teachers of religion in church-related colleges and schools, who have been expected to be precise teachers of approved books. They have been expected to indoctrinate students from approved books, with the denomination's general interpretation of the Bible and theology. Many students have been indoctrinated, more or less; questions from students have been kept in a limited range; and the answers of professors have varied little from year to year.

At the other end of the spectrum there has come a group of teachers of religion, who often seem to have little to do with Christian vocation or Christian doctrine. These have been well-trained people, learned and able, who have treated religion with skepticism or adverse criticism. Their courses have often been very interesting. Some students welcome these courses, while others say that their traditional concepts of religion have been greatly altered, and still others say their religion has been destroyed.

Between these schools of thought are conceptions and ideals held by many religious officials with respect to the teachers of religion in church-related schools and colleges. Church constituencies are showing a high degree of interest in the teaching of religion in the institutions which they support. Church bodies also contribute, sometimes generously, to their educational institutions. They ask the teachers of religion to be scholars who have the respect of others in their professions, who present religion in full perspective in a mood of inquiry, and who witness to the truth and faith that is in them in ways appropriate to the teachers. Many officials also ask that Christian vocations, such as are described in this book, shall be presented systematically to the students.

One study has revealed that 247 Protestant-related colleges received over $100 per year per student from churches as support in their institutions in the academic year 1954-55. No later study of this kind seems to have been made.

PERSONAL QUALIFICATIONS. Just as the personality of a person influences his style of writing, so *who* is teaching religion will largely determine what is taught and how. Religion is a difficult subject to teach, even in a church-related college or school. While there is good evidence of much interest in religion among students, there is also good evidence of wide indifference. Students at times express their rebellion against much about religion that they have heard from their parents and in local churches. Thus it has been remarked that some college presidents and deans select their teachers of religion with more care than other faculty members.

Two accents that students seem not to like in courses in religion are dullness and pretense of special cleverness. They do respect careful scholarship (See Education and Training below). Love of learning, love of students, and reasonable ability in communication are talents sought in all parts of the nation for school and college teachers of religion. To possess all three may be an ideal, but its implementation should be sought.

Men and women do not teach religion in school or college in a vacuum. Every academic community has its ways of revealing its attitude toward the teacher of religion. Some other teachers are much influenced by their memories of former teachers of religion. The teacher of religion will necessarily and desirably have many contacts with other faculty members. There is frequently prejudice —open or concealed—against ordained ministers who teach religion. This may be based on the theory that the ordained person will be more of a preacher than a teacher, a theory that has some support in experience. "Glad-handing" is not nearly as important as unmistakable evidence that the teacher is a person of learning who is seeking truth, and also is one with deep convictions who respects persons with findings other than his own. Thus the teacher of religion has, by his personal contacts and otherwise, to prove his competence to fellow teachers. To his students he is required to display learning and conviction in a setting of inquiry that is different from the climate of the local church.

EDUCATION AND TRAINING. A Bachelor's degree at a liberal arts college, plus a Master's degree or a Bachelor of Divinity degree, seem to constitute the educational background of many teachers of religion in schools and colleges. In the colleges, the Ph.D or the Ed.D. enable persons to offer the more advanced courses. Critics of the Ph.D. as a prerequisite for teaching religion argue that it involves too great an emphasis on specialization, including a dissertation in which a student must write more and more about a narrowed field or a small aspect of religion. The Ed.D. requirements apparently usually are such as to permit a more practical study of problems, issues, and programs on the part of students of religion.

Numerous summer conferences, courses, and consultations offer opportunities to college and high-school teachers, and prospective teachers, to become acquainted with current developments within religious bodies.

As in all vocations today, specialization may be emphasized early in the years of study. In the smaller colleges, the courses are fewer in number and permit little concentration. Thus if one hopes to teach religion at one of the larger schools or colleges, it will be well to find out what courses will be offered at these institutions.

WHAT DO THEY TEACH? Traditionally, teachers of religion have offered courses in the Bible, such as Introduction to the Old Testament, Introduction to the New Testament. They have often taught the Bible as literature, a subject that has also been assigned to departments of English. Comparative religion is frequently taught, perhaps too often by means of texts written by theologians for other theologians, rather than for students. It is also sometimes taught with presuppositions that prevent the full presentation of values and developments in the non-Christian religions.

Ethics or distinctly Christian ethics may be taught in departments of religion or in those of philosophy. (See Ethics.) Christian doctrine may constitute a course, or part of one. A history of Christian thought may make up a course or a portion of one. At the larger institutions, where more than one person teaches religion, one may find courses in philosophy of religion, sociology of religion, religion and public issues and affairs, including international and interracial relations. The teaching of religion may be as controversial as any in an institution. The New Testament has been regarded as a most radical tract as well as a source of conservative theology.

Knowledge of points of view of prominent theologians and of major theological positions (fundamentalist, conservative, liberal, neo-orthodox, natural humanist) always serves the teacher well. And in institutions where there are Roman Catholic, Eastern Orthodox, and Jewish students, it is only fitting that their general history and development shall be known to the teacher and at times interpreted to the students. This is also done where the student body is usually only Protestant.

OTHER INFORMATION. For further information one may consult

with school and college teachers of religion with respect to opportunities for training. *The Journal of Bible and Religion* office Wilson College, Chambersburg, Pa., is an undenominational resource for prospective teachers, as well as for those already in the profession. Pertinent information on religion in higher education may be secured from publications of the Council of Protestant Colleges and Universities, 1818 R St., N.W., Washington, D.C. 20009; those of the Commission on Higher Education, National Council of Churches, 475 Riverside Drive, New York, N.Y. 10027; and the National Association of Biblical Instructors, Hartford Seminary Foundation, Hartford, Conn. 06105.

(For many of the emphases in this Chapter, I an indebted to William Spurrier, in a treatment of the teaching of religion in a symposium edited by Paul M. Limbert (*College Teaching and Christian Values,* New York: Association Press, 1951).

## *Sociology*

Sociology is the science in which the many groups of men are studied. Sociologists study families, tribes, communities of all types from neighborhoods and villages to nations; also the numerous relationships and interests of mankind such as professional, business, social, educational, and religious organizations. They inquire concerning the origin, growth, and behavior of these groups, and the influence of group activities and standards on the lives of the individuals who take part. The proliferation of accumulated knowledge and the developments of modern culture, have led to a great deal of specialization. For example, some sociologists study rural communities—others, the urban. Still others concentrate on the family, relations between races, population trends and characteristics, or analyses of public opinion on various issues or policies. There are also sociologists who specialize in methods of research. Some with a bent toward social problems concentrate on the application of sociological knowledge to delinquency, penology, correction, education, community planning. A relatively small proportion give their full attention to the sociology of religion, while larger numbers give part of their time to this branch. A recently developed specialty is medical sociology.

Most sociologists are teachers and research workers in colleges and universities.

PERSONAL QUALIFICATIONS. The general personal qualifications of teachers of sociology in church-related colleges are the same as in other disciplines. (See Teaching in Colleges.) The sociologist is a scientist and educator. He may be interested in developments within religious groups, relationships between religious organizations, and in the practical application of sociological knowledge.

He comes into contact with social reformers and their aims. This may result in cooperation, indifference, or conflict. The sociologist works with data concerning which people in the churches have strong emotional attitudes. The institutions of religion may welcome, reject, or ignore his findings. His problem is the more difficult because of the growing complexity of modern institutions, and their relationship to one another. This becomes evident when discussing race relations, and the role of religious organizations in communities where a position must be taken on these problems. How shall the sociologist deal with these matters in the classroom? Does he voice an opinion about the "sit-ins" and the "kneel-ins"? Does he comment on the exclusion of persons from a place of worship because of their color or race? Of all the institutions in the U.S., churches are frequently observed to be among the most rigidly segregated. Does the sociologist advocate that church-related institutions shall admit applicants without regard to race or color? What is his attitude toward "action research"? Does he simply point to alternatives without making a choice or recommendation? The sociologist is thus in the midst of discussion of what constitutes human welfare.

The sociologist in a church-related college is probably called upon to avoid two extremes, both frequently encountered. First, he is not asked to be only a cold dissecter of society as the tissue of animals is dissected. Second, he is not called upon to deliver sermons in the classroom.

But the sociologist may be asked to speak to crusading groups within churches or others in the community. If he becomes only a reformer, he may lose the respect of his professional colleagues. If he dissents too much from the simple solutions of widely approved propaganda, his speaking engagements may be few in number. Probably, one of his roles is to point to the complexity of social and economic forces in the community, to the low value of extremely simple solutions, the difficulties involved in evaluating any program or institution or personality in modern society.

EDUCATION AND TRAINING. Young people with Bachelor's degrees may be able to secure positions in research projects administered by departments of sociology in colleges or by religious organizations that have research programs. Such employment may be conditioned by agreement to do graduate study.

A Master's degree with a major in sociology is now usually required for college teaching, with which research may be combined or alternated. The Ph.D. is increasingly required for teaching the more advanced or specialized courses.

Summer schools and evening classes offer opportunities for pursuit of graduate education. Part-time employment of students in programs related to sociology will enable them to test their interest, and to acquire knowledge and practical experience.

Professional journals and meetings of professional organizations are valuable for the continuing education of both students and persons professionally employed. Numerous church conferences, denominational and interdenominational, often enable the sociologist to contribute his knowledge and findings, and also to learn about current trends and interests in religious circles.

WHAT DO THEY DO? Sociology is taught in most institutions of higher learning. A small church-related college may employ one teacher. Sociologists are found mainly in the larger university communities, where graduate courses are offered and there are opportunities for research. A number of theological seminaries have sociologists on their faculties, where they may combine teaching and research.

Teachers of sociology offer courses ranging from introductory or general or survey courses to highly developed specialties. Among these, in church-related colleges, are probably those on family life, population, community organization. In departments of education, or in cooperation with them, may be courses in educational sociology. Some of the larger colleges offer courses on the sociology of religion, or the relation of the churches to the community. Research methods in sociology are sometimes the subjects of advanced courses or seminars.

Beginners in this field often start with a research assignment and later shift to teaching. The more experienced teachers often combine teaching and research, or alternate the two.

Sociologists are employed as full-time research workers in denominational boards, councils of churches, and other national church agencies. (See Research Workers.)

In high schools, sociological findings are usually included with general courses named social studies or social problems. (See Teaching in Secondary Schools.)

OTHER INFORMATION. Information on this social science may be had from publications of the American Sociological Association, 1755 Massachusetts Ave., N.W., Washington, D.C. 20036.

## TELEPHONE OPERATORS

Large numbers of women are employed as telephone operators. Many of them work in offices of the larger religious organizations, in church-related colleges, hospitals, and social-welfare institutions.

This is a vocation being greatly affected by technological changes, which enable fewer operators to handle more calls and other services. In spite of these changes, large numbers of telephone operators are needed.

There are many times when the voice of a telephone operator is the first contact between a person and an organization. The direct and indirect impression made by the operator is of significance in "public relations," broadly defined.

PERSONAL QUALIFICATIONS. Among the personal qualifications are courtesy and good judgment in all contacts with the public; willingness to cooperate with other employees; a good handwriting; alertness; capacity to act with speed in emergencies. Often applicants are given physical examinations that include tests of eyesight and hearing. For general personal qualifications, see the descriptions under Office Positions.

EDUCATION AND TRAINING. Women who have graduated from high school are usually preferred to those who have not received a diploma. Some local telephone companies employ students and former telephone operators on a part-time basis. Companies generally provide training for beginners, who practice the handling of ordinary calls on dummy switchboards, and then are given experience in more difficult assignments. Usually when they have had from one to three weeks of training, they are ready for positions on an ordinary switchboard. Operators learn much by doing their duties on the job, or by instruction in new techniques during their employment.

WHAT DO THEY DO? Most telephone operators help employees and those who use the services or publications of religious organizations in making connections for special kinds of calls. Most local calls and a large proportion of long-distance calls are now "dialed" directly by callers throughout the nation. Thus the main duties of most operators consist of giving out information requested or by assisting persons in the making of long-distance calls. For example, they give service when a caller has difficulty in dialing and in emergencies. They keep records of these services.

In the larger organizations there are usually a chief operator and several assistants. The chief operator is responsible for supervision of the assistants and for the over-all efficiency of the office.

Telephone operators at times have opportunities to transfer to other units of an organization, mainly to business service departments.

## YOUNG MEN'S CHRISTIAN ASSOCIATIONS

The Young Men's Christian Associations employ many professional people. There are over 1,800 local associations; new departments, branches, and facilities are constantly being opened.

The Y.M.C.A. is an independent organization with a Protestant heritage, which now has both Protestants and others as members. It cooperates with Protestant churches and offers employment to many Protestants, and for these reasons is included in this book.

The Y.M.C.A.'s strive to develop Christian leadership through a wide variety of social, recreational, physical, educational, and religious programs among their members. Activities for youth include clubs, camping, hobby units, physical exercises. Activities for young adults include social and recreational clubs and groups, formal and informal education, physical education, opportunities for community service.

The officially stated purpose is: "The Y.M.C.A. in its essential genius is a world-wide fellowship united by a common loyalty to Jesus Christ for the purpose of developing Christian personality and building a Christian society."

POSITIONS FOR COLLEGE GRADUATES. The Y.M.C.A. offers positions for college graduates, as follows, all described in some detail below:

> Youth program secretary.
> Adult program secretary.
> Physical education secretary.
> Administrators of business operations.
> Membership secretary.
> General or executive secretary.

PERSONAL QUALIFICATIONS. In order to secure professional employment, a person is expected to be familiar with the Y.M.C.A. movement's purposes, through his own experience. A person who has completed his college education should also have achieved for himself: systematic thought and experience with respect to a Christian philosophy of life; commitment to the task of working with people toward growth and religious service; social awareness and capacity for social leadership.

The Y.M.C.A.'s now employ both men and women for professional work, and some local branches have both men and women as members. An applicant for a position must pass a standard health examination, and either be a member of a Christian church

231

or sign a statement of faith and purpose as authorized by the National Council of the Y.M.C.A.'s.

Volunteer work in a local Association or a summer job in group leadership, church work, camp counseling, and community service will be helpful to a person interested in full-time professional employment.

EDUCATION AND TRAINING. Applicants are required to have a B.A. or B.S. degree with major study in either religion, philosophy, psychology, sociology, education, physical education, business administration, personnel administration, recreation, or closely related fields. Specific courses of value are those in group work, camping, youth leadership, counseling, guidance, accounting, community planning, community organization. Short and intensive professional training is also required, which may in many cases be obtained after employment begins.

Practically all persons enter the Y.M.C.A. profession as junior executives for the purpose of orientation and indoctrination over a two-year period. Associations often offer opportunities for in-service training, and even for formal academic study after employment. On completion of two years of professional work and academic requirements, candidates are eligible for certification.

Two professional training institutions offer special graduate and undergraduate curricula designed to prepare persons for Y.M.C.A. work. They are Springfield College, Springfield, Mass.; George Williams College, Chicago, Ill. 60615.

## Brief Descriptions of Positions

GENERAL OR EXECUTIVE SECRETARY: Directs the work of the local (or branch) Y.M.C.A. according to the general policies determined by the Board of Directors; responsible for general community relations; enlists, trains and supervises staff; develops the lay organization; guides committees as they develop plans and carry forward their responsibilities; recommends an annual budget to the Board of Directors and administers the authorized program of activities in accordance therewith; responsible for financial and business operations and for contribution income to sustain the program; maintains plant and equipment appropriate to the program, frequently including housing and food services.

MEMBERSHIP SECRETARY: Secures and maintains a membership; guides the committee responsible for membership policies; interprets Y.M.C.A. to members and public; organizes volunteer groups for membership service; maintains relationships with community agencies; counsels with individual members and groups as the basis for developing programs meeting members' needs; keeps membership records.

ADULT PROGRAM SECRETARY: (Sometimes called young adult secretary, men's secretary, general program secretary): Responsible for program with persons 18 and over other than physical education and formal schools; aids them to achieve understanding concerning religion, vocations, health, recreation, social life, family and marriage relationships and to express themselves in Christian service, enlists and supervises volunteer and group leaders in the various programs; counsels individuals regarding personal problems; conducts vocational guidance and employment services; organizes and directs committees, clubs, citizenship classes, religious and social study groups, hobby interest groups, recreational activities, dramatics, music groups, co-ed activities; maintains adequate records and reports.

YOUTH PROGRAM SECRETARY: (Sometimes called boys' work secretary, community boys' secretary): Aids boys and girls through organized groups and informal education to develop attitudes and social habits consistent with Christian principles; integrates programs and activities with efforts of parents, school, church and community leaders; guides the Youth Program Committee and sponsoring committee of parents; counsels with individual boys and with their parients; organizes group programs according to individual and community needs; enlists, trains and supervises volunteer group leaders; surveys community situations affecting youth; cooperates with others to create community interest in the needs of youth; interprets Y.M.C.A. to members, parents, and public; manages business aspects of the youth department; generally responsible for camping program; maintains adequate records and reports.

PHYSICAL EDUCATION SECRETARY: (Sometimes called physical director): Directs the program of physical education in accordance with policies of the Board of Directors and Physical Education Committee; keys program to health, physical fitness, recreation, and character education needs of members and community; consults and cooperates with local medical, health, recreation, and sports leaders in respect to members' health and recreation needs; arranges for physical examinations and follow up to aid members' health and physical fitness; counsels with individuals regarding health and personal problems; conducts classes in gym work, swimming, life saving, and first aid; organizes and conducts recreation groups, games, athletic teams and leagues, both in the Y.M.C.A. and in connection with church, school, industry, and occupational groups; enlists, trains, and supervises volunteer and paid leaders for this work; supervises the work of physical department; carries on a program of interpretation, and keeps adequate records and reports.

SOME OTHER POSITION TITLES, DESCRIPTIVE OF THE WORK PERFORMED OR CONSTITUENCY SERVED, ARE: community secretaries, industrial secretaries, secretaries conducting programs among women and girls, public relations secretaries, business secretaries, residence secretaries, student secretaries, armed services secretaries, and transportation secretaries. (From text published by Personnel Services, National Council of Y.M.C.A.'s.)

OTHER INFORMATION. Decisions with respect to employment are made by the local Associations. In addition to Social Security coverage, there is a Retirement Fund in which an employed secretary may participate. Life insurance is available at low cost. Vacations depend on policies of local Associations. Further information, including that on fellowships and scholarships available, may be had from Personnel Services, National Council of the Y.M.C.A.'s, 291 Broadway, New York, N.Y. 10007. Students may also consult with secretaries in local Associations, and in regional offices.

## YOUNG WOMEN'S CHRISTIAN ASSOCIATION

The Young Women's Christian Associations of the U.S. offer programs in some 5,400 centers of the U.S. and 16 other nations.

There are many persons in professional and managerial positions. The Y.W.C.A. is an independent organization of individuals of Protestant heritage, which now has Protestants and others as members. It offers employment to Protestant young women. The purpose of the Y.W.C.A. is "To build a fellowship of women and girls devoted to the task of realizing in our common life those ideals of personal and social living to which we are committed by our faith as Christians. In this endeavor we seek to understand Jesus, to share his love for all people, and to grow in the knowledge and love of God."

The Y.W.C.A. employs college graduates for the following professional positions, all described in detail below:

Program director, working with youth and adults.

Health, physical education, and recreation program director.

Assistant directors in the fields above.

Executive director in community association.

Executive director in college or university association.

For the last two, only candidates who already have professional experience are considered.

PERSONAL QUALIFICATIONS. From the Bureau of Personnel and Training of the national Board of the Y.W.C.A. comes the following statement: "For the complex task of the Y.W.C.A. you will need the ability to work creatively with people—imagination, adaptability, sensitivity, enthusiasm, maturity. A desire to express Christian ideals in daily living is basic. The Y.W.C.A. expects of you specialized knowledge acquired through professional training in one of a variety of fields—social work, psychology, social science, religious education, physical education, recreation, human relations."

More specific qualifications for all Y.W.C.A. positions are described as follows: "Belief in the Christian purpose of the Y.W.C.A.; understanding and warm acceptance of people, belief in their capacities for growth and ability to work democratically with others; ability to analyze and interpret social forces as they affect the lives of human beings; positive and developing social attitudes on international, interracial, economic, and social affairs; ability to reach decisions objectively, to assume responsibility, and to carry through; good health, physical and mental; initiative and resourcefulness; capacity to enjoy life—a sense of humor and proportion . . .

"A Y.W.C.A. job is more than a job. Those who work for the Y.W.C.A. do so because of the kind of people they are. They believe in the worth and dignity of every human being. They want to help others learn and grow and be happy, expressing their highest and best through faith in God, and responsible action in their daily lives. They want to be at the center of life, part of the great adventure of their time—heads, hands, and minds dedicated to building the kind of lasting peace which can come only through the mutual respect and understanding of all people."

EDUCATION AND TRAINING. Preparation should begin in high school. A girl in high school should join a Y-Teen club; meet the director of the local Y.W.C.A. and discuss interests and concerns; take part in local Y.W.C.A. group activities; try to develop skills in such as crafts, music, drama, dancing, writing, or public speaking.

In college, a prospective employee will need to work toward the degree of B.A. or B.S.; pursue major or minor study in religion, social science, education, or philosophy. One seeking to become a director of health and physical education needs a major in physical education. For one aiming to become director in a college Y.W.C.A., a graduate degree in religion, social work, education, or a social science is essential.

In addition, for background and experience, summer jobs in camp counseling, assisting in playground activities, or community service projects are recommended. Local Y.W.C.A.'s often offer summer jobs.

The Y.W.C.A. School of Professional Workers, 600 Lexington Ave., New York, N.Y. 10022 offers "basic agency training, orientation institutes, on-the-job training, and special seminars in certain subjects."

## Description of Positions

PROGRAM DIRECTOR. The program director has a three-fold task: leader, teacher, adviser. A program director may have responsibility for teenagers; young adults; or health, physical education, and recreation clubs. A program director works with groups or clubs through volunteers and lay advisers, and helps to discover ways of meeting the needs of each individual. She shares with a committee of volunteers the participation in a particular program. She recruits new members of groups or clubs. She recruits, trains, and supervises volunteer leaders and part-time workers for their specific program activities.

She interprets the program for which she is responsible to the board of directors of the Association, to the community, to parent-teacher associations, churches, and other organizations. She helps to develop publicity materials for local newspapers, radio, TV, magazines. She administers the budget of her department, keeps the necessary records, and makes financial reports as needed.

A program director cooperates with other staff members in planning the total program in the community. She consults at intervals with her supervisor or executive concerning plans, methods, and evaluation of her work. She must keep informed on trends and developments in the Y.W.C.A. and elsewhere in the field of her activity.

DIRECTOR OF TEEN-AGE PROGRAMS. This director is responsible for Y.W.C.A. activities among youth of junior and senior high-school age in those Associations with resources for this specialization. This program provides recreation and fellowship; develops thoughtful discussion of attitudes toward personal and family relations, work, health, and social responsibilities; deepens convictions concerning the Christian way of life. Teen-age clubs and groups meet in Y.W.C.A. buildings and elsewhere. Their interests include hobbies, camping, conferences, canteens, and recreation. The major duty of the program director, as already stated above, is recruiting, training, and supervising adult leaders. She works with school teachers and administrators. She cooperates with other youth-serving agencies in the community.

DIRECTOR OF PROGRAM WITH YOUNG ADULTS. This director works with women aged about 18 to 35, both the employed and those who are home-makers. The local program is designed to provide opportunities for creative leisure-time activities, for growth in understanding and assumption of responsibilities of citizenship, for leadership development, for study and action on social and economic problems, and for other means of applying Christian ideals to daily living. The methods of work are essentially the same as those indicated in the descriptions of program directors above.

DIRECTOR OF PROGRAM FOR HEALTH, PHYSICAL EDUCATION, AND RECREATION. The Y.W.C.A. program in a community includes such emphases as are locally needed, and as resources are available, in health education, physical education, and recreation. It is developed through individual, group, and community contacts. The functions of the director may include adaptation of a health program to a variety of age groups; discovery of needs and determination of those activities that will be helpful; sharing of the program with members and volunteers. The specific methods of a program director have been indicated in the first two descriptions of positions above.

ASSISTANT PROGRAM DIRECTOR. Assistant to program directors in the fields of Teen-Age, Young Adult, and Health and Physical Education is a position frequently open to beginners. They are employed for some of the same functions as the directors as outlined above, but with less responsibility for supervision and administration. An assistant in health and physical education usually has major responsibility for teaching groups, clubs, or classes.

EXECUTIVE DIRECTOR. The executive director of a community Y.W.C.A. has responsibility for giving direction to the whole organization, members, board of directors, committees, and employed staff. She has the task of drawing them all together into a cooperative working group. She handles the usual "top" administrative duties. She correlates the various programs, manages the total budget, selects and trains the paid staff members. She works with other agencies of the community and their leaders. She furnishes the "tone" to the entire organization under her direction. Much of her work is in cooperation with the board of directors and committees. Only persons with considerable experience in administration and supervision, and of maturity, will qualify for the position of executive director. Frequently program directors with the qualifications are promoted to executive director.

U.S.O. DIRECTOR. The Y.W.C.A. cooperates with the United Service Organizations, which have special responsibilities for service to persons in the armed services of the U.S. and their families. The directors of U.S.O. operations for which the Y.W.C.A.—or the other cooperating organizations—assume responsibility must be persons with considerable experience in the organization and development of programs, in administration of clubs and buildings, in staff relationships, and in community organization. The age range for all U.S.O. staff is 25 to 55 at the time of employment.

STUDENT DIRECTOR. The executive director of a college or university Y.W.C.A. works in a special kind of community—the campus—with a special group of persons—students. There is here an atmosphere of inquiry different from that of a local community. Many questions are raised about religion, yet the major function of the student director is religious education, broadly defined. This is related to the objectives and total program of the Y.W.C.A., and to the social needs of the national and world situation. The Y.W.C.A. often stands at a strategic point between the college and the church. The student director must understand both.

The director uses the techniques of group organization in religious education, and in administering a membership organizaton of students with a Christian purpose. At some institutions the student program is carried on in close cooperation with the Y.M.C.A. (which see). At other places there is an interreligious program that includes a number of student groups and organizations. To qualify for consideration for a position, one should have, in addition to the general requirements mentioned above, knowledge of the history and philosophy of work among students.

OTHER INFORMATION. Decisions with respect to employment are made by the local Y.W.C.A. The Bureau of Personnel and Training of the National Board of the Y.W.C.A., 600 Lexington Ave., New York, N.Y. 10022, receives and reviews applications and refers credentials of applicants to local associations. The Bureau has publications available to interested applicants.

In addition to coverage under Social Security, there is a retirement fund in which professional workers may participate. The local Associations have the policy of offering staff members a 12-month contract (9 months for student work), written job descriptions, a month's paid summer vacation plus a week in winter, sick leave and maternity leave provisions. Many Associations grant leaves of absence for graduate study. Periodic increases of salary are the general rule.

# III
# Summaries of Church Statistics

The selected statistics that follow are a generous sampling of the more comprehensive officially reported figures appearing in the Census of Religious Bodies; the annual *Yearbook of American Churches* published by the National Council of Churches; publications of the religious bodies; and other sources, all indicated.

## NUMBER OF CHURCHES AND OF MEMBERS, BY SIX FAITHS

| Religious Group | No. of Bodies Reporting** | No. of Churches | No. of Members |
|---|---|---|---|
| Buddhist | 1 | 55 | 60,000 |
| Old Catholic, Polish National Catholic, and Armenian Church of North America, Diocese | 7 | 348 | 597,372 |
| Eastern Churches | 20 | 1,454 | 3,001,751 |
| Jewish Congregations* | 1 | 4,079 | 5,509,000 |
| Roman Catholic | 1 | 23,412 | 43,847,938 |
| Protestant | 222 | 289,892 | 64,929,941 |
| Totals | 252 | 319,240 | 117,946,002 |

\* Includes Orthodox, Conservative, and Reform.
\*\* No. of Bodies Reporting Membership.

## CLERGY, BY FAITHS

| Religious Group | No. of Bodies Reporting** | No. of Pastors with Charges | Total Number of Clergy |
|---|---|---|---|
| Buddhist | 1 | 75 | 90 |
| Old Catholic, Polish National Catholic, and Armenian Church of North America, Diocese | 7 | 321 | 422 |
| Eastern Churches | 19 | 1,309 | 1,857 |
| Jewish Congregations* | 1 | 3,790 | 5,120 |
| Roman Catholic | 1 | 17,298 | 56,818 |
| Protestant | 202 | 223,807 | 300,168 |
| Totals | 231 | 246,600 | 364,475 |

\* Includes Orthodox, Conservative, and Reform.
\*\* Number reporting pastors with charges.
(SOURCE: *Yearbook of American Churches,* 1964. New York: National Council of Churches. Data are mainly for 1962.)

## GROUPS OF RELIGIOUS BODIES: CHURCHES AND MEMBERSHIP

A tabulation of the latest information on churches and membership is given for *groups or families* of religious bodies, arranged below. In the parenthesis following the name of the group or family is the *number of bodies reporting figures.*

## MEMBERSHIP AND POPULATION

The latest thoroughly reported Federal Census of Religious Bodies was for the year 1926, and this year is often used as a base for comparison of later figures. Since that date, too, there seems to have been no major change in the methods of counting members. Roman Catholics, Eastern Orthodox, Jewish Congregations, Old Catholics, Lutherans report on an inclusive, or population basis. Most Protestant bodies report as members only those who attain the status of full membership, usually at about age 13.

# RELIGIOUS AFFILIATION, BY FAITHS

The following are figures on religious affiliation, by major groups, reported to the YEARBOOK OF AMERICAN CHURCHES, from 1951 through 1962.

| Year | Total Membership | Buddhist | Old Catholics* and Polish National Catholics | Eastern Orthodox | Jews | Roman Catholics | Protestants |
|------|------------------|----------|----------------------------------------------|------------------|------|-----------------|-------------|
| 1951 | 88,673,005 | 73,000 | 337,408 | 1,858,585 | 5,000,000 | 29,241,580 | 52,162,432 |
| 1952 | 92,277,129 | 73,000 | 366,956 | 2,353,783 | 5,000,000 | 30,253,427 | 54,229,963 |
| 1953 | 94,842,845 | 63,000 | 366,088 | 2,100,171 | 5,000,000 | 31,476,261 | 55,837,325 |
| 1954 | 97,482,611 | 63,000 | 367,370 | 2,024,219 | 5,500,000 | 32,403,332 | 57,124,142 |
| 1955 | 100,162,529 | 63,000 | 367,918 | 2,386,945 | 5,500,000 | 33,396,647 | 58,448,567 |
| 1956 | 103,224,954 | 63,000 | 351,068 | 2,598,055 | 5,500,000 | 34,563,851 | 60,148,980 |
| 1957 | 104,189,678 | 10,000 | 468,978 | 2,540,446 | 5,500,000 | 35,846,477 | 59,823,777 |
| 1958 | 109,557,741 | 10,000 | 488,246 | 2,545,318 | 5,500,000 | 39,509,508 | 61,504,669 |
| 1959 | 112,226,905 | 20,000 | 484,489 | 2,807,612 | 5,500,000 | 40,871,302 | 62,543,502 |
| 1960 | 114,449,217 | 20,000 | 589,819 | 2,698,663 | 5,367,000 | 42,104,900 | 63,668,835 |
| 1961 | 116,109,929 | 60,000 | 572,897 | 2,800,401 | 5,365,000 | 42,876,665 | 64,434,966 |
| 1962 | 117,946,002 | 60,000 | 597,372 | 3,001,751 | 5,509,000 | 43,847,938 | 64,929,941 |

* Since 1957, Armenian Church of North America, Diocese, included in this column.

*Number of Churches and Inclusive Church Membership, By Groups of Religious Bodies, According to the Most Recently Reported Figures, Mainly for the Year Ending December 31, 1962.*

| | Number of Churches | Inclusive Membership |
|---|---|---|
| Adventist Bodies (5) | 3,813 | 372,972 |
| Baptist Bodies (28) | 92,242 | 21,643,490 |
| Brethren (German Baptists) (4) | 1,413 | 250,227 |
| Brethren (River) (3) | 183 | 8,698 |
| Christian Churches (Disciples of Christ), International Convention, and Churches of Christ (2) | 26,473 | 4,029,046 |
| Churches of God (11) | 9,570 | 485,010 |
| Churches of the Living God (2) | 379 | 45,922 |
| Churches of the New Jerusalem (2) | 73 | 5,854 |
| Eastern Churches (20) | 1,454 | 3,001,751 |
| Evangelistic Associations (9) | 554 | 66,717 |
| Friends (8) | 1,096 | 128,495 |
| Latter Day Saints (5) | 4,796 | 1,846,841 |
| Lutheran Bodies (11)* | 17,092 | 8,356,656 |
| Mennonite Bodies (12) | 1,746 | 164,440 |
| Methodist Bodies (21) | 54,813 | 12,739,925 |
| Moravian Bodies (2) | 185 | 67,807 |
| Old Catholic Churches (5) | 134 | 159,961 |
| Pentecostal Assemblies (12) | 5,223 | 404,611 |
| Presbyterian Bodies (10) | 14,578 | 4,361,344 |
| Reformed Bodies (6) | 1,594 | 507,751 |
| Spiritualists (3) | 419 | 173,001 |
| United Brethren Bodies (2) | 329 | 22,214 |
| All *other* bodies (69) | 81,081 | 59,103,269 |
| Total: 252 bodies reporting | 319,240 | 117,946,002 |

* Total includes also figures for Negro Missions, maintained by the synodical conference of Lutheran bodies.

(SOURCE: *Yearbook of American Churches,* 1964. New York: National Council of Churches.)

Since 1926, the average size of congregations of all faiths has increased from 235 to 370, or a gain of 57 per cent, according to reports appearing in the *Yearbook of American Churches,* 1964, the latest figures being for 1962.

Protestants officially reported were 31,511,701 in 1926, and 64, 929,941 in 1962. They were 27.0 per cent of total population in 1926, and 34.9 per cent in 1962.

Roman Catholics reported 18,605,003 persons in 1926, and 43,847,938 in 1962. They were 16.0 per cent of population in 1926, and 23.6 per cent in 1962.

The Church of Christ, Scientist, does not publish figures of affiliation. The Federal Census of Religious Bodies, 1936, reported 268,915 members of that body.

## RELIGIONS REPORTED BY AMERICAN CIVILIANS

The question, "What is your religion?," was asked in 1957 of a sample of persons over 14 years of age in 35,000 households with about 100,000 persons, by the Bureau of the Census, Washington D.C. 20233. The replies received about religion from the persons 14 years of age and over were then "extrapolated" for the entire civilian population over 14, estimated to be 139,330,000 persons in March, 1957. "Related children under 14 years old by religion reported for the family head and his wife" were also enumerated. A summary follows:

| Religion | Persons 14 years old and over | Per cent Distribution |
|---|---|---|
| Total | 119,533,000 | 100.0 |
| Protestant | 78,952,000 | 66.2 |
| Roman Catholic | 30,669,000 | 25.7 |
| Jewish | 3,868,000 | 3.2 |
| Other Religion | 1,545,000 | 1.3 |
| No religion | 3,195,000 | 2.7 |
| Religion not reported | 1,104,000 | 0.9 |

| Religion | Related Children under 14 with family head and wife reported in same religious group | Per cent Distribution |
|---|---|---|
| Total | 44,397,000 | 100.0 |
| Protestant | 30,558,000 | 68.8 |
| Roman Catholic | 11,757,000 | 26.5 |
| Jewish | 1,107,000 | 2.5 |
| Other Religion | 388,000 | 0.9 |
| No religion | 502,000 | 1.1 |
| Religion not reported | 85,000 | 0.2 |

Only those in the four large Protestant families or groups of denominations were separately tabulated. The total of 78,952,000 persons was divided as follows:

| Bodies | Number | Per cent of Population 14 years and over |
|---|---|---|
| Baptist | 23,525,000 | 21 |
| Lutheran | 8,417,000 | 7 |
| Methodist | 16,676,000 | 14 |
| Other Protestant | 26,676,000 | 21 |
| Presbyterian | 6,656,000 | 6 |

(SOURCE: *Current Population Reports,* Series p. 20, No. 79, 1958. Bureau of the Census, Washington, D.C. 20233. The question was not used in the Population Census of 1960.)

## ATTENDANCE AT WORSHIP

Reports from a sample of civilian adults in the U.S., who were asked if they had attended a church service the week prior to the interview, have been made at various times by polling organizations. Those of the American Institute of Public Opinion, Princeton, N.J., which are syndicated in many newspapers, are summarized as follows:

| Year | Per cent of adults attending church |
|------|-------------------------------------|
| 1939 | 41 |
| 1940 | 37 |
| 1942 | 36 |
| 1947 | 45 |
| 1950 | 39 |
| 1954 | 46 |
| 1955 | 49 |
| 1956 | 46 |
| 1957 | 47 |
| 1958 | 49 |
| 1959 | 47 |
| 1960 | 47 |
| 1961 | 47 |
| 1962 | 46 |
| 1963 | 46 |

For some of these years figures were published indicating that women said they attended more frequently than men; and Roman Catholics more regularly than Protestants or Jews.

## CHURCH-RELATED SOCIAL WELFARE AND HEALTH INSTITUTIONS

Estimates indicate that the following numbers of institutions are church-related, according to definitions made by the officials of religious bodies:

247

|                                  |     |
|----------------------------------|-----|
| Hospitals                        | 600 |
| Homes for Aged                   | 700 |
| Homes and Agencies for Children  | 800 |

(SOURCE: *Social Work Yearbook*. New York: National Association of Social Workers, 1963.)

## CHURCH-RELATED COLLEGES AND UNIVERSITIES

There are some 450 colleges and universities related to Protestant churches, according to definitions made by officials of these bodies or their boards of higher education, and as compiled by the Commission on Higher Education of the National Council of Churches, New York. Most of them are liberal arts colleges. The list was first published in Information Service of the National Council of Churches, February 3, 1962, and has since been updated by the Commission on Higher Education.

### Church Gifts to Colleges

With reports from some 250 church-related colleges, the Council for Financial Aid to Education, New York, reported financial support from churches of $104.05 per student in 1957. These colleges had over 240,000 students at the time. The figures have not been updated.

## CHURCH-RELATED ELEMENTARY AND SECONDARY SCHOOLS

Among Protestant bodies there were reported 1,353 kindergartens, 2,849 elementary schools, and 592 secondary or high schools, as noted in Information Service, National Council of Churches, New York, January 3, 1959.

Enrollments were 18,058 in kindergartens, 286,839 in elementary schools, and 76,842 in secondary schools.

These schools were reported mainly by Lutheran bodies, the Seventh-day Adventists, and the Christian Reformed Church. The

248

National Association of Christian Schools, Wheaton, Ill., publishes a list containing the names and addresses of many of these schools.

## SUNDAY SCHOOLS AND RELEASED-TIME CLASSES

Protestant Sunday schools originated in England, the one started by Robert Raikes, a layman, at Gloucester, in 1780, being often cited as the first. In the U.S. total enrollments of Sunday and Sabbath schools of all faiths, including pupils, teachers, and officers, as reported by officials of denominations to the *Yearbook of American Churches* were as follows:

| Year | Total Enrollment |
|------|------------------|
| 1952 | 32,638,879 |
| 1962 | 44,615,962 |

Teachers in Sunday and Sabbath schools are usually unpaid volunteers.

In weekday religious education about 500 teachers are paid by cooperating local churches to serve in classes held on "released-time," that is the time released by public school authorities for this purpose, according to estimates of the Division of Christian Education, National Council of Churches, New York. There are also a few supervisory positions.

## MISSIONS OVERSEAS

Protestant churches of the U.S. have developed, from modest beginnings, a large number of missions overseas. There were 26,-390 Protestant foreign missionaries in 1960, sent by 312 agencies of Protestant churches. The figure represented an increase of 80 per cent since 1950. There was an increase of 8.6 per cent between 1958 and 1960. These persons worked in most nations of the world, although there were none reported in Afghanistan, the People's Republic of China (Mainland or Communist China); and very few in the Communist nations of Eastern Europe and

249

some Arab states. To both India and Japan 108 foreign mission agencies had sent out workers; while Hong Kong and the Philippines had persons from 58 societies of the U.S. The income of all foreign mission agencies was reported to be almost $164,000,000 in 1959, an average contribution per Protestant member of $2.75 that year. The missionaries from the U.S., 26,390, as noted above, were over 60 per cent of the 42,250 missionaries of the world sent out by Protestants of all nations.

(SOURCE: Missionary Research Library, New York, Occasional Bulletin, Vol. XI, No. 9, November 23, 1960.)


## CHURCH FINANCE

The churches of all faiths receive about one-half of the total philanthropic gifts of the American people, according to rough estimates made from time to time, but not for recent years.

Forty-two Protestant bodies reporting for the years 1962 and 1961 to the National Council of Churches indicated finances of slightly over $68.00 per year per member. There are no figures on the proportion of members contributing. The total amount reported in 1962 was $2,799,670,577, of which about 82 per cent was for local congregational expenses. The other 18 per cent was for foreign and home missions, education, social welfare, relief abroad, and other benevolences.

(SOURCE: For 42 bodies, Statistics of Church Finances. New York: National Council of Churches, 1963.)


## CHURCH BUILDINGS

About 90 per cent of the parishes or local congregations of all faiths reported owning their own houses of worship, the remainder meeting in rented halls, other churches, homes etc., according to the Federal Censuses of Religious Bodies, 1906, 1916, 1926, 1936. Although there has been no general reporting of the number of buildings since the enumerations above, it seems probable that many new congregations start their operations without an edifice of their own, and the percentage of the past could be reasonably accurate now.

Estimates of the annual value of new construction of religious buildings, 1925-1962, are found in *Construction Volume and Costs,* a statistical supplement to *The Construction Review,* a periodical of the Department of Commerce; and in the monthly issues of the periodical itself. The published figures at five-year intervals and for 1961-63 follow:

| Year | Value |
|------|-------|
| 1925 | $ 165,000,000 |
| 1930 | 135,000,000 |
| 1935 | 28,000,000 |
| 1940 | 59,000,000 |
| 1945 | 26,000,000 |
| 1950 | 409,000,000 |
| 1955 | 736,000,000 |
| 1960 | 1,016,000,000 |
| 1961 | 984,000,000 |
| 1962 | 1,035,000,000 |
| 1963 | 995,000,000 |

## WOMEN IN THE MINISTRY

Some 80 Protestant bodies in the U.S. ordain or license women to carry on a ministry. However, the number of women ordained is relatively small and may be no more than 3 per cent of all active ordained persons. Also, only a small proportion of the women ordained have charge of parishes or congregations. They tend to have employment as associate or assistant ministers, as directors of religious education, teachers, missionaries, and in many other positions in boards and agencies.

Among the well-known Protestant bodies that ordain women are the Methodist Church, the United Presbyterian Church in the U.S.A., the United Church of Christ, the Christian Churches (Disciples of Christ), Baptist Churches, and the Unitarian Universalist Churches.

251

The number of women ordained is not reported regularly, but reports of some published denominational statistics appearing in *Information Service* of the National Council of Churches, March 6, 1954, indicated 5,791 ordained women.

# INDEX